STAND UP STRAIGHT
AND SING!

JESSYE NORMAN

Stand Up Straight and Sing!

Mariner Books

Houghton Mifflin Harcourt

Boston   New York

First Mariner Books edition 2015
Copyright © 2014 by Jessye Norman

For information about permission to reproduce selections from this book,
write to Permissions, Houghton Mifflin Harcourt Publishing Company,
215 Park Avenue South, New York, New York 10003.

www.hmhco.com

Library of Congress Cataloging-in-Publication Data
Norman, Jessye.
Stand up straight and sing! / Jessye Norman.
pages cm
Includes index.
ISBN 978-0-544-00340-8 (hardback)   ISBN 978-0-544-48405-4 (pbk.)
1. Norman, Jessye. 2. Sopranos (Singers)—United States—Biography. I. Title.
ML420.N736A3 2014
782.1092—dc23
[B]
2013046581

Book design by Victoria Hartman

Printed in the United States of America
DOC 10 9 8 7 6 5 4 3 2 1

I am honored to dedicate this book first to my parents,
Janie and Silas Norman Sr., then to my siblings, Elaine, Silas Jr.,
Howard, and our beloved angel, George.

And lastly to our big, bountiful family, with every single one of whom
our ancestry is shared, as well as those who compose an extended,
multitudinous group. As Richard Bach wrote:

"The bond that links your true family is not one of blood,
but of respect and joy in each other's life."

Blest be the tie that binds.

CONTENTS

STAND UP STRAIGHT
AND SING!

INTRODUCTION

In the summer of 1972, at the first rehearsal of what became a thrilling concert performance of *Aida* with the Los Angeles Philharmonic at the Hollywood Bowl, I met a young soprano who was making her American operatic debut and about whom I had heard much—but whose voice I had not heard at all. Friends who had had told me, "Just wait!" Fortunately I did not have to wait long; nor did I have to wait to discover that this brilliant young woman was well on her way to a fully realized career as one of the very rare sovereign artists.

Over the more than forty years since that day I have had the joy and privilege of making music with my friend, Jessye Norman. Indeed, we have evolved a simple and all-but-tacit language in our collaborative process so that we are able to react to one another instantly on stage. She is an extraordinarily dedicated artist, extremely disciplined, but at the same time deeply expressive, lively, and spontaneous in response to every detail demanded by the composer of whatever music is at hand. Our work has encompassed an especially diverse repertoire for voice and instruments —opera, oratorio, and *songs*!—dozens of small masterpieces of words and music for voice and piano; perhaps the most astonishing repertoire of all. Not every great composer wrote operas or oratorios but they all wrote songs—*glorious* songs: Beethoven, Schubert, Strauss, Mahler, Wagner, Brahms, Ravel, Debussy, Poulenc, Berg, Schumann, Schoenberg, Wolf, Ives, Copland, to name a few, and of course, "Anonymous," the most prolific of all, over many centuries, an incredibly vast collection of the world's folksongs and spirituals.

All of these composers provided us with far too many memorable collaborations to describe in this short introduction. That may have to wait for my memoir! But the shortest possible list of my favorites would have to include:

1. Our first "Recital with Orchestra" with the Chicago Symphony Orchestra, in which Jessye sang the entire program, just as she would in a recital with piano.
2. Beethoven's *Missa Solemnis* with the Vienna Philharmonic at the Salzburg Festival.
3. Mahler's Second Symphony with the Vienna Philharmonic at the Salzburg Festival on the occasion of Jessye's Salzburg debut.
4. Her performing as soloist in the first of what became an ongoing series of concerts with the Met Orchestra playing as a symphonic ensemble at Carnegie Hall.
5. The time Jessye sang both Cassandra *and* Dido in the same performance of *Les Troyens* at the Met.

6. The concert of Spirituals, with Kathleen Battle at Carnegie Hall.

7. Strauss's *Vier letzte Lieder* and Wagner's *Wesendonck Lieder* on the same program with the Berlin Philharmonic.

8. The rehearsals, performances, and recording sessions for Schoenberg's *Erwartung*.

9. The recording sessions for *Die Walküre, Parsifal,* and songs of Beethoven, Wolf, Debussy, and Schoenberg.

10. Lots of recitals, especially in Vienna, Salzburg, Chicago, and New York—and the unique Songbook series at Carnegie Hall.

Over the years at the Met, I was lucky to work with Jessye in dozens of exciting rehearsals and performances, starting with her unforgettable debut in *Les Troyens* on the opening night of the Metropolitan's one hundredth anniversary season. The excitement never flagged as she gradually built her singular Met repertoire: *Die Walküre, Parsifal, Tannhäuser, Erwartung, Bluebeard's Castle, Oedipus Rex, Ariadne auf Naxos, The Dialogues of the Carmelites, The Makropolus Case* ...

The book you hold in your hands is Jessye's latest work of art. Not a career chronicle like so many ("and then I did . . .") but the story of her magnificent life written in her own words—not the words of a "ghostwriter," and, of course, in her own voice as well. Her mastery of language goes hand-in-glove with her mastery of music and singing, and her work ethic is ideal! Would that it were a model for every singer.

In this fascinating memoir, you will feel Jessye's unique presence on every page—her passion, her sense of humor, and her full-scale zest for life. I recommend it as a "must-read," not only for her legion of admirers but also for the layman, for students of every age—everyone who cares about the artistic life.

James Levine
New York City
February 2014

PRELUDE

*I*t was a beautiful autumn when I found myself in Europe for the very first time, in bustling, stylish Munich. While completing a master's degree in vocal performance at the University of Michigan, I had been among the students selected from around the country by a special committee of the United States Information Agency to participate in international music competitions. I was thrilled to be taking part in the prestigious Bayerischer Rundfunk Internationaler Musikwettbewerb, the Bavarian Radio International Music Competition. Julius, a great friend and fine pianist whom I knew from my undergraduate days at Howard University, had traveled with me as my accompanist. There was electricity in the air: the whole city seemed to be involved in the events at the Bavarian Radio. All of the performances during the competition were to be held before a live audience.

The country Julius and I had left behind for these few weeks was on fire. The assassination of Dr. Martin Luther King Jr. the previous spring had sparked riots all over the States. Classes at

Berkeley had not taken place in months. Los Angeles, Detroit, and Newark were ablaze with the passion for peace and justice. Protesters marched, organized sit-ins, and took over administration buildings on college campuses. Attacks on Dr. King's legacy were as vicious as the trained-to-kill dogs, fire hoses, and smoke bombs directed at American citizens exercising their civil rights. Those sworn to protect and serve stood quietly on the sidelines or, worse still, joined the chorus of hate emanating from those sidelines.

The war in Vietnam had surely and steadily lost support, and no half-truths or presidential speeches beginning with the words "My fellow Americans" could douse the flames of revolution visible just across the street from the White House, in Lafayette Square. The country roared in opposition to the status quo. Europe was no less a hot spot, particularly in Paris, where student protests against university tuition payments and other concerns made for significant unrest. The world was most certainly in a state of evolution and revolution.

I had participated in mass meetings and protest marches, carrying signs exhorting NO JUSTICE, NO PEACE, and lending my voice to the song concluding almost every gathering, Pete Seeger's "We Shall Overcome." I understood that many organizations, with varying approaches to the fight for justice, were needed. No single civil rights group could channel every frustration, or rally everyone to stand tall in the face of those who would just as soon see us crawl away in defeat. Every voice needed to find its own place, its own platform from which the cry for freedom and equality could be heard.

Even though I was engaged increasingly in politics and social issues back home, I was enthralled by gorgeous Munich, and had few worries about my participation in this important competition. I felt that I was there to offer what I had been trained to do, first at Howard, then the Peabody Conservatory, and now at Michigan, with these very words from my mother in my ears from my earliest memories: stand up straight and sing!

Shortly after our arrival, Julius and I received the time slot for our appearance in the first round of the competition. All was well. Our performance time in hand, we went into a rehearsal room to make our final preparations, mindful of the wonderful honor that had been bestowed on us. Yes, we were here to represent ourselves, but more importantly, we were representing the United States of America in an international forum. We took this to heart.

Julius and I moved through the first round of competition with appreciation for all the work we had put into rehearsing and studying for this moment. We felt compelled to do even more, and work even harder in the next round. This was a serious event and an important time in our young lives, and we were grateful that we felt prepared.

Round Two.

A different kind of electricity surfaced in the second round of competition. Almost as soon as the names of those who had made it to the second round were announced, I was called into a room far away from the performance hall, without my friend Julius. There, the adjudicators of the competition suggested that having my own accompanist in Round One had given me an unfair advantage over the other singers. The fact that some of the other singers were participating with their pianist spouses or their coaches was not part of the discussion.

This was unusual behavior for a jury—and most assuredly against its own rules. Normally, there is absolutely no interaction between an adjudicator and a competitor. I was told that I would need to give up my accompanist and sing with one of the piano accompanists provided by the organizers. I did not know quite what was afoot, but I knew enough to request that the new pianist, Brian Lampert from London, should rehearse with me every single song and aria on my list, before I went forward in Round Two.

In the first round, competitors may make their own choices from the list of music approved at the time of their acceptance into the competition, as long as this does not exceed the performance time limit. In the second round, the jury chooses from that same list what the competitor will perform. In still another unusual move, the adjudicators summoned me a second time to discuss my second-round performance. This time I was advised that the jury wished me to sing something that was not on my previously submitted list of repertoire. To my knowledge, no other contestant was being offered such creative treatment.

Now, I had reviewed the requirements carefully for this competition and knew them by heart. I was therefore very comfortable in stating my case: "I am sure that you are not permitted, according to the rules governing the competition, to ask me to sing anything that is not on my list," I said. "And why would you want me to sing something I have not prepared, in any case?"

"Well," one judge said, "you have performed the second aria of

Elisabeth in *Tannhäuser* during the first round. We would like to hear you sing the first aria." I stated that I of course knew the first aria as well, but that my vocal professor and I felt that the first aria did not lend itself as a performance piece with piano nearly as well as with an orchestra. That was why this aria was not on my list.

To say that these adjudicators—an impressive slate of singers, accompanists, and music critics from around the world—were surprised by my response to their "request" would be something of an understatement, but I was not concerned. The audience had been advised already that I would be among those performing in the second round. I surmised that no one on the jury wanted the responsibility of having to explain that a change in the regulations of the competition, created especially for me, might well prevent my further participation in the event.

After a few more fruitless attempts to change my mind about singing the wonderful aria "Dich, teure Halle" ("You, dear treasured hall"), with piano, and with no small amount of intimidation, the jury members relented. I would sing what I had come prepared to sing.

The second round of the competition was completed, and more of the original eighty singers were eliminated. I was so happy to make it through to the final round. Not even the questionable behavior of the jury members had caused me to lose focus or concentration.

Round Three.

The third round of the competition was with orchestra, in Hercules Hall, the best of the concert venues in Munich at the time. The support I had from brand-new friends in my very first

European city, singing in the third and decisive round, was cause for even more giddy excitement.

With the thrill of being in Munich, I had not expected my participation in this competition to be met with the kind of challenges presented by the members of the jury. Julius and I had been more concerned with how our artistic readiness would compare to others from the different countries represented in Munich. I found a determination and a guiding spirit within myself in defending what I saw as my rights in this competition, the same clear guidance that drove my personal political growth and understanding.

I would sing what I had come prepared to sing. Whether in spite of or because of the judges, I was not the same young woman who had left the States just a few weeks earlier.

In the Beginning

"GREAT DAY!"

Great day, great day, the righteous marching,
Great day; God's gonna build up Zion's walls.
Chariot rode on the mountaintop,
God, He spoke and the chariot stop.
This the day of Jubilee,
God done set His people free!
Take my breastplate, sword in hand,
March out boldly through the land,
Want no cowards in our band,
Each must be a good, brave man.
Great day, great day the righteous marching,
Great day; God's gonna build up Zion's walls.

I am the joy and the pride of my maternal grandmother, looking out over a front yard overflowing with grandchildren. I am the steady and stern glance of my paternal grandfather, and the upbeat whistle pushing past my father's lips as he enjoys a ride in his very first car, that green, two-door Chevrolet. I am the warmth of my mother as she speaks the letters of the word *Mississippi* in rhythm, her special way of making spelling lessons more fun. They are all in my DNA: their beautiful blood, rich with the determination, the songs, the hope, the heartbreak, and the strength of my people, stretching back past the cocoon of my childhood home in Augusta, Georgia, beyond the most storied of concert halls, beyond the earth's surface, beyond, even, the nurturing glow of the African sun. Because they were, I am.

My ancestors' gift of song rustled the leaves of gnarled southern oaks and pines, whispered between the rows of the fields they tilled, danced in the winds just beyond the ocean's ripple, above the waters that brought my people and my blood to these shores. I am all who have made me: Mother Africa, the hills of Georgia, and these United States. My gift is uniquely my own, and yet it is also all of this. I pay homage to those who nurtured and nourished me. I stretch out and wrap my arms around them all.

There was always music, always. When we were small children, we would visit my mother's parents on their farm, where Grandma Mamie's voice would fill the quiet spaces. I loved to hear her sing. She had songs for every time of the day. Of course, when we kids were there, the quiet spaces were few, especially if we found our way to the organ. My grandparents were the only people I ever knew who had one — a grand pedal organ, or more accurately, a harmonium — right there in their house. It lived over in the corner of the front room, and I remember thinking that it was the most exotic thing I had ever encountered in my entire life. As far as I can recall, we were never stopped from playing it, nor admonished for disturbing the adults. My brothers Silas Jr. and Howard and I were too small to play the keyboard and work the pedals all at the same time; there just wasn't enough body on any one of the three of us to do so. But that did not stop us from trying. The knobs that indicated various stops were new to us, and that was part of the fun. By pulling one of them out, we changed the sound coming from the keys. It was too good to be true. We had all begun our piano lessons, so the keyboards of the instrument were familiar. There was something for each of us to do with that majestic box of wood and veneer, and the two rows of ivory and ebony that produced such magic. So we would split the duties: the boys would be responsible for the keys and I took the pedals, with the grand promise of reciprocation once it was my turn to finger a tune (or more likely simply press the keys down in no particular pattern, just for the thrill of it). I worked hard. I made sure the boys were having a great time on the keys while I stooped at the bottom of the bench and used my hands to make the pedals work and work. Of course, when it came time for me to play the keys, my brothers always found a reason to be somewhere else. No surprises there. Grandma Mamie, five feet ten in her stocking feet, with a mass of glorious white hair and Native American beauty dancing across her strong cheekbones and chestnut-colored skin, would just laugh; she never chastised the boys for leaving me on my own. And I did not really mind, either, as I could then have "the magic box" all to myself!

One could tell Grandma Mamie's mood by the songs she sang or hummed. It was very easy to do, even as a child. I always say that young children are as sensitive to mood swings as family puppies. Whatever you are feeling, they can sense it. I could tell just from her choice of song whether she was having a happy morning or whether her thoughts were uneasy. Happy moods brought offerings that were more spry, such as "In That Great Gettin' Up Morning, Hallelu, Hallelu." If you woke up from a peaceful slumber and heard her humming a tune like that, you knew instantly that this particular morning was good. Things were going well. By contrast, a slower, deeper, more mournful song, such as the hymn "Precious Lord, Take My Hand," indicated that Grandma Mamie was thinking about something, and that something was not bringing her joy at that particular moment. Whether happy or melancholy, whether we rejoiced with her or worried for her, Grandma's singing was always beautiful, deeply soulful, and right.

I was much too young to understand fully the depth of influence her singing had on me. All I knew was that I loved to look at her and to hear her voice. Years later, my heart and, perhaps, a bit of cellular memory made clear that the songs and phrases that lived in Grandma Mamie's breath, and the passion and emotion that flowed from her very core, had found their way into my young spirit. This became wonderfully apparent during a performance in 2000 of my production of the sacred music of Duke Ellington that I call *Sacred Ellington*. This took place in the beautiful Episcopal Cathedral in Philadelphia. I was accompanied on the piano by Mark Markham, a fine jazz band, and the dancer Margie Gillis, and was having quite a marvelous time with the audience when I decided I would add a couple of Spirituals as encores. That afternoon, I offered one of my favorites: "There's a Man Going 'Round Taking Names," a song popularized in the early twentieth century by the folk singer Lead Belly.

There's a man going 'round taking names.
There's a man going 'round taking names.
He has taken my father's name,
And he's left my heart in pain.
There's a man going 'round taking names. . . .

To this day, I have no idea what came over me when, without thinking, I walked down from the stage and began moving through the aisles, taking in the faces of all who were there and really connecting with each individual as I sang and glided through this deeply sacred space.

I had never done that before in my life.

It was not until after the concert, as my family and friends gathered to celebrate the birthday of my older brother, Silas Jr., that it was revealed why, exactly, I had broken with normal protocol and left the stage and gone into the aisles. It was Silas who made me understand. "There's no way that you could possibly remember this," he said simply as we sat together at dinner. "You were too young."

"Remember what?" I asked.

"That Grandma Mamie would get up from her pew at the church on Sunday mornings and sing Spirituals as she walked around the entire church," Silas said, referring to Hilliard Station Baptist Church in Washington, Georgia. "She used these moments to greet her neighbors and just enjoy offering her singing so freely to everyone."

For a moment, we were silent. You can imagine that this revelation sent chills through me. I truly had no recollection of this magnificent woman walking around the church while she sang. I could not have been more than about four years old at the time, but Silas would have been about eight—old enough to have that lovely memory. To me, he was divinely ordered to be at that performance in Philadelphia, and to connect me with our beloved grandmother. She was speaking through me then. She speaks through me now.

My mother, Janie King Norman, had that singing spirit in her as well. She sang all kinds of songs, most of them Spirituals and offerings from the church. She taught me to sing one or the other of them, for programs at the church, or at Girl Scouts, or wherever I would sing in the community. She had such a beautiful voice. As a young woman, she performed frequently for church and community functions with three of her seven sisters. As a group, they were well known around Washington, Georgia.

Songs were my mother's friends—her confidants. They accompanied her while she did whatever she was doing during the course of the day, from tending to the many details of running a busy household, to keeping the financial books of the church, to, it seemed, serving as the secretary for every organization of which she was a member. It was from her that I learned a true appreciation of music and of the beauty of filling the whole house with it. It was with her and through her that I felt free to sing with as much joy and power as was within me. I was never told that I should "be quiet."

If you ask me outright, I always say singing and speaking became a part of me at the same time. My brothers had a lot of fun teasing me about this. "Soon," they laughed, "you'll be telling everyone you were singing in the womb." All joking aside, I cannot recall a period in my life when I was not singing—when music was not at the very center of all that I enjoyed. But it was the radio that informed this little girl in Augusta, Georgia, of a much wider world —made me know, for sure, that music was bigger than the voices I heard in my house, on my grandparents' farm, or in my town. I was all of ten or eleven years old when this revelation flowed through that brown and beige radio, my very own radio in my very own bedroom. There were the voices of Nat "King" Cole, Ella Fitzgerald, and Dinah Washington, the music of Duke Ellington, Dizzy Gillespie, and Louis Armstrong, the Tommy Dorsey band, Sister Rosetta Tharpe, and Mahalia Jackson. They all spoke to me—captivated my ears and my senses. I can still remember a day when I heard Nat "King" Cole sing the beautiful song "Stardust." I asked my parents to purchase the sheet music for me, and they obliged happily. The cover of the sheet music was cloud-blue with an image of the great singer. I was quite proud to have my very own copy. I wanted to sing "Stardust," too!

Surely, those early years marked the beginning of my abiding love of music—all kinds of music. And this was most revelatory on Saturday afternoons, when it was time for my weekly chores. There was cleaning to be done in the kitchen and in my own room, tasks that, when performed with proficiency, would have taken no more than a couple of hours for the average child who wanted to get out of the house and bask in the light of the sun or conquer the tallest limb of the biggest tree or go off exploring on a bike. But because I really felt that I was being put upon when asked to contribute in this small measure to our housecleaning, I made my duties stretch the entire length of the opera broadcast that I discovered on that magic box, my radio. My program of choice: the

Saturday-afternoon broadcasts of the Metropolitan Opera. Lucky for me, my mother entertained this preference of mine, in part because she simply wanted the work done, and perhaps also because, deep down, she adored having a daughter who was developing a love for beautiful music. Neither she nor I paid much attention to all the fun my brothers had at my expense. They thought my listening to opera was too grand for words. I mean, they thought it was simply comical that I pretended to understand opera—to really like the voices, the orchestra, and the drama, along with all the various languages that were sung. But I wasn't pretending at all. You see, anyone who is anywhere near my age and had the great fortune to listen to those broadcasts on Saturday afternoons knows that Milton Cross, long the voice of the Metropolitan Opera, told you everything you needed to know about that day's performance. So it did not matter whether or not you had ever heard or seen the opera being performed. Milton Cross made sure that his listeners knew what the singers looked like, what they were wearing, what the set looked like, the entire story of the opera as it proceeded—everything you needed and wanted to know. You saw all of this in your mind's eye, and your imagination took care of the rest.

One of the first operas I recall hearing was *Lucia di Lammermoor,* in the late 1950s. This would have been with Roberta Peters in the lead, and other times with Mattiwilda Dobbs. Later, in the early '60s, the role of Lucia was taken over by a soprano new to me: the great Joan Sutherland. The well-known ensemble from this luscious opera stayed in my mind, and I remember humming the melody to myself rather often. At some point, I even enjoyed a cartoon showing animals on a tree limb "singing" this very melody. It is amazing how such beautiful music can enter the spirit and simply live there.

This is to say that I simply loved the whole idea of an opera performance. And as the dreams of children know no bounds, I thought about singing this music—certainly not as a profession, but simply singing it because it was beautiful to me and I loved it as much as I loved listening to the music of everybody else on my radio. I remember thinking that opera stories were not very different from other stories: a boy meets a girl, they fall in love, they cannot be together for some reason, and most of the time it does not end happily ever after. For me, opera stories were grown-up versions of stories that were familiar to me already. The way that I felt about the opera as a child was no different from how I feel about opera now. Duke Ellington once said these words, which I find just as profound today as when I first heard them: "There are two kinds of music: good music and the other kind." Some of that good music was written by Mozart and Beethoven and Bach. Thank goodness, too, that some of that good music was written by Rodgers and Hammerstein and George Gershwin and Ellington himself. The good music that I sang as a child included children's songs, hymns learned at the church, and, of course, Spirituals. My enthusiasm for good music only increased in the choir stands of Mount Calvary Baptist Church and in the school choruses at C. T. Walker Elementary, A. R. Johnson Junior High School, and Lucy C. Laney High. I sang in the assembly halls of local community groups and all types of organizations, even in the living rooms and yards of our neighbors. I was part of a small group of kids who were interested in the arts and were invited to give performances. Some of us sang, some played piano, some gave recitations and acted in plays and such. It was just something that we all did and loved.

When I say now that we were completely interchangeable as performers, I mean we were completely interchangeable. This is absolutely true. Aside from the fact that I knew I could sing with more power than some of my peers, there was no acknowledgment whatsoever that my voice was any more special than that of any of my friends who sang. I realized early in my professional life—and I still celebrate it now—that I was very lucky to have that part of my life unfold in such a way. None of us children were given reason to consider ourselves more special than the other. Yet collectively, we were special in the eyes of the community that nurtured and supported us. We were lucky to have had the support of our parents, teachers, and other influential adults in our lives. They understood the importance of these meaningful interactions, both to our early socialization and to the development of our communication skills, the ability to express ourselves in front of others comfortably and confidently—skills that would turn out to be extremely valuable later.

My parents were constant observers of how my siblings and I deported ourselves, what our school responsibilities were, what we were meant to be doing on any given day. I can still see myself standing in the hallway, with my mother getting herself ready for the day and my father preparing to take us to school, reciting a poem that my school's class was charged with presenting on Monday mornings. My father would say, "Now, you've got your poem ready?" And I would say, "Yes, of course, Daddy." And I would recite it, stumbling all the way, and my mother would say what she always said: "Stand up straight, honey." I can still hear her voice. *Stand up straight.* And even on this day, I am sure she is looking down on me, saying the same thing, particularly when I fall into resting in my right hip, a lifelong tendency. When I realize I am doing it, I do my best to correct my posture. *Stand up straight.*

The act of standing in front of crowds, large and small, and offering a performance of some kind, was as natural as passing around the Ritz crackers with pimiento cheese at the end of a program. I do not remember my first solo performance (though there are a number of stories circulating, purporting to know what my first song was), but I do know that my big numbers around age five were "Jesus Loves Me" and "Jesus Wants Me for a Sunbeam."

Church gatherings on Sunday afternoons were held often in the living rooms of members of the congregation, and there were many times when this took place in our home. My mother would play the piano and I would sing something, and then I would go back outside to continue playing with my friends. (I was particularly fond of playing jacks with the girls of the neighborhood.) Even though being called into the house to perform interrupted my playtime, I was always happy to do the actual singing. I would be rewarded with cookies and juice from the grownups' dessert plates. Those Sunday-afternoon gatherings were called silver teas, as the funds collected for the church's activities were not expected to be grand sums of money, so "silver" could be offered, rather than dollar bills. They were far more important as social occasions than as fundraisers.

I sang my first opera aria in junior high school, under the direction of the choral director, Mrs. Rosa Sanders, who had decided that I should learn a special song: "My Heart at Thy Sweet Voice," from the opera *Samson and Delilah* by Camille Saint-Saëns. Of course, I knew the story of Samson and Delilah from Sunday school, but I did not speak French, the language in which the opera was written. Instead, I learned the song in English and sang it at various churches, recreation centers, and even at a supermarket opening around the Augusta area. After we had done that for a while, Mrs. Sanders decided that I could move on to singing the aria in French. We found a recording of the great mezzo-soprano Risë Stevens performing it and I mimicked her, singing it precisely as she did. I would listen to the recording over and over again, sing a bit, and then listen again. When it was time to sing the aria in French in front of my middle school peers, with the school band accompanying my performance, I was excited. I do think that if you can stand up and sing in French in front of an assembly full of middle-schoolers, then you can do just about anything. Can't you just see the unchecked expressions of boredom on the faces of the boys, most particularly the popular boys who participated in athletics? I took absolutely no notice. Mrs. Sanders was happy, my other teachers were happy, my group of pals supported me, so all was well!

This kind of recollection reminds me to acknowledge the presence of grace in our lives. I sing and I truly enjoy doing so and have done so practically all of my time here on this earth. I live a blessed life, filled with the sounds of music. I take enormous pleasure in seeing the effect that music can have on the emotions and the spirits of people. It is wonderful to hear from music lovers that they listen to a particular recording on occasions special to them or that they feel a kinship with my music because it has come to mean something important in their lives. I do not take such sentiments for granted. I know that making music that means something to someone else is a privilege.

I noticed this as a youngster in church on Sunday mornings. The pastor would preach the Gospel, and with every crescendo, the parishioners cried a little louder, their tears flowing freely. I thought there was something very special about being a preacher. I came to understand and to appreciate that this wonderful exchange of energy from person to person is something that is alive. A similar kind of thing happens on the musical stage when we are very lucky.

Widmung • ROBERT SCHUMANN • Dedication

Du meine Seele, du mein Herz,	You, my heart and soul,
Du meine Wonn', O du mein Schmerz,	You, my happiness and woe,
Du meine Welt, in der ich lebe,	You, the world in which I live,
Mein Himmel du, darin ich schwebe,	The heaven to which I rise,
O du mein Grab, in das hinab ich ewig	You, the deep well into which I place
Meinen Kummer gab.	my troubles.
Du bist die Ruh, du bist der Frieden,	You, the calm and peace,
Du bist vom Himmel mir beschieden,	My gift from above.

Dass du mich liebst, macht mich mir wert,	Your love leads me to value myself,
Dein Blick hat mich vor mir verklärt,	Your glance gives me understanding of myself,
Du hebst mich liebend über mich,	Your love raises me to a greater height,
Mein guter Geist, mein bessres Ich.	My best spirit, my best self.

A Mother's Joy

"I WANT TWO WINGS"

> *I want two wings to fly away,*
> *I want two wings, to be at rest.*
> *I want two wings to veil my face,*
> *I want two wings to be at rest.*
> *Lordy, want you help me,*
> *Lordy want you help me to run this race.*

*I*t is, perhaps, the scars on my legs that tell the story of sticky hot days in the Georgia sun, playing tag and hide-and-seek in the schoolyards and at home in Augusta or amid the thick stalks of corn on my maternal grandparents' farm. Those scars tell tales, too, of roller-skating—unsteady, more than a little wobbly—on the L-shaped pavement over at Liberty Baptist Church, and riding bicycles down the bumpy, graveled streets of our neighborhood (our streets were not paved until I was about twelve years old). The scars remind me of those glorious days when the games that boys played together held my sharp attention. I was not at all good at them, but I wished much more to play softball and basketball than partake in the activities and events reserved solely for a girl child of the 1950s. I never learned to sew properly, or crochet or knit. I could never sit still long enough to pick up those skills. None of that was nearly as interesting to me as what was happening on our street, where the boys swathed themselves in fun, adventure, and, above all else, a delicious freedom to just . . . be.

Of course, I had a mother who, with two rough-and-tumble sons to usher into manhood, was happy with the shot of estrogen that came with having a little girl. Every bit of that desire played itself out in the way she dressed me. She was the architect of my most fancy wardrobe. There were dresses with Peter Pan collars, and pintucked tops, and organdy for Sunday, and great big bows that tied perfectly in the back, with black patent leather Mary Jane shoes shined with a little petroleum jelly just so — bangs and pigtails coaxed straight on Saturday nights with the scorch of the hot comb and a few fingerfuls of Royal Crown hairdressing, then gathered neatly with ribbons. Nothing pleased Janie Norman more than to see her little girl looking like, well, a little girl.

I LIKED DRESSING UP, and I would oblige my mother's wishes for me to walk instead of run, and to stop and recover should my sash get caught on the door handle, rather than just pull away, torn sash and all, in my mad rush hither and yon. But really, I was fascinated with what my brothers and their friends were allowed to do. Alas, wearing sneakers and climbing trees and skinning my knees on the hard pavement was but a dollop of salve for my independent spirit — the spirit of a baby boomer whose generation had yet to even begin a serious conversation about the liberation of girls and women.

Girls were born, given a certain amount of schooling, then they were married, were mothers and homemakers and, if they worked at all, were limited to very specific kinds of jobs, not meant to leave a real mark on the world outside of their homes. Too few of our elders seemed to imagine a bigger world for us.

I craved bigger. And I found it hard, even at an early age, to fit my mind, body, and spirit into the too-tiny box carved out for girls and women of my generation. After all, I was raised by the hand of Janie Norman in a family full of strong women. There was my maternal grandmother, my mother, her seven sisters, and my four paternal aunts—each firm in their stance that none of us should be hampered by the limitations saddled on the shoulders of women. Each of them provided daily inspiration to simply "get on with it" —to grow into the best woman I could be, no matter the hurdles, despite the odds. My aunt Veronia, for example, was an ordained minister who would dress up, complete with heels, a handbag, and gloves, just to go the grocery store, because she felt one "ought to do so." She also wrote books and held such glamorous events as "book signing parties." One of my paternal aunts was named Cleopatra, and though we called her Aunt Cleo, she wore her full name splendidly, majestic and proud! Another paternal aunt, Louise, traveled often to Ghana, and wore fabulous African clothing that on someone else would have resembled a costume. They were amazing women.

My mother was the very embodiment of a woman who worked through gender limitations—a person who made no excuses, stood up for herself with the perfect mixture of strength and grace, and who managed to be much more than her country had come to expect of an African American woman raised on a farm in Washington, Georgia. Janie Norman was educated and an educator—a middle school teacher who found a career long before she found a husband (she married my father, Silas Norman Sr., when she was twenty-seven, which, in that era, meant that she was in danger of being labeled an old maid by the time she said "I do"). It was not easy for women—mothers, in particular—to have careers, when veterans were heading back to the States to reclaim their jobs and the media continually spread the message that women should be keeping the home and raising children while the men earned their keep. My mother followed her passion and poured her very soul into the betterment of African American children who, at the time, counted on their own communities to give them what segregation denied them: a fighting chance in a country that had yet to allow those of African descent to participate fully in the pursuit of the American ideal. Great progress has been made, yet still there is so very much to do. My mother and countless others are counting on us.

Still, being black and a woman and a mother had its limitations. It was not really an option for most women, no matter their skin color, to work full-time, willingly, and raise children, and this was true for her. So she relinquished teaching for the joy of raising and teaching her own family. Fortunately for her, my father was a determined provider. He was also a man who saw himself absolutely as the head of our household. His job as a manager at the North Carolina Mutual Life Insurance Company's branch office in Augusta, and his Saturday evenings spent with other deacons from our church looking after the grooming of the locals in our community barbershop, made it somewhat easier for my mother to be at home, pouring her love of books and words directly into my siblings and me.

She spent an incredible amount of time with us—nurturing, disciplining, teaching, encouraging, loving. By the time we were four years old or so, we all knew how to read, thanks to my mother, who employed rhythm and movement to help us learn how to spell and understand language. This was long before we were calling this kind of thing rap or hip-hop, mind you. To this day, I still spell *Mississippi* in the rhythmic way my mother taught me. With a nod to my mother's efforts, I entered first grade only to find myself bored silly with my teacher and fellow students. I remember coming home from school one day, absolutely indignant after long hours dealing with youngsters who could not so much as recite their ABCs, let alone read a book. "Mother, do you know that those children don't know how to read?" I asked, exasperated. In my very young mind, any child in first grade who did not know his ABCs and was not reading books had wasted five good years of learning. Little did I know that what I had at home—a mother who saw bigger things for me and who had, too, the ability to pour that foundation of knowledge into me with sure intensity—was something quite special.

It was during the summertime that other children got to experience the wonder that was Janie Norman, the teacher, in their own lives. She volunteered as an instructor at Vacation Bible School, with a special interest in what she used to call her "juniors"—what we know today as middle-schoolers, or students between the ages of eleven and fourteen. She was committed to the idea of grabbing hold of children in that particular age group, just when their hormones are going crazy and they stop being lap children and do not want to be cuddled so much in public. Yet they are not as grown-up as they like to think and still need that cuddle, though they hesitate to ask for help because they don't want to seem like babies. Others might compare teaching this age group to running toward a wildfire. But Mother truly believed that if you could get juniors, particularly the girls, to develop a sense of themselves, their own worth and that of their bodies—specifically, that they have the right to all that the world has to offer—that they would have this understanding forever. She knew, too, that there was only a relatively small window of time in which to reach this age group, to fuss and advise and answer questions and really help them gain that sense of their complete selves, before they found themselves burdened with trying to fix those parts of themselves they could not accept or understand, for the rest of their lives. I thank my mother for that gift—for showing me the importance and beauty of self-worth.

PRACTICING ONE'S SENSE of oneself outside the home, though, could prove challenging, since speaking one's mind and railing against the expected path, if you were a girl, was not really acceptable, not really the thing to do. Indeed, on the other side of our front door, girls and women were supposed to accept the limitations placed on them by an inflexible society, and they were expected to make the best of it. This much was made clear by the time I was thirteen and not only old enough, smart enough, and bold enough to have an opinion, but foolish enough to actually express it out loud. It was my home economics teacher, Ms. Reynolds, who was the focus of my complaint. School schedules and rules notwithstanding, I simply did not understand why, when I finally made it to middle school, there was such a rigorous effort by the grownups in my life to guide my thoughts and actions, particularly where this teacher and the course that she taught were concerned. Our differing points of view were apparent almost as soon as my body connected with the little wooden desks in her home economics class—around the same moment she announced that we girls were going to learn how to prepare meals and sew the perfect stitch, so that later in life we could be useful, or some such. Well, I had sense enough to keep my opinions about these things to myself during class; after all, I was not a difficult child or a revolutionary or anything like that. But I did allow myself to have a word with my teacher after class, out of earshot of my classmates, to let her know that I was not in the least interested in learning how to sew and cook. "What I would prefer to do is take shop," I said simply. "I would like to learn how to make a table. Could you arrange that, please?"

There was method to my madness. I didn't just want to get out of home economics; learning how to make a table seemed like fun. My father fancied himself a weekend carpenter and I would watch him with his nails and his hammer and his insistence that he was going to build something and make it work. I was impressed by it all, even if my father seldom had time to complete the numerous projects he began. Often, it would end with his calling in another deacon from the church to help finish whatever it was that he had started. But really, there was a joy he had when he swung that hammer, no matter to whom the credit of completion was awarded. I wanted to experience that—much more so than I wanted to take time to study something that I imagined I would "pick up" in life somewhere along the way.

I thought my request was quite simple. But for dear Ms. Reynolds, a girl who wanted to bend the rules was quite complex— much too complex, surely, for her taste and sensibility. "Girls," she responded, "do not take shop."

For her, that was the end of the discussion. For me, it was the beginning of my own little one-girl war against home economics and the teacher who insisted I learn to prepare meals and sew. The battlefield was the classroom, where I made a point of showing up to class and reading while Ms. Reynolds taught my fellow students the art of "setting the perfect table" or some other important (to her) lesson. It did not take long for me to find myself in the principal's office.

Now, the sight of a Norman child in the principal's office did not usually signal trouble. Mr. Reese, the principal, was my father's good friend and so all of us knew him well. He took great joy in seeing us, good students who had respect for our elders, who loved school and had the ability to participate in school activities and still get good grades. This, however, was not a friendly visit. As you can imagine, Mr. Reese was surprised to find out that I had been sent to his office by one of my teachers. Explaining why I was there and making my request to switch from home economics to shop class only made matters worse. "Oh, we can't do that," Mr. Reese said confidently. "There are only boys in the class."

"Oh, I'll be fine," I said matter-of-factly, thinking he was just concerned that I would be uncomfortable in a classroom full of boys. "I have brothers. Uncles. Cousins. I'm surrounded by boys."

Let's just say Mr. Reese and I did not see eye to eye. My parents were summoned to the school to assist in my getting it through my head that table making was for male students and learning to sew was the province of girls and that I would remain in home economics because this was as it should be. And so I stayed. But I did my best to avoid any heavy lifting of sewing needles, fabric, spatulas, pots and pans, or anything else that had to do with housekeeping. And my mother was my willing accomplice. She even helped me complete one of my sewing assignments—the one in which I had to make my own apron. It was a project I started in class but had neither the interest nor the inclination to spend days on something that I knew my mother could complete in all of about fifteen minutes. So I took my half-sewn apron home with me one day. My mother sewed it all up in, quite literally, minutes, and I took it back to school and turned it in on time.

Ms. Reynolds was not fooled. "This stitch didn't come from our sewing machines," she said, holding the apron up to the light.

"No, it did not," I said without hesitation. "My mother did it. It is finished."

Of course, this spelled more trouble for me.

The absolute last straw for me was the day Ms. Reynolds announced that we were going to learn how to prepare breakfast and set a breakfast table and then let the boys come into the home economics class and enjoy the fruits of our labor. Now, to understand how insulting this was to my young being, you must first digest how I felt about boys at this time in my young life: I thought they should have their own planet. I did not see why they needed to be here, spoiling all the fun. My brothers and male cousins and their friends had a habit of "borrowing" my things and then not knowing where they were when I asked to have them back. I may have envied them their games and their freedoms and, yes, their shop class, but boys themselves, not very much. It would take only a very short time for my feelings toward them to change, however. But I interpreted Ms. Reynolds's lesson plan as making the girls subservient to the boys in our class and I did not want any part of that.

I did not say this out loud, though. Instead, I asked to arrange the flowers for the breakfast tables. I have always loved flowers —big, bountiful blooms like the ones that grew on the fruit trees in our backyard and the rosebushes so beloved by my mother and our next-door neighbor, Miss Daisy, and in the fields on my grandparents' farm. Flower arrangements were fun for me and I was happy to do this, but my refusal to participate in the cooking part of the breakfast event did not endear myself to the home economics teacher.

This landed me back in the principal's office. And once again, my parents were summoned as well.

"Little Norman," Mr. Reese scolded, "this kind of behavior is going to bring your grade average down. You don't want to do that."

"I do not want to do that," I agreed.

The lecture was never ending, and my parents were none too pleased with it all. Yet when that meeting with Mr. Reese was over and my parents were leaving, my mother took my hand into hers, squeezed it, and said, ever so quietly, "Good for you."

· · ·

JANIE NORMAN DID not raise me to take a back seat to anyone. However, as a girl child there were restrictions that drew clear distinctions between the freedoms my brothers and their friends enjoyed that were not extended to me. There was no staying out playing in the street after dark. No leaving the house without letting someone know where I was going. Girls needed protecting. My mother understood instinctively that, even in what we considered a safe community, no good came from letting a young girl roam about without her parents knowing exactly where she was, who she was with, and when her feet would cross the threshold of the front door and usher her into the warmth, comfort, and safety of her parents' home. At age twelve or thirteen, one cannot see the fairness in the fact of a younger brother having more freedom than his big sister, but then, at such an age, one can also be completely unaware of the danger that lurks, or that gender has anything to do with it.

Still, despite the physical restrictions, my mother had the wherewithal to encourage me to be independent—to square my shoulders and know, really know, that I could do anything well if I put my mind to it. My siblings sometimes laugh about the "propaganda" we heard in the house at the time (we had learned that word and thought we were being clever in applying it to our parents' disciplinary habits behind their backs). Their concern, of course, was firmly rooted in a specific place and time in the history of our nation, in the Deep South, where our people marched, bled, and soldiered their way through the civil rights movement. Every image of African Americans being run down with water hoses and chased by dogs brought long lectures from them about how each of us was born a child of the Creator and that we were just as good as anyone who breathes on this planet. I can still hear their voices, clear as a Sunday-morning church bell: "You may have to work twice as hard to show that you are as good. That is a fact of life," they would say. "But you can do it. And you must. And you must always do your best. You must always show your best side."

These lectures carried over into absolutely everything we did. "You must practice your piano lesson so that next time you can play better than you played the last time you were there." "You must practice reciting that poem every day instead of waiting until the very last minute to learn it by heart." Such things were said all the time. I thought otherwise because in my young mind, having to work twice as hard was simply unfair. The very idea of having to work harder than someone else in order to receive the same reward did not seem right to me. But I understood what my parents were saying on a practical level, and I knew that if this was what I had to do, then this was what I would do. It was a pleasure to make our parents happy; they rejoiced in good grades at school and in compliments from other adults who thought well of something that one of us managed to accomplish.

The civil rights of my people did not become linked to those of women, for me, until much later. There were just so many marvelous women in my own family, my community, the schools, my church, and our social clubs, seemingly unhampered from moving mountains and lifting their voices, that the connection between racism and sexism was not immediate. I admired, for example, the social studies teacher who had been a member of the Women's Army Corps during the Korean War, and who was instrumental in making sure that we girls understood our womanhood and that it was something to be cherished and respected by our boyfriends. I did not consciously consider the importance of her presence in my life as a youngster, or that of all my amazing aunts. Understanding the groundbreaking work of the likes of Betty Friedan and Gloria Steinem would not come until later.

It is said often that the world might be a more loving and kinder place if there were more women at the head of governments. I surely feel that a more equitable presence for women in governing bodies worldwide would make a difference. Sexism plays out in different ways in different parts of the world, due in large part to a lack of understanding of history, and the way women of old moved and molded their world. I recall a conversation with a terrific woman president of an American university who stated that at the time that she was being interviewed by the school's board of trustees, one member stated that she, being a woman, would most surely not require the services of a full-time cook, although such a provision had always been offered by this very institution to all of her predecessors, all of whom had been men. Sexism is still very much a part of our culture, to say nothing of sexual and domestic violence against women and the current backlash against long-fought-for and hard-won civil liberties for women. Oh yes, a great deal has been accomplished, but much work remains.

It is remarkable that still today, there are so few female orchestral conductors, and that I have worked, astonishingly, with only two: Jane Glover and Rachael Worby. Jane Glover and I presented a celebration of women in history as a Great Performers from Lincoln Center production in the mid-'90s. Not only did we have Jane as conductor, but our first violinist, always referred to as "the concertmaster," was also female. The repertoire chosen for the production reviewed legendary women characters and roles: Delilah, Berenice, Dido, Carmen, and many more. It was an undertaking that has not been repeated, to my knowledge, in which a singer offered a performance with orchestra, singing every single piece of music on the program. I remain very proud of this and the tremendous ease and pleasure with which we all worked together.

With Rachael Worby, I have performed a very varied repertoire, combining the music of George Gershwin and Duke Ellington in the same programming as Mozart and Saint-Saëns, for example. Our work in Europe, Africa, the Middle East, and Asia has provided a magnificent opportunity for many to experience a female conductor for the very first time and we find that orchestras and audience members alike are delighted to have such an experience. At her home base with the orchestra, MUSE/IQUE in Pasadena, California, it is wonderful to witness the fun that they all have together. The mutual respect and the joyful music-making are evident in every moment of preparation and result in performances that remain in the spirit for a long time.

I am blessed not to have had a thought of allowing myself to be held back, no matter my color or gender. I have simply become an adult version of that budding teenager who was more interested in cabinetmaking than in cooking. I do not take a simple path in my professional life. I was cautioned early on that I would have an easier time of it were I to follow the unwritten rule of African American female opera singers—and we do not comprise a very long list—in concentrating my stage life on the works of Italian composers rather than pursuing my interests in the music of the French, Germans, and Austrians. Still, I follow my own path, one that is filled with challenges, which I meet and accept, sometimes joyfully, sometimes reluctantly, but which I confront nonetheless.

For instance, it seems that society in general and the media in particular take great pleasure in holding women to almost impossible standards of physical attractiveness, then using that meager yardstick to assess intelligence, worth, and capabilities. I have not been spared this foolishness. One of the most egregious instances of it in my own life came during a *60 Minutes* interview with Morley Safer.

Now, preparing for this particular national television show was no mean feat, considering that I was then in the midst of a demanding schedule, appearing in Robert Wilson's production of Gluck's masterpiece *Alceste* at the Chicago Lyric Opera. The day of the interview, I woke and nourished myself, did my hair and makeup, arranged my clothing, and prepared to be interviewed by a person who was completely new to me, all while recovering from a performance the evening before. As it turned out, I arrived for the interview uncharacteristically late. (I had tried to have the interview moved to an hour more suitable to my obligations of the moment, but this was to no avail. Morley Safer had scheduled it at this particular hour so that he would be able to return to New York that evening.)

In agreeing to do the interview, I had only one stipulation which was brought forward by Philips, the recording company that had made the arrangements with CBS and accepted, I was told, by the *60 Minutes* team. I wanted the piece to be centered around my performing, rather than my personal life. I did not want cameras invading my middle school, high school, churches, or other places in Augusta, Georgia, inventing an idea of my past. I had seen interviews of this type previously and found them rather painful, if not completely embarrassing for all involved. I was assured that my wishes would be honored.

I should have known that the *60 Minutes* interview would be a challenge when Morley Safer skipped my performance the previous evening. While speaking with him as we prepared to shoot, with microphones being arranged and camera positions and lighting tested, I could see that he would be guided by questions written on three- by five-inch index cards, none of which had been offered to me as a courtesy beforehand. (Neither was I given access to the edited product prior to its being telecast in the early part of 1991.)

Imagine my utter surprise, then, when I gathered with my friends in a hotel suite in the city, where we thought we would make a party of watching the telecast, only to find a portrait marked by incomplete thoughts, misleading editing, and, much to my dismay, footage of Augusta. Against my stated wishes, *60 Minutes* had visited my hometown. They had filmed at Mount Calvary Baptist Church, where our family worshipped, describing my smart-as-a-whip sister, Elaine, as the choir director, without bothering to add that she also has an MBA and was then a student at the Medical College of Georgia School of Nursing, with intentions of becoming a nursing supervisor, the profession she practices to this day. Surprises like this one kept coming, with the biggest of all eliciting a concerted gasp from my pals and stunned silence from me when Safer announced that the opera *Carmen* was my favorite role. "Jessye Norman's majestic proportions," Safer intoned in a voice-over during footage of me singing the role in question, "have kept her from performing on the opera stage the role she may love most." I have to admit, I am not sure what he said after that, because the room erupted in indignation: "What on earth is he talking about, Jessye?" my friends demanded. "When would you have said such a thing?"

The answer to this question is very simple: Morley Safer never posed the question of my favorite role; he had asked me nothing about my performing in *Carmen*. Had he bothered to ask, I would have responded in the way that I always do: I sing only the roles that I love, and my favorite opera role is the one that I am singing at the moment. If I'd had the opportunity, I would also have informed him that I am not one to equate dress size and artistic performance.

As it happens, I had only recently declined an invitation to appear in a new production of *Carmen* in a leading European house. I was very pleased to have received this invitation, and the conductor had even offered me the opportunity to discuss with him the question of who would direct the production. I explained at the time that whereas several of my colleagues, two or three of them African American, were singing this fabulous opera, not one American and surely not one of my race was engaged in the female leading roles of Wagner, the operas on which I was concentrating my performance life during that period. My dress size did not influence my choice or my opportunities to perform onstage.

What is clear is that Morley Safer steered clear of engaging me in a discussion about body mass, and that more than likely his statement about *Carmen* was included in the segment by a producer as a way of addressing "the issue" without eliciting any commentary from me. Not that he would have gotten it had he asked: I am comfortable speaking about myself when the conversation is conducted with respect and the understanding that I consider my health a personal matter and not a social issue. When I happened to have run into Mike Wallace later that year, I did not feel the need to pretend that I had been pleased with the segment. Because he was a professional and this was surely not the first time he had come across a "dissatisfied customer," he did not seem to take any offense at my statement of unhappiness. We soon found ourselves in conversation about other things, including the sheer beauty of Martha's Vineyard.

I, like too many other women, have also experienced financial shenanigans due to gender. Such was the case in one of my favorite European cities. It is a very old custom practiced in a number of theaters in Europe to offer performing artists their payment in cash, in small envelopes doled out by a member of the staff, most often during the intermission of a performance. This is not something that I enjoy, as I am often less than careful with my handbag, and most of my friends will tell you readily that I hardly ever carry cash. On this particular occasion, the person responsible for these payments appeared dutifully backstage and began his job of handing out the pay packets to the soloists. Mercifully, he had waited until the completion of the performance of the great *Requiem* of Giuseppe Verdi.

No sooner had I begun to peek inside the envelope he'd offered me than this man circled back to say, "Oh, I made a mistake. I gave you the tenor's large fee." And with that, he pulled the fat envelope out of my hand and pushed a second, thinner envelope in my direction. "This is yours."

Rather surprised, I mustered, "I beg your pardon?"

Confusion flooded his face. It was clear that he did not understand my question. Even though I did not raise my voice or furrow my brow, I made it plain that I perceived an injustice. I have no idea how much more the tenor was being paid, and I had not been unhappy with my own fee. What I cared about was that this organization had offered a male performer a larger fee and felt this to be proper behavior. Need I state that I have never performed with this organization again?

My sense of self was inspired and nurtured by Janie Norman, her mother, her sisters, and the women who came before them—the people of whom I am fearlessly and wonderfully made. They taught me to speak out when necessary and to act, always. That is the "get on with it" that is steeped deep in my soul. It is my legacy as a "Little Norman"—a legacy of strength. A reverence for honesty and a will to speak to inequity when it rears its head, even in the form of a thinner envelope.

Ave Maria · FRANZ SCHUBERT · Holy Mother

Ave Maria, Jungfrau mild,	Holy Mother, mild
Erhöre einer Jungfrau Flehen,	Hear the virgin's prayer
Aus diesem Felsen starr und wild	From the untamed rocky ground
Soll mein Gebet zu dir hinwehen.	This prayer comes to thee.
Wir schlafen sicher bis zum Morgen,	We rest protected until the morning

Ob Menschen noch so grausam sind.	Although we people are unfaithful to Thy laws.
O Jungfrau, sieh der Jungfrau Sorgen,	Oh Virgin, look upon the virgin's sorrows
O Mutter, hör ein bittend Kind.	Oh Mother, hear a praying child.
Ave Maria, unbefleckt,	Holy Mother, pure
Wenn wir auf diesen Fels hinsinken	We rest upon this hard ground,
Zum Schlaf, und uns dein Schutz bedeckt	To sleep under Your watchful care
Wird weich der harte Fels uns dünken.	The hard ground seems smoothed
Du lächelst, Rosendüfte wehen	Your joy brings the fragrance of roses
In dieser dumpfen Felsenkluft,	To this dark and rock filled ground
O Mutter, höre Kindes Flehen,	Oh Mother, hear the prayer of a child
O Jungfrau, eine Jungfrau ruft.	Oh Virgin, hear a virgin's call.
Ave Maria, reine Magd.	Holy Mother, sacred of women,
Der Erde und der Luft Dämonen,	On this earth, we are protected from the
Von deines Auges Huld verjagt,	dangers of life
Sie können hier nicht bei uns wohnen.	Which cannot harm us.
Wir wollen uns still dem Schicksal beugen,	We take gladly the good fortune
Da uns dein heiliger Trost anweht;	That your holy strength gives to us
Der Jungfrau wolle hold dich neigen,	The Virgin's regard of this bowed head
Dem Kind, das für den Vater fleht,	Of the child who prays for the father.
Ave Maria.	Holy Mother.

3

A Father's Pride

Ev'ry time I feel the Spirit movin' in my heart, I will pray.
Upon the mountain, my Lord spoke,
Out of His mouth came fire and smoke.
Down in the valley, on my knees,
I asked the Lord, Have mercy, please.

Jordan river, chilly and cold,
Chills the body, but not the soul,
I looked all round me, looked so fine,
I asked the Lord if all was mine.
Now, ev'ry time I feel the Spirit movin' in my heart, I will pray.

I often joked to my father, uncle, and brothers that I would never forgive them for refusing, when I was a child, to allow me to go fishing with them at three thirty in the morning. It didn't matter how many different ways they insisted that sitting at the edge of a lake, fishing poles cast, was solely a man's domain. I wanted to be there. There was something so exciting about their getting up in the middle of the night, food packed, thermos bottles filled with coffee, fishing poles at the ready. It seemed as though I was missing something really wonderful. I mean, if there was something to be done at three thirty in the morning, it had to be fun. I wanted to be with them there in the mist before sunrise, in the cool of the morning breeze, floating in shadows, folded in the silence, and then emerging into the hot summer sun with a bucket of triumph. Or, as my mother called it: dinner.

Alas, it would be many years later before I would have my first fishing experience, as an adult, sans my brothers and father and uncles. This adventure was taken with a few friends of mine from New York who, while we visited with one another, talked of taking a break from a very busy year to go on a fishing trip in the mountains of Quebec, where brook trout, sturgeon, walleye, bass, and muskie are in abundance. "Ah, that sounds wonderful," I said wistfully. "I should like to go fishing, too." And I did. Right there in beautiful Quebec, in some of the most stunning land and water this earth has to offer, on a boat—nothing fancy—with one hearty fisherman in charge of steering and another responsible for getting the bait onto the hooks for my friends and me, trying our best to coax the fish onto our lines for our catch-and-release conquest. There were others charged with catching proper-sized fish that would adorn our dinner table later. It was a wonderful time. I felt inspired to sing one of the many songs about being on the water, because, well, this is what happens when nature and beauty and friendship fill my heart and my spirit.

I sang quietly to myself. And I noticed that with every note of Schubert's "Auf dem Wasser zu singen" ("Singing on the Water"), the fish drew closer to the boat. Fairly soon, I was catching fish — a lot of fish. There is a scientific explanation that speaks to how water transports sound and why the fish would have therefore been attracted to our boat. But I remember my father and uncles saying that one had to be absolutely quiet and still while fishing so as not to scare the fish away. Had I found particularly musical fish?

My sudden fishing prowess and my singing did not go unnoticed by the captain, who had not the faintest idea of who I was, or what I did for a living. As I with a song on my tongue reeled in yet another fish for him to release back into the beautiful waters, he turned to me and said, "You should take that up! I'll bet you would be asked to sing somewhere. I've heard lots of singing in my time and you're pretty good."

I laughed so hard, I was weeping, my makeup completely ruined. "Do not say a word," I told my friends through tears of pure delight.

AS A HIGH SCHOOL STUDENT I had made certain that I obtained the requisite credits for entering a liberal arts college from which I could move on to medical school. I loved singing, I loved music; all this gave me great pleasure. However, I saw no clear path to becoming a professional singer. My parents, being who they were, gave me space and time to come to my own decision. They focused, instead, on making sure that my siblings and I understood that whatever we chose — physician, singer, teacher, whatever — we should use every ounce of our ability to be the best at it. Their parenting skills and their sheer dedication to us were demonstrated in countless ways. My father was president of the PTA for over twenty years (he was still in this position at our elementary school when the youngest of my siblings was entering college). He drove us to school every morning not because it was too great a distance for us to walk, but because it gave him a moment to visit with us. He would check to see if we had finished our homework, and find out what afterschool activities we might have planned.

In addition to being an excellent provider and a God-fearing, curious man, he was attentive—something I could notice easily by the way my father did something as simple as help my mother descend steps. He was always there with his hand at her elbow, a kind gesture that I noticed even as a very young child. He opened car doors and made sure she was settled in the seat next to his— the driver's seat—long before seat belts became the requirement of the day.

My siblings and I speak now about this parenting, which we took completely for granted at the time. As children, it is not altogether clear how one's upbringing compares to others in one's community. It is easy to see material differences, perhaps, and to say, "Well, this person has a new school bag and I want one like that," but one cannot necessarily tell how that person with the new school bag is being nourished at home, as compared to what one is receiving in one's own home. Janie and Silas Norman were incredible parents. They were present at every performance of mine and of my siblings; no matter if we were reciting the Twenty-Third Psalm at a church function or starring in a Greek play at college, our parents treated each performance with the same importance. They got us up and ready for Sunday school and church services, and for community and church-related duties during the week. They were each rooted in their faith and a determination that all five of us were going to "make something of ourselves," and wanted us desperately to live a purposeful life with distinction. Bringing home report cards with anything less than an A merited the uncomfortable question: "Well, who received the A?"

When I brought home a report card for the first time in my life that was just shy of putting me on the dean's list, there were many questions. "How did this happen?" my father asked. I countered by listing all of the extracurricular activities that were taking my attention. I was fascinated by a brand-new school, was participating in the math club, the Future Teachers of America club, and the chorus. Plus, I had a close friend in the band, and would find myself at his rehearsals, and the football games. I was busy. But in my father's mind, certainly, I was not too busy to bring home better grades than this.

It was not a request; it was an expectation.

This was the prevailing sentiment of many African American parents of the time. Despite the often desperate hand they'd been dealt, despite a government-sanctioned caste system that denied them basic rights, and despite the constant threat of danger, these parents dared to dream of and plan for brighter futures for their children—futures they held dear even if they had never experienced anything like this for themselves. I recall a conversation with my maternal grandfather on such a subject. We talked as we stood looking out over his land, a farm that he and my grandmother owned outright. They had worked it to sustain themselves and their hefty family of fourteen, some years after my grandfather's first farm had been lost in the Depression, when he, like all too many black landowners, had fallen behind on his taxes. Unbowed by this setback, my grandparents did all that they could to save enough to purchase another farm — land they walked proudly, sometimes with me trailing not far behind. I was only seven or eight years old when, during one of these walks, I discovered that my voice could produce an echo if I stood looking out over the ridge down into the valley. This seemed very big to me at the time. I heard my voice rise high into the sky and then rain down over the treetops and back toward me. "God willing," my grandfather said simply, as I stood in wonder, "I'll be able to cut down some of these trees to send you to college one day."

This was a wonderful thought at the time, though I couldn't quite make the connection between those giant trees and college tuition payments. But even at that tender age, I knew that college was an expectation. It was not a matter of "if," but "where." This man had seen all twelve of his children graduate high school — a thirteenth, Samuel, had died in a tragic horse-riding accident — in a place and at a time when segregation assured inadequate teaching materials, inadequate facilities, and low teachers' pay for black schools. Yet he saw nothing but better things for those who carried in their veins both his blood and that of the sainted ancestors. With him, the sky was blue, the well was full of water, birds flew merrily above, and all of his grandchildren were going to make a good life for themselves. Yes, expectations were high, but really, it was so very easy to make my elders happy, especially my parents. Nothing pleased them more than having their children make it all the way through a memorized rendition of a passage of Scripture or a poem without missing a word or two.

My siblings and I recognize this now as a true blessing, because the world is full of parents who offer a different level of attention to their children—mothers and fathers who are intent on choosing what their children will be and pronouncing them prodigies before they can barely walk. I have run into quite a few mothers who push their way backstage, children trailing in their wake, to pronounce their kids the ninth wonders of the world, possessing unparalleled talent and skill—at age eight. These children are pressed through a mill of voice coaches and vigorous singing schedules that do nothing more than make it impossible for them to thrive when they are adults and their bodies are finally ready for the rigors of singing professionally. Nothing is sadder for me than to meet a twenty-year-old who has been studying voice since the age of thirteen or so and to find that young voice now ruined. I have gone out of my way to frighten my very young colleagues intent on early training by saying, "Listen, the vocal cords must be protected. They can help you produce an extremely powerful sound, but they are themselves very delicate." And the thing about this is, as is true of any ligaments in the body, once you have stretched them, once you have put them out of their natural expansion and retraction, they will seldom return to their natural state of flexibility and strength.

This is simply a matter of understanding human anatomy, how the body functions. With all athletic performances, whether running a marathon, playing a strenuous game of tennis, or singing on a stage in front of an auditorium full of people, one uses the body and muscles in ways that one would not do normally. The body must be trained to do these extra things and can do them very well with the proper tutelage. And whether or not a person has a wonderful wingspan perfect for tennis, or long legs perfect for running, or a voice perfect for the stage, those special abilities and the required control cannot reveal themselves fully until the physical body is ready and strong enough to withstand the demands of the discipline in question. It takes training and a certain respect for one's body to be a professional singer whose voice can withstand the demands of preparation and rehearsal, and the travel, and everything else involved in a performance. One can train a voice to have greater projection, just as one can train to run a two-minute mile or perform a front pike somersault on a gym floor, but in each of these cases the correct technique is crucial. Children's bodies are just not suited to the demands of serious vocal training. The torso muscles used for singing are still developing in youngsters. It is not until one is past puberty and well into the teenage years that serious voice training should begin. The entire vocal apparatus has to develop along with this growing body—and has to be left alone to speak and sing naturally while this amazing physical development is taking place. When it is ready, it can be trained to do more.

This is why I am so grateful that instead of being sent off to voice lessons when I was eight years old, my parents made it possible for me to study the piano. Rosa Sanders did not try to teach me to sing. Instead, she taught me songs. Vocal technique was far from our thoughts at the time; the focus was on encouraging me to enjoy my music, to excel in school, to honor my elders, to be comfortable in front of crowds, and to be sociable—all things that, at a young age, were important to the building of the solid foundation that ultimately shaped the musician I would become. By the time I entered Howard University and began vocal training, I was lucky indeed that I did not have to unlearn an incorrect way of singing. The sound that came from my mouth, from my body, was just what came out naturally.

It was Mrs. Sanders who came up with the idea of my participation in the Marian Anderson Vocal Competition in Philadelphia when I was but fifteen years old. My parents were eager for me to have this experience, but traveling all the way to Philadelphia in the middle of the school term was quite a different thing to consider. Of course, I was gung ho!

It was a heady time. The principal of our high school, the long-suffering Lloyd Reese, with whom I had had my frequent meetings as a middle-schooler, was now at Lucy C. Laney High School. It was he who came up with an idea that to this day warms my heart and brings happy tears to my eyes. At one of our weekly school assemblies, Mr. Reese announced that I would be attending the competition in Philadelphia and that he wanted the whole school, hundreds of students, to participate by choosing one day on which, rather than going to the cafeteria and paying twenty cents for a hot, well-balanced lunch, they would contribute that money toward travel expenses for me and Mrs. Sanders. To be certain no student went hungry, the PTA paid for all school lunches that day. It was a novel idea and a beautiful gesture. Wonderful.

Mrs. Sanders and I prepared my songs for the competition. And soon enough, we were on a train heading from Augusta to Philadelphia. I was more than excited about this adventure; it was utter joy. All of my father's siblings and their families lived in the Philadelphia area and so I had made this particular journey with my family on a few occasions. But this was different; somehow, even more exciting.

The age group for the Marian Anderson competition was sixteen to thirty, a very wide span, and I was on the way to being sixteen, but not quite there. So I should not have been allowed to participate, and I was competing against singers who were up to twice my age, some of whom were already singing professionally. Others, too, had a great deal more experience than I did. But I was too excited and happy to worry about these things. When my time to perform arrived, with Mrs. Sanders at the piano, I sang Schubert's "Leise flehen meine Lieder" ("My songs lie gently on the wind") in English—I had not yet studied German—and "Stride la vampa" ("The rising blades of fire") from Verdi's *Il Trovatore,* since one of the requirements was to include a Verdi aria in the presentation, and the sheet music for this aria happened to be available at the local music store in Augusta. I promise, this was why this particular aria, about a woman burned at the stake, found its way into the repertoire of a fifteen-year-old. I laugh out loud at the thought! I can still see the orangey-red and white cover of that sheet music.

Needless to say, I did not win a prize at the competition, but I was fortunate in meeting the sister of Marian Anderson, who told me that she "wished to keep an eye on me," and encouraged me to reenter the competition once I had had vocal training. This was good enough for me. I was much too delighted by the whole experience to feel any disappointment at failing to win a prize.

Since the day following the competition was a Friday, we decided that on the way back to Augusta, we would stop in Washington, D.C., where we both had relatives and where Mrs. Sanders was acquainted with the associate dean of the School of Music at Howard University. As it happens, Dean Mark Fax had been chair of the music department at Paine College in Augusta when Mrs. Sanders was a student there. Upon our arrival in Washington, we went straight from Union Station to the Howard University campus, where we met with Dean Fax in the school's College of Fine Arts building.

After meeting for a few minutes with Dean Fax, he suggested that we visit with the head of the voice department, and he ushered us upstairs, where the renowned professor Carolyn V. Grant was in the middle of a graduate class on vocal anatomy and pedagogy. Too excited to be nervous, we waited outside her classroom until Professor Grant, no doubt wondering who we were, came to the door. After she received an explanation from Dean Fax, she welcomed Mrs. Sanders and me into her classroom, and suggested that perhaps I would sing one of the songs I had performed in Philadelphia. There was a piano in the classroom, and I had no thought of warming up or concern as to whether or not I was dressed properly for the occasion, and without further ado, I offered one of my songs. I was ever ready for a performance. Afterward, Professor Grant thanked us and asked that we wait for her outside the classroom.

It was not long before her class ended and Professor Grant was standing before me, saying that she had been pleased with what she heard. She asked my age, and whether or not I was a good student. "Oh, yes," I answered enthusiastically. "I am on the dean's list in high school." Then and there, as amazing as it sounds, she told me that if, indeed, I had good grades in high school—and my high school transcript would have to bear this out—then after I completed high school, she wished to teach me at Howard. To say that I was flabbergasted would be the understatement of all time.

We called my parents with this amazing news, and without seeing a single relative, we took the train back to Augusta.

The train ride home was a blur of excitement and anxiety. What had just happened? I had been to Philadelphia, had an enlightening time of it, had not won a prize, but then had met Dean Fax and Professor Grant at Howard University, all within a very short period of time. My mind was swimming. Had I truly been invited to become one of this storied professor's students? Dean Fax had told us how revered she was as a teacher. Oh my, it was all too wonderful.

I was so happy, the following Monday morning, to tell Principal Reese all that had transpired on our trip. He was no more disappointed than I that I had not won a prize at the competition. The invitation to Howard, he said, was a far better prize for me.

Now, even in the midst of all this excitement, I was still harboring the desire to pursue a career in medicine. But I decided not to bring this up with Principal Reese. It did not seem a good time to speak about it.

My parents were, of course, thrilled at the prospect of my going to Howard University, and totally overjoyed when, just a few weeks later, word arrived that not only would I have the opportunity to attend, but that on the recommendations of my two new best friends there, Dean Fax and Professor Grant, I was being offered a full-tuition scholarship. I did apply to other universities in the course of my senior year in high school, just for the fun of it. I found myself in happy disbelief that I was accepted wherever I had applied, though none of the others offered me the scholarship assistance that Howard had.

The summer before I entered the university, I spent a great deal of unnecessary time packing my trunk. My mother would walk through my bedroom while I pretended to have so much to do to get ready to travel to Washington. She knew well that I was feeling torn. Part of me wanted to study in the College of Liberal Arts at Howard, in preparation for medical school. Yet I also held the "bird in the hand" prize of the College of Fine Arts. In her typical fashion, my mother stated something like "I'm not trying to tell you what to do, dear, but you do have a full-tuition scholarship to the School of Music." We both had a little laugh at that.

I'm most grateful for that not-so-subtle nudge. You have to wonder how many parents would have encouraged a child to pursue music over medicine.

AT LAST, THE FALL of 1963 approached. I would arrive again at Union Station in Washington, this time accompanied by my father, only a few days after the great March on Washington and one of the most renowned speeches of all time, Dr. Martin Luther King Jr.'s "I Have a Dream." Even then, the irony of this now historical speech's title and my arrival in Washington was apparent to me: a dream.

At Howard, I arrived to find that even though I had been accepted to study vocal performance, I would still have to sing for the entire voice department, as only Professor Grant and Dean Fax had heard me sing those many months ago. This is a normal part of the entrance process there. First-year music students present themselves before faculty in determining their two primary courses of study. I recall my uneasiness when waiting for my appointment outside the door to the audition room, I spotted another student holding a stack of music scores in what seemed to be about eighteen different languages.

"Do you know all those songs?" I asked nervously.

"Yes," she answered confidently.

"Are you going to sing your Schubert songs in German?"

"Oh, yes!" she said matter-of-factly.

I thought I might as well go home right then and there. I still knew only the one Schubert song, and I was not going to sing it in German. I didn't know that anyone expected me to. When the time came, I sang the music I had prepared, including my Schubert song in English. The faculty was pleased with me and asked me all kinds of questions about my education in Augusta. I was happy to talk about the many teachers who had supported me throughout my public school education. I also sat for an initial piano examination, which went so well that I was allowed to choose piano and music education as my second subjects.

It was Carolyn V. Grant who helped me to find and know my own voice. She had been teaching for about forty-five years when I came to her, and there was nothing about singing that had not come across her desk at some point. It was so wonderful to work with a person who, though a trained singer herself, was dedicated to teaching, who *wanted* to be a teacher, rather than a performer. Professor Grant was a person who, from the time she was a student studying music, wanted to teach other people to sing and to sing properly because she felt very strongly that, somehow, we were getting away from the understanding that the sounds we make as singers should be produced naturally. She insisted that there were not any tricks to the understanding of the science of one's own physiology as it relates to breath control, posture, and the functioning of the whole body in support of the respiratory system. For her, it was essential for singers to have this understanding and knowledge, and to draw from it over the course of their careers.

I remember her saying to me after my first lesson: "Hmmm, underneath all that breath is a rather good instrument, and I am going to help you find it." Those were her exact words.

Professor Grant's understanding of vocal production remains with me to this day. It was she who taught me that the only "mystery" to singing has to do with the fact that each and every singer has a different sound, one that's personal and unique. I was absolutely amazed when she explained to me that the timbre—the "color" of the voice—is fixed practically at birth. This has to do with our own physiological makeup—the shape of the nasal cavity, the lung capacity, the singer's strength and stamina, the height of the inside of one's mouth, the natural position of the roof of the mouth, the height of the uvula, the width of the nose, the distance between the end of the chin and the beginning of the nose, the distance between the end of the chin and the beginning of the collarbone, and the height of the cheekbones and their position near the eyes. All of these things with which you are born determine the timbre of your voice. Each of these things, when paired with one's intelligence and musical understanding, is what sets us apart as singers, one from the other. It was this that Professor Grant insisted that I understand—that I learn to trust. And I was an eager student. I was especially taken with the anatomy component. I consoled myself with the fact that I was learning a little science even though medical school was not in my future. But it was equally important that I was not trying to collect a string of opera arias and operatic roles, goals that seemed to occupy the thoughts of my fellow students to no end. Instead, I wanted to know what Professor Grant knew.

And so we spent a lot of time learning how to take in a breath and allow it to come out slowly and evenly, in the same way practiced by singers of the eighteenth and nineteenth centuries, particularly in Italy. One such exercise involved standing with a lighted candle about fifteen inches from the mouth. If you could exhale without blowing out the candle, you were thought to be breathing with control and evenly. As you can imagine, this is not an easy thing to do, but I did it for months with Professor Grant. I still work on breath control all these many years later, I assure you. My colleagues often laugh at me when they recognize the vocal exercises I use to warm up prior to a performance—exercises developed by nineteenth-century master teachers they know from their own studies, such as Panofka and Francesco Lamperti. These vocal gymnastics work for me in preparing for a performance. So does the practice of hatha yoga. These are things I have done all of my performing life, and I still practice them on a daily basis. They are the core of my vocal strength. I have Professor Grant to thank for this.

She was a real Francophile, so my repertoire was full of the music of French composers. There was still more to learn after my four wonderful years at Howard, however, and it was Professor Grant who encouraged me to study with someone new. She promised that I would always be her student and she would always be my teacher, but she wished me to broaden my musical training beyond her studio. This was a generous and thoughtful consideration on her part, and during the summer semester that followed my graduation from Howard, I was very fortunate to find myself under the tutelage of Madame Alice Duschak at the Peabody Conservatory. It was she who helped develop my interest in the great German and Austrian romantics, music that would become an integral part of my repertoire. Mme. Duschak was happy that I had, as she called it, a "classical vocal line" in my singing, but she wanted to see more drama, more daring. And so she set about helping me explore repertoire that would call on me to employ new aspects of the craft of singing.

One of the first songs she assigned to me was Johannes Brahms's "Auf dem Kirchhofe" ("In the Cemetery"). The first part of the song describes a rainstorm, before giving way to an almost hymnlike rendering of thoughts of eternal peace. Dramatic, indeed. I also have Mme. Duschak to thank for assigning me the second aria from Richard Wagner's *Tannhäuser*. "You already have the breath control for it," she insisted. This aria would become the basis for every vocal competition that I entered in my early twenties. It is nothing as flashy as the character Elisabeth's first aria, "Dich, teure Halle," but most singers would admit that this second aria, "Allmächt'ge Jungfrau" ("O Holiest of Virgins"), is a more difficult aria to sing due mainly to the fact that one is accompanied in the orchestra only by the brass section, and the breath control required is significant.

An aside: It happens that in my first year at Howard University, as a member of the concert choir, I participated in a performance of Beethoven's *Fidelio* at Constitution Hall, the largest concert hall in Washington, D.C. The women members of the Howard choir were singing in what is actually a men's chorus, an effort to produce the fuller sound required in such a vast performance space. Both of the lead singers, Hans Beirer, performing Florestan, and Gladys Kuchta, in the role of Leonore, were from the Deutsche Oper Berlin. There is no way that anyone could have so much as dreamed that less than seven years later, I would make my operatic debut at this very opera house, with this very tenor, in the lead of Wagner's *Tannhäuser,* and that I would perform the female lead role of Elisabeth!

I thank Professor Elizabeth Mannion, with whom I worked at the University of Michigan, for showing me that agility in the voice is necessary, regardless of the type of voice one possesses. The ability to sustain a long phrase, keeping one's breathing in absolute control, is the basic requirement of all singing. The ability to keep one's vocal apparatus agile is one of the many things that make for a long performance life.

I do believe that we come to this earth understanding the naturalness of breath, and then we come across those who try to change the way we sound, or maybe, if we're lucky, improve the way we sound. We can become confused about the fact that singing is actually—and should be—a very natural process, supported by torso muscles that are there for that purpose, as opposed to the muscles in our necks, shoulders, and jaws.

To point up this fact, I have often asked nonsinging music lovers to try something with me: sit or stand and just breathe deeply—very, very deeply—for five minutes. It is a long time to do this, long enough to experience that your body chemistry changes. You feel differently after only five minutes, refreshed, more relaxed. With this small action it is possible to begin to understand what it must be like to have a flow of breath for two or three hours in the course of an evening's performance. You can feel as if you are floating or flying when everything in the body is working as it should and added to that the flow of adrenaline in the bloodstream!

Truly, one of the most joyous things that I do in preparing for a performance is the warming-up part. Any singer will tell you that a voice is hardly ever in the same place every day, meaning that since the instrument lives in one's own body, it is governed to a great extent by how well, or not, one has slept, dined, and all else. We need to understand and accept these vagaries of the physical self as a gift of nature, and work with them rather than against them. After decades of experience, with a few minutes of deep breathing I find that I am able to move forward in my warm-up routine no matter the circumstances prior to my entering the dressing room.

Often I find that preparation is simply allowing my breath to flow naturally so that singing happens naturally. And when it is right, when it is sweet, singing, for me, is a physical, emotional, spiritual, and intellectual expression of my breath that allows me to connect with myself and with an audience in ways that I would find difficult without the aid of music. Some of the texts I sing were written by people with a deep, broad intelligence and understanding of mankind. I revel in being able to sing the words of a Virgil, a Racine, a Goethe, and other such masters of words.

Nothing pleased me more than when, after singing a recital in London recently—quite a few years after I had first stood in front of that candle with Professor Grant—some friends of mine told me they overheard an audience member say, "Isn't this amazing? That woman's breath control?" After singing for four decades, I found this comment, coming from someone in the audience, to be special indeed. I said silently to Professor Grant, whom we lost years ago, *Thank you for insisting that I should learn and appreciate the very basis of this craft.*

Isolde's Liebestod, Tristan und Isolde · RICHARD WAGNER · Isolde's Love-Death and Transfiguration

Mild und leise wie er lächelt,	Gently and quietly he smiles
Wie das Auge hold er öffnet —	How the eyes open so tenderly
Seht ihr's, Freunde? Seth ihr's nicht?	Do you see this, my friends? You see this not?
Immer lichter wie er leuchtet,	His spirit shines with still brighter light
Stern-umstrahlet hoch sich hebt?	The stars illuminate his being
Seht ihr's nicht?	Do you not see this?
Wie das Herz ihm mutig schwillt,	How his heart throbs so strongly
Voll und hehr im Busen ihm quillt?	Completely and boldly in his breast
Wie den Lippen, wonnig mild,	How his lips so gently release

Süsser Atem sanft entweht —	the sweetest of breath
Freunde! Seht!	My friends; look at this.
Fühlt und seht ihr's nicht?	Do you not feel and see all of this?
Hör ich nur diese Weise,	Is it only I who hears this melody
Die so wundervoll und leise,	so magnificent and quiet
Wonne klagend, alles sagend,	Cries of delight which tell all
Mild versöhnend aus ihm tönend,	Gently calling forth the sound of him
In mich dringet, auf sich schwinget,	Which enraptures me, carrying me upwards
Hold er hallend um mich klinget?	His resonance surrounds me gently
Heller schallend, mich unwallend —	Clearly resounding and embracing me
Sind es Wellen sanfter Lüfte?	Are these billowing waves the softness of air?
Sind es Wogen wonniger Düfte?	Are these the fragrant vapors of pleasure?
Wie sie schwellen, mich umrauschen,	How they invade my senses and capture me
Soll ich atmen, soll ich lauschen?	Should I breathe, should I listen?
Soll ich schlürfen, untertauchen?	Should I drink my fill
Süss in Düften mich verhauchen?	And succumb to the sweetness
In dem wogenden Schwall,	of this essence
In dem tönenden Schall,	In this storm, in this resounding of him
In des Welt-Atems wehendem All —	In the eternal breath of all that there is
Ertrinken, versinken —	Overcome, engulfed completely
Unbewusst, höchste Lust!	Overtaken, the highest of pleasure.

4

Church, Spirituals, and Spirit

"THERE IS A BALM IN GILEAD"

There is a balm in Gilead to make the wounded whole,
There is a balm in Gilead, to heal the sin-sick soul.
Sometimes I feel discouraged and think my work's in vain,
But then, the Holy Spirit revives my soul again.
If you cannot sing like angels,
If you cannot preach like Paul,
Go and tell the love of Jesus,
And say, He died for all.
There is a balm in Gilead to make the wounded whole,
There is a balm in Gilead to heal the sin-sick soul.

My faith informs my life. I consider myself to be religious, as I subscribe to a particular belief system, the Judeo-Christian doctrine, and consider its tenets to be the foundation of my philosophy for living. Even though I was raised in the Baptist Church, as a child I enjoyed attending services in other churches with my friends, Catholic churches, synagogues, as well as what I found to be one of the most beautiful small churches in Augusta, St. Mary's Episcopal Church.

I am also deeply spiritual in the sense that I revel in those things that make for good — the things that we can do to shed a little light, to help place an oft-dissonant universe back in tune with itself and with ourselves. There is spirituality in saying good morning to a stranger. There is spirituality in sending a daughter off to school with the words: "You are just the best little girl. I am so glad you are mine and I am yours." Spirituality can be as simple as saying hello to the person who is cleaning the floor when you walk by in an office building. Spirituality is everywhere I turn, and it manifests itself in all ways — in performance, in my studying, and in the work that it is my privilege to offer to charitable organizations. It is present in my love of family, friends, and community. I have faith in the universe and in its goodness and believe that goodwill moves through space and time and comes into my life when I least expect it, and certainly when I need it most.

I have my parents to thank for introducing me to and guiding me to a place of faith and trust. So many things I remember about my childhood are rooted firmly in the foundation of their faith, gleaned from their parents and, surely, their parents' parents, as well. My father was raised in the front pews of Twin Oaks Baptist Church, in Wilkes County, Georgia, a sanctuary founded by his grandparents that stands to this day. It is a perfectly beautiful church, the style of which can just as easily be found in any number of quaint New England towns. Today, there is a paved main road that fills in what was once a quiet country path, but it still looks exactly like the thing it should be: a white clapboard church with a little steeple. It is a wonderful sight and a joy for our family and the entire congregation that it serves. On the occasions when my family and I visit, I feel a beautiful surge of warmth as I enter the church, understanding the deep connection between my spirit and that of both my great-grandparents and my grandparents, whose images in the vestibule grace this proud, small, sacred space. The faith of my forefathers and foremothers sustains my own.

I learned early in life that God is somewhere beyond the sun and the clouds and the moon and the stars, looking after us. But I also had other ideas about God that stretched far beyond what was being taught as I understood it in Sunday school, namely that God was all around us down here, too. And at about age five, I found Him often in the backyard of our home, in a lovely tree that stood sentry over the garden. I loved that tree because some of its limbs were low to the ground and swingy and you could climb onto them easily and jump on and dangle from them and, with a bit of kindergarten imagination, you could turn those huge branches into a majestic leaping horse, or a fancy car full of magical people, or a train as real as the ones that made their way through our town on a regular basis, sounding their lonesome horns as they moved along the tracks.

One afternoon, while playing on this favorite tree as my father was busy taking care of something having to do with our house, I proclaimed, "When I come back to earth I would like to be a tree, because everyone has fun with trees. You can sit in trees, sometimes trees have fruits, and that would be a great thing to be."

I do believe that just for a moment, the birds stopped chirping, the bees stopped buzzing, the wind stopped blowing, and the earth stopped on its rotational axis. Or maybe it was just that my father, a devout Christian who served as the chairman of the board of deacons at Mount Calvary as well as head of our Sunday school, became very, very quiet—and just a bit perplexed by my ideas and thoughts about the afterlife.

"I want you to understand that we are Christian people," he said in a measured voice, "and when we die we go to Heaven if we have been good, and when we have not been good, we go to that other place."

"But no, Daddy, we come back!" I insisted. "We come back as other things."

My father shook his head in wonder. That was the end of this particular dialogue. My father did not go on to explain the holy doctrine that shaped the very foundation of his faith and belief system of the resurrected Christ and a place for believers in Heaven, after one's earthly journey. Coming back to life in another form after death was not a part of the tradition. My father must have wondered how his five-year-old daughter, from a deeply religious Christian family, had come across, let alone chosen to believe in, the concept of reincarnation. Or maybe he convinced himself I had no idea of what I spoke, just youthful musings in the backyard on a beautiful day. I, on the other hand, stood firm in my belief that I could return to earth and be a tree if I wanted to, and that I could be that specific tree and this was a kind of secret that God and I shared. I guess that you can say that I found my version of faith in my own backyard!

Certainly, faith was the center of our familial visits to my maternal grandparents' farm, which they worked themselves and of which my siblings and I are the grateful owners today. When we were children, about once a month, we would drive to Wilkes

County, go to church with Grandma Mamie and Granddaddy, and then retire to their house for big Sunday dinners with them and my uncle Floyd and aunt Esther and my many cousins, whose land was contiguous to that of my grandparents.

Our cousins were our best pals. There could be as many as twenty people at these after-church dinners, prepared by the able hands of my grandmother, my mother, and various aunts and older cousins—each of them amazing cooks with the uncanny ability to prepare enough food for an army in an incredibly short amount of time. My sister, Elaine, has that magic touch: she can go into her kitchen and take things out of the fridge and freezer and assemble enough food for twelve, alongside the most delicious fresh biscuits one can find this side of the Mason-Dixon Line. I, on the other hand, can cook lots of things, but even with my full concentration, I cannot make a southern-style biscuit that anybody would want to eat. The ability Elaine possesses is in her DNA; it flows directly from my grandmother, our mother, and aunts, who made magic on those Sundays on the farm, where sharing food and laughter and play was a spiritual act. There would be baked ham and lots of chicken, whether roasted or pan-fried, and many serving bowls of vegetables, because they grew them right there on the farm, which, to this city child, was on a par, surely, with what the Garden of Eden must have been like. You could walk around the farm and see peaches and melons and collards and beans, all kinds of delicious things growing on shrubs and trees and on the ground, and you could pick them and eat them right off the vines. I remember my uncles bringing my grandmother milk, produced from the cows on the farm, and watching her seated with a tall wooden barrel between her strong knees and something that looked like a tall pole, as she churned the milk into cream and then butter, by hand. This deliciousness bore no resemblance to the same kind of products purchased at the grocery store. It was not until many years later, when I was invited to sing in Normandy, in northern France, that I tasted butter that pure and sweet again—truly a Proustian moment.

It was nourishing on every possible level to be seated at my grandparents' table, to have someone offer a long prayer over the food, and to have everything served family style from this glorious presentation laid out in front of us. This family fellowship would continue long after the plates were cleared and the kitchen was cleaned as the men settled into conversation on one side of the front porch and the women watched out for us children, who, dressed in our Sunday best, played out in the yard. They knew that red clay and grass would have to be cleaned from our shoes and socks, and must have hoped that our clothing survived the games of tag, hide-and-seek, and softball. Perhaps I didn't fully understand it then, but I do now: that time together laughing, walking, playing, sharing, loving, truly was food for our souls and spirits.

Of equal importance to my spiritual foundation was the enlightenment, ritual, and sense of community I enjoyed as a child in what was truly the center of our lives, our church. I learned fairly early on that the learning of Scripture and attending Sunday school and the church service that followed were valuable and significant. But so, too, was the bonding, the friendships that came to us through our worship services and social hours. Those friendships were not reserved for Sundays but carried on through the week — at chorus rehearsals and children's circle meetings, in the deacon board and missionary club meetings my parents attended, and in the barbershop, which my father and several deacons from our church counted as their personal discussion hall for social and political matters and the airing of church concerns.

In the African American community of my youth, the barbershop served not only as a place where men and boys could go to get their hair cut on Saturdays, but as a gathering place where they could discuss politics, news of the city, prevailing social matters, and the like. The happenings of the church were discussed often as well, because in the case of the barbershop in our neighborhood, all those with "chairs" were members of the board of deacons at our church. Private matters of the church were discussed during lulls in the shop's activity.

I remember vividly the younger men and boys gathering in the shop beginning early on Saturday afternoons to listen to those all-important discussions — to listen to the older men simply talk.

Just a few years ago, I encountered one of these young men — Roscoe — and he wished me to know what a wonderful philosopher he thought my father had been, how he encouraged people to look at things from different points of view and to be able to defend their own thoughts on what was being discussed. Roscoe stated that my father believed firmly that a contrarian opinion should be informed. This lovely man stated that he had learned more from my father and those deacons in the barbershop than he ever did at university. Roscoe went on from the teachings of the barbershop to become a college professor.

That sense of community came, too, at Vacation Bible School and the many afterschool activities in which we participated. There was an unspoken competition on those occasions when our church would be the guest of another church in Augusta, or in a nearby Georgia or South Carolina town. Which choir was better? Would our preacher bring the congregation to its feet? At every turn, we found ourselves in the company of our neighbors and fellow church members in living rooms throughout Augusta, full of ease and comfort, not from luxurious surroundings, but from the soul-sustaining presence of true amity. This is where our spiritual lives flourished, alongside the deepening core of our social lives. These activities rooted in the church and community provided a wonderful opportunity for people to get together, to talk about things that were important to all: raising children, maintaining stable marriages, ensuring the proper education of the children, politics, staying safe in a segregated climate that made life demanding and, yes, dangerous, for our people.

It was really an amazing time, because although we all led distinctly individual lives, this strong sense of community bound us together. Everybody was interconnected and naturally supportive of one another. Everybody knew everybody else, what the parents did for a living, which church member failed to show up for Sunday service, and the like. There was much talk about the cooking skills of the church ladies, and everyone knew which of the women on the usher board made the best casseroles and which deaconess you could count on to bring the perfect lemon pound cake to share after Bible study. Our corner of the world was, in the purest sense of the word, a true village "raising children," and I learned from the best the importance of protecting that village—being there for one another.

We kids took those cues and applied them to our own inter-actions with one another. We moved as a unit, my little group of friends. It was composed of boys and girls, and no one gave it a sec-ond thought. We did everything together—chorus rehearsals and club activities in school, youth social clubs at our various churches, and surely in Scouts and Y-Teens. The friendships were uncompli-cated because, in spite of the indignity of Jim Crow laws and the hostile atmosphere created by the desperate and often despicable behavior of whites who continued to rail against those of us "in the struggle," we felt an unerring sense that "this was our country, too," because our communities and our parents and our history said so. Our very lives were protected by a deep sense of belonging, by our friendships, our parents, the village. Gender differences played little role in those bonds, even when we reached the age when boys and girls started to have different kinds of friendships and some in our group began to date. The funny part was that until it was stated otherwise, we all expected to accompany the friend from our group and his or her new love interest when they went out as a couple. It seemed completely normal to us to be together and share every-thing. When I think of this, it is really quite hilarious. But we were innocent of any jealousy or anything of that kind; our tight-knit group was built on a foundation of immeasurable trust—the kind we saw amongst our parents and the adults in our community and in our clubs and church pews.

My siblings and I speak of this often and wonder how the parents of the day managed it all: raising children and taking care of a home and tending to all of their various responsibilities within the community and the church and the many different organizations to which they belonged. My mother's responsibilities as the church auditor alone took up a huge portion of at least one of her Saturdays every month. She was tasked with publishing the names of every member of the church and every club in the church and what financial support they'd contributed to Mount Calvary that month. She did this on a manual Remington Rand typewriter. I can recall so easily the smell of the typewriter ribbon, and of the red rubber eraser with the little plastic tassel at the other end. I used to marvel at how she never looked at her fingers on the keys as she typed. When I think about the technology available today, I imagine how much easier it all would have been for my mother to manage if she'd had one of these fancy word processors with the newest of software. But even using what today we consider rather ordinary tools, her reports were never late. She and my father would go over to the church on Saturday, open the glass doors that housed the bulletin board in the lobby, and post the information, page after page, for everyone to see when they arrived at church the next morning. Since you could look at this and see what every member and every club donated for the month, it was probably a good incentive to pay your tithes! But my mother's work and intentions were concerned fully in that she had a job to do and she felt it her responsibility to do that job to the best of her ability because doing so honored God and her church. Mind you, this was a volunteer position, as was every other position in our church, other than that of our pastor's.

My mother's work ethic and dedication to her faith extended, too, to our personal lives and those around us. She felt it her duty to God and her community to be there for those who lived around us, and I know for sure that she was not alone in this thinking. There were many people on our street who were older than my parents —people whose children had grown up and moved away and who were getting on in age and having a difficult time taking care of themselves. Medicare and Medicaid were yet only dreams in our country at the time. These neighbors needed help with managing their lives, and it never would have occurred to the younger parents on the street to leave them to fend for themselves. I remember clearly when Mrs. Hubert, one of our favorite older ladies, who lived directly across from us, was not really feeding herself properly. She had lost the ability to cook for herself, so the women in the community simply got together to work out on which day of the week each of them would be responsible for making breakfast, lunch, and dinner for her. It was understood that this was something they would do. There was no discussion other than of the logistics of providing Mrs. Hubert the care she needed: food and a little company during the course of the day. No one said anything like "Gee, I don't have time." I loved taking my turns bringing breakfast over to Mrs. Hubert before going off to school; she was always so happy to see me and made a point of asking if my grades were still good in school and if I had time to sing her that song she had heard I'd sung at church last Sunday. I was always happy to oblige; she was just the best audience.

Today, we can live next door to someone for years and not recognize them in the grocery-store queue. But that simply was not the case in our community. Indeed, more than twenty years ago when I became involved with City Meals-on-Wheels in New York City, one of many such organizations around the country that deliver nutritionally balanced meals to thousands of seniors. I noted that what we were doing on a very large scale was, in many ways, what my mother and our neighbors did while I was growing up in Augusta. As neither the federal, state, or local governments provide food to our older citizens in need on weekends or holidays, many of whom are unable to avail themselves of the physical and spiritual nourishment of a senior citizens' facility, it is essential that community efforts and privately funded organizations fill the gaps.

In our community, it was absolutely natural, too, for our neighbors to look after each other's children, and for the children to extend the same respect and consideration they gave their own parents to all the adults in their lives. It was perfectly acceptable for any adult entrusted with the care of a child to call that child to account for bad behavior. A parent would be comfortable in saying to a neighbor, "I've got to go to the supermarket—just keep an eye on the children there in the backyard." And were any child to be questioned by an adult in the neighborhood, the child's response would have had to include the words "Yes, ma'am," or "Yes, sir."

Being neighbors meant something—and doing the right thing by those neighbors had meaning. There was a spiritual element that compelled the neighbors to help one another, because they knew these actions to be a part of serving their faith and their Creator. My parents believed in this wholeheartedly and demonstrated their belief in the most tangible of ways. The Mrs. Huberts of our community had nothing to fear.

The church informed my journey into adulthood. It was there, too, that I learned to share and work in cooperation with others. Singing in the chorus meant I had to learn to blend my voice with everyone else's, an ability that carries through in my professional life. There is a great deal of ensemble singing in operas and oratorios and the greater the harmony among the singers, the more thrilling the presentation.

We also learned how to take constructive criticism—how to stand up in front of our peers, which surely was not simple, and, after doing whatever it was that we were charged with doing, to have the humility to listen to the person in charge who offered comments on our presentation and ways it could be improved. "No, try that again," or "Next time, do it like this." We accepted the suggested changes because we understood that we were learning, and that those adults cared about us and wished us to be good at whatever we found ourselves doing. Of course, when I was six years old, I was not thinking of these things as learning experiences; I was doing as I was told. All that I did in the church and my community gave me pleasure, which was a plus, but I was not thinking beyond that place and time. Yet, less than twenty years later, on an opera stage in Germany, those teachings from my youth would come in handy, because in many important ways, I was already well rehearsed.

In other words, leading prayer, singing with my mother at the piano, or in Sunday school, performing in Christmas pageants, reciting the Twenty-Third Psalm or a Walt Whitman or Langston Hughes poem, all of these things were more than just ritual. The elders, the parents, the Sunday school teachers, the choir directors, the teachers at our schools, all of them understood that they were preparing us to move about in this world. They understood how very important it was to support and nurture us—to teach us how to walk onto a stage, look around and smile, and say in our minds, *I'm glad to be here, and now I would like to sing for you.*

The training ground of my community was as crucial to my performance life as to my spiritual journey. Music has always been an essential part of the African American worship service, and this was no less true in my community. The church choirs were phenomenal. There were gospel singers, young and more mature, who could easily have had professional careers as they were truly that good.

I used to enjoy in particular listening to the deacons "line a hymn." I'll explain: Just as in Mother Africa, with the tradition of the call-and-response in group singing, in our churches, lining a hymn meant that a person, most of the time a deacon, would offer the name of the hymn to be sung and announce the meter that the hymn would take. "We'll now sing 'Amazing Grace,' a song in common meter," the deacon would say. Just as in Africa, common meter is a song in three-quarter time. The deacon would say the words, one line at a time: "Amazing Grace how sweet the sound that saved a wretch like me," followed by the congregation's singing of that phrase. Then the deacon would follow with more text: "I once was lost but now I'm found, was blind but now I see," and the congregation would sing that phrase, the melody always led by the same deacon who lined the hymn.

At the time, I had no idea that this kind of practice had anything to do with my ancestors, but once I became aware of the connection, I felt a special pride in it.

In any church, it was possible to find at least one star singer, most often a woman. In our church, the senior choir was anchored by one Mrs. Elizabeth Golden, with a voice that equaled her name. She had easily a three-octave range, with some extra high notes at the top of her magnificent voice. She was marvelous; her voice was strong yet gentle, and she clearly enjoyed the joyful noise she made. Her pride of place in the senior choir was the end of the first row on the right-hand side as one faced the choir stand. We all admired her. It was she who guided the children's chorus. We all wanted to grow up to be able to sing like Mrs. Golden.

Our church's missionaries group had their own star, Sister Childs, who would bring forth a song at any point in the service that suited her, whether she was on the printed program or not. I admired this immensely. She simply acted "as the Spirit moved her," and no one ever dared to ask her not to interrupt the proceedings with her singing. The spirit seemed to move her most especially on Communion Sundays, the first and third Sundays of the month. This meant that on top of the already long regular service, extra time was given to the ritual of bread and wine in remembrance of the Last Supper of Christ. I can still see Sister Childs in my memory's eye, in her white dress worn by all the missionary ladies, sitting over in the corner just below the children's chorus platform, and beginning her singing from the seat in which she sat, always. She would begin first with a bit of rocking back and forth in her seat. When she was truly taken over by the Spirit, she would rise and sing. That was all there was to it. She had the floor and would hold it until she felt like sitting down again. With one hand waving a white lace handkerchief in the air, she would throw her head back in ecstasy and sing: *In the morning, soon in the morn-*

ing, when the clouds shall roll away, I'll be happy, soon in the morning, when the clouds shall roll away. Soon there would be the clapping of hands in rhythm to her singing and the congregation's encouragement to "go on and sing, Sister Childs, tell the whole story!" She was happy to do just that.

We could all well do with a little Sister Childs inside of us from time to time.

THAT IS THE BEAUTY of music. No matter the genre, it is spiritual —a ministry—and the rhythms, the lyrics, the pacing, the dramatic content, the delivery, each of these things has the exquisite power to touch people, to bring them immense joy. I was about twelve years old when I began to understand this. It happened as I was beginning to understand the Christian religion more deeply. I came upon the principles of Hinduism in the school library, right there in the pages of a Childcraft encyclopedia, which I read voraciously. I thought that Hinduism sounded like a really interesting religion, and found within its tenets the idea from my backyard a few years earlier: reincarnation. Perhaps I could come back to earth as a tree after all. As I understood it from my very young perspective, practicing Hinduism meant embracing the idea that God wants us to be happy and that our reason for being on earth is to be happy and to share that joy with everybody we meet. I thought it sounded really wonderful, particularly since in our church, happiness didn't always seem to be the point of Sunday-morning services—at least not after the pastor had his way in the pulpit. It seemed to me that the minister thought his service was a success only if everybody in the congregation was in tears and the sermon ended with everyone incredibly emotional. And I thought I wanted this other kind of faith, the happier state that I thought Hindu practice produced, as my own. And so, as was my wont when there was something on my mind, I brought this new idea up at home, during dinnertime.

There is no doubt that some Christian parents, upon hearing something like this from their child's mouth, would have had an unmistakably negative reaction. But my parents were very patient; they had a lot of children who had a lot of ideas. My mother and father always encouraged us to say what we were thinking. Pronouncements such as mine were accepted, but they had to be accompanied with solid information and an opinion, the latter being of utmost importance to my father. I can remember many instances when we would sit in the living room listening to him give a long sermon about some social or political subject that was upsetting him, only to have him take a breath and look into a six-year-old's eyes and say something like "Now what do *you* think?" Be clear: one needed to have an answer, which could never be "I don't know." We were expected to have an opinion and to be able to express it as best we could. We didn't have to agree with every part of the sermon, should we have had enough courage to say so, but we did have to have some thought on the matter.

So my parents were not surprised that I had discovered Hinduism and thought it would be a fine religion for us. They were curious to know, though, just how much I knew about the subject. "Now, what do you know about Hinduism?" they asked. "And where in the world, particularly, is this practiced?" I didn't hesitate to head back to the encyclopedia for more information, and in my research, I learned a little about India but also about that state of

joy—that wonderful feeling that God wants for us. In my own innocent way, I wanted joy to be expressed in a way that I could understand. I did not know anything about crying with joy; I thought
tears always indicated sadness.

Though I certainly came to have much more knowledge and
understanding of the subjects of Christianity and Hinduism, reincarnation and joy, than I did when I was on the cusp of being
a teenager, I've never stopped being curious about spirituality, religion, and cultural differences that seem to prompt the way we
interact with one another. Energy is alive. On those occasions when
there is that exchange of positive energy between myself and what
is happening onstage and those watching and listening and receiving it, it is in those moments that my spirit thrives. The connection
with the audience is there as clearly in the depth of silence that exists as in the applause.

I was encouraged to trust in this energy, in the secret of that
silence, the power of stillness and slow movement, in my first production with Robert Wilson, which was called *Great Day in the
Morning*, and took place in Paris in 1982. It was here that I learned
the "for a lifetime" lesson not to allow the audience's response to
determine the tempo of my presentation.

Great Day in the Morning was, in many ways, a piece before its
time. The aim of the production was to demonstrate how Spirituals were created in the lives of the enslaved—in the course of
a day's work, on a long walk to church, during a moment of joy
with one's family and loved ones. Alas, the audiences that came
to view our work in the first nights of the performance were not
pleased. Either they were there to see what they had come to expect

of a Robert Wilson production, sans someone singing, or to witness a recital of mine. Of course, this production was neither of these things, and word spread in Paris as to what was truly afoot at the Théâtre des Champs-Élysées and how unhappy our early patrons were (which Parisian audiences have no difficulty at all expressing: cue Stravinsky's *Le sacre du printemps* and the riot that occurred at its 1913 premiere in that very theater).

But by the end of the run of *Great Day in the Morning,* the audience had turned their own stillness, their own listening, into eruptions of approval following the final song in our presentation, "Amazing Grace." Under Bob Wilson's direction, I sang this unaccompanied while pouring, over the course of a full four minutes, a pitcher of water, lighted from above and below, onto a Lucite table, the water and light flowing seamlessly from pitcher to tabletop to floor, the audience becoming a part of that continuous stream. We had, in the end, become one.

One still encounters people who believe mistakenly that "Amazing Grace" is a Spiritual. While discussing the song with a journalist in London recently, I was stunned to find that he knew nothing of the eighteenth-century British slave-ship captain John Newton, a devout nonbeliever, who saw the transportation of a free people from their own land into bondage in the United Kingdom and beyond as a means of making a living. Newton's human sensibilities were kept apart from this endeavor. As it happens when the universe is determined to teach us a lesson once and for all, a mighty storm developed on the sea during one of the captain's crossings from Africa to Europe. John Newton was certain that he would not only lose his precious cargo, but his own life as well.

In that moment, in that instance of clarity with himself and with his trade, he wrote the words that the entire world now sings:

> *Amazing grace, how sweet the sound, that saved a wretch like me.*
> *I once was lost, but now I'm found; was blind, but now I see.*

Some claim the melody for "Amazing Grace" to have originated in John Newton's home country of Scotland. I choose to think that the meter, the shape of the melody itself and its resemblance to so much West African folk music, rose from the bowels of a slave ship, with human beings arranged so as to accommodate as many as possible on a single crossing, but still living and breathing through the miracle of a song, a melody, humming, as there was often no common language, yet making music from the deepest parts of their beings. Living energy, undimmed by even such circumstances, from one human being to another.

WHEN WE REALIZE that energy is truly a living thing and that it travels a room as easily as it does a whole town—or an ocean—we come to understand that our thoughts have power and consequence, that we can extend loving kindness through positive thoughts, through openness of mind and spirit. And well we should! When an audience is engaged truly in a performance, this offering of positive energy can make all the difference in elevating the level of the performance from something that is merely good to something that is extraordinary. I do think that a performer, in order to remain at a high level of artistic achievement, must feed the spirit continually. The exchange of energy between performer and audience replenishes both.

I am having a wonderful time with music that has been playing in my ear practically all my life but which I, until six or seven years ago, hardly ever performed.

The wish to add more music to an already long list of repertoire became apparent to me during my research in preparing the festival for Carnegie Hall that took place in March of 2009: *Honor! A Celebration of the African American Cultural Legacy*. The idea of the program, as suggested in the title, was to honor the cultural contributions of African Americans to our world. From the time that Clive Gillinson, the artistic and executive director of Carnegie Hall, extended this amazing invitation to me in autumn 2006, I spent goodly amounts of time listening to recordings of the greats —in a range of musical genres—and decided then and there that I wanted to feel this music in my very being. Thus was born my first solo CD in about ten years, *Roots: My Life, My Song*.

I thought it vital to share these songs with an audience. Studying and performing the music of the great Europeans is a grand pleasure in my life, an honor and a privilege. Adding jazz and songs from the American musical theater simply expanded and enlivened my own artistic growth. Offering even wider attention to the Spiritual was natural to me and relevant, as I'd grown up hearing my grandmother, my mother, and my aunts humming and singing these songs to themselves as they tended to their daily lives. When all is said and done, I am African, and I cannot think of a single reason why I should not celebrate this to the hilt. So when I sing a Spiritual, I am telling a most personal story. These cries, these longings, these testaments of faith are a part of my own DNA, and my goal is always that the audience understands the music in the same way that I understand it.

In addition, I wish to help audiences appreciate the difference between a Spiritual—I use a capital *S* on purpose—and a gospel song. Whereas the whole world is filled with music of a sacred or spiritual nature, a Spiritual can only have been created by my ancestors, the slaves brought to a new land starting in the early 1600s, and their descendants up until 1865, the historical period of slavery in the United States. There were no trombones and Hammond organs to be had by them and no composers other than the heart longings of a people in bondage singing their way through the most challenging of human experiences. "Singing through," not "singing themselves out" of the horror.

The blues came next, and then more instruments helped bring jazz into being. These new instruments, first abhorred by churchgoers, soon found their way into the church, where Spirituals, in a new presentation, became the first gospel songs. Therefore, it is possible to take a Spiritual and turn it into a gospel song, but one cannot do the reverse. The Spirituals came first. The gospel song is often a modern version of a well-known Spiritual.

If we are lucky as performers, the music and spirit together reveal themselves before our audiences, creating an added dimension to the performance—an added dimension over which we have absolutely no control. For any undefined reason one can be ill at ease during a performance, or maybe the connection with the audience can be so visceral, so powerful, that some are inspired to come backstage and say something like "I know that you were singing that song especially for me tonight. I really felt that you were looking straight at me," when in fact, you had been conscious of no such thing. When this happens, I am grateful for it. We are human beings, and this kind of connection sustains us in our humanity, and we are better for it.

Indeed, such connections become all the more profound when the presentation is in a sacred space. Growing up, churchgoing and church activities made up the fabric of my daily life, and so I have always found singing in a church, in the great cathedrals of the world, to be experiences at once awe-inspiring and wondrously comforting. The grandeur of the spaces has never overtaken the sense of joy of being there. I seem to always know my way around these wonderful places. There are not the usual dressing rooms, and the pulpit more often than not serves as the stage. Lighting rigs are not often used, nor diffusion gels to flatter the face. And yet, somehow, the rector, pastor, or other church officials always feel compelled to make remarks prior to the performance. In other words, it's just like home. My experiences in some of the world's most beautiful, sacred spaces are every bit as treasured as they are memorable. In some, I sing, in some, I take part in fellowship, in others still, I mourn. I count each experience as a blessing.

Some church edifices are so celebrated, so historic, that seeing them only from the outside can be a very moving experience. I will not soon forget the time I talked my way into the Sistine Chapel, in Vatican City, Italy, after visiting hours. When, finally, a security guard allowed me through those doors, I stood motionless for a long while just taking in the whole of it all. Through streaming tears, I looked up at a ceiling that was far larger than my art history books had led me to understand: the colors, the majesty of the frescoes, the detail. I can see this as clearly in my mind's eye today as I did up close that fine afternoon. The security guard understood what I was experiencing and left me to my heightened emotions, my gratitude, and my even higher regard for one Michelangelo.

I recall those same feelings the first time I performed an orchestral concert in the Cathedral of Notre Dame de Paris. I was standing on the built-up stage in front of the altar, at a great distance from but still directly in front of the famous Rose Window, the fifteenth-century masterpiece that had also been such a part of my art appreciation studies. The sight of it was so moving that I found it difficult to focus on anything else. The same goes for the flying buttresses of the cathedral's exterior. Somehow, I managed to remain quiet in our rehearsals and concentrate on the work at hand.

In England, the historic Canterbury Cathedral was the sacred space where I performed my first televised Christmas concert. I remember visiting the cathedral prior to our first rehearsal there and coming across a stone plaque in the floor, which read 1687. I thought, *My word, here we have a church that is older than the United States!* There was something magical in that.

So, too, was the way that this particular Christmas concert came to be. I had a great deal of work to do in Europe and wanted a base from which to travel, and so I chose England. Knowing that I would be in Europe during Christmastime, I decided to rent a house in the country where friends might gather and we would have a lovely celebration of the holidays.

Christmas magic is real.

We gathered on Christmas Eve—had a fire ablaze in a large fireplace, and a huge, beautifully appointed tree standing in one corner, feathered underneath with beautifully wrapped packages. We had read some of the New Testament account of the Christmas story, and were planning to sing Christmas carols with the lovely piano that was just there next to the Christmas tree. Dinner was delicious, and some of us were off busily preparing coffee and dessert afterward when, suddenly, someone started playing the piano. The melody was unfamiliar to me, but those of us in food-preparation mode kept to the business at hand.

In no hurry at all, we emerged finally with the last part of our meal prepared. It was then that Jane, a writer, and Don, a composer and arranger, announced that they had written a new Christmas carol, and that it would be called "Jessye's Carol." I did not take them seriously, but I was understandably curious as to what they had actually done. Indeed, in the time it took for us to prepare dessert, they had created this song:

> *Green and silver,*
> *Red and gold.*
> *And a story borne of old;*
> *truth and love and hope abide, this Christmastide.*

The dessert waited as we all gathered around the piano to sing this new song! Afterward, I announced to those present: "Okay, from this song, we shall make a Christmas CD."

And we did; it is called *Christmastide.*

The Canterbury Cathedral was a poignant choice for filming this work for television, as it had been an important landmark for American air pilots in World War II; the building gave them a precise calculation of their proximity to the sea and an absolute certainty of their location in the United Kingdom. So an American singing in this cathedral, sparked by a song created by two Brits, had a rather lovely symmetry to the circle of life. I was joined by the American Boychoir of Princeton, New Jersey, and the cathedral's boys' choir, who worked so wonderfully well together, with the cathedral's gothic interior providing several beautiful places in which to record different segments of the program.

We filmed in July, but with these massive edifices and their stone walls—in some places they are more than two feet thick—one could feel the chill, even in high summer, so our saying "Happy Christmas" to one another during that week of work did not seem in the least out of place. The plan was to perform the concert for a live audience and, if necessary, do retakes following the performance, the manner in which many such programs are prepared for television broadcast, generally. Preparation is key, so it goes without saying that our schedule was packed with rehearsals. On one particular day, I was in my "dressing room" during a rehearsal break, going over the words to oh so many songs, when I heard what sounded like a relatively tentative rap on my door. Then a slightly bolder one. I called out for the person to enter, and in walked about five of the young boys from the American boys' choir. Immediately, I asked if anything was wrong. Right away, one of them answered, "Oh, no! We just wanted to come to visit you."

Flattered, I invited them in and tried to find enough chairs for everyone. Then one of the boys said, "Um, could we have a hug?"

"Of course!" I said.

So we all gathered around and gave one another big, strong hugs. Mind you, these youngsters were traveling with their chaperones and choir directors, but given their ages—between about seven and twelve—they had most probably not spent an entire week away from familiar surroundings or their parents. It was a perfectly delicious moment—one that will remain in the memory bank always.

This beautiful story has a coda. Fast-forward ten or eleven years: there I am in the Lord & Taylor department store on Fifth Avenue in New York, with two or three days at the most before Christmas, trying to get all of my shopping done in this one afternoon. It was during the traditional workday and offices hadn't yet closed for the holiday, so the store was not desperately crowded at the time, allowing for two salespeople in the men's accessories department to help me find classic ties, gym socks, and all those other sundries that one wraps in pretty Christmas paper and places under the tree. In my shopping flurry, I spotted a beautiful young man in a lovely winter coat, carrying a briefcase, and to my surprise he was headed straight for me. He stopped just a few feet from where I was standing, placed his briefcase on the floor, and asked, "Do you still give hugs?"

Now this, coming from such a gorgeous young man, caused me to have to gather my composure. "Now, this isn't fair," I said finally. "Tell me to which of my pals you are related. Come now, whose son are you?"

That beautiful smile reached across his face. "No, it's not that. The time that I had a hug from you was in your dressing room in the Canterbury Cathedral in England."

I beamed. And he and I had a grand, grand hug, this old acquaintance, who was now at university with his eye on attending law school. After more talk of our memories of Canterbury, he took his leave.

Talk about the magic of Christmas!

I have had similar emotional experiences singing in St. Paul's Cathedral in London, and in the Cathedral of St. John the Divine and Church of St. Ignatius Loyola, both in New York City, though the latter two were for much more somber occasions. My memory of St. Ignatius Loyola begins in the basement level of the church, where we gathered early one crisp, sunny morning. There were logistics to be reiterated and technical checks to perform. Media crews were everywhere. Organizers were busy behind the scenes, making sure that protocol was followed in every detail, as befitting a state funeral. After all, America's very own "royal" was to be memorialized: the stunning Jacqueline Kennedy Onassis.

It was her sister, Lee Radziwill, who had contacted me on behalf of the family: they were well aware of my fondness for Mrs. Onassis, and wished me to sing Schubert's "Ave Maria." Mrs. Onassis loved music, and dance most particularly, and adored talking with artists and being present for performances. Naturally, I was honored to have been asked to be a part of this celebration of the life of such a beloved person—one who had offered her kindness and friendship to me in ways that still make my heart sing.

I had rehearsed "Ave Maria" with the church organist, and was thankful for my practice of yoga, which helped me so very much in maintaining focus and concentration in the midst of all the activity in preparation for the service. Nothing was hurried or breathless; it was just very busy—quietly and methodically so. But I had to draw on something deep, something powerful, to make it through the emotional service. The church was hushed. I remember the presentation by Maurice Tempelsman, Mrs. Onassis's longtime companion, of the Constantine Cavafy poem "Ithaka." I still read it from time to time. I will always remember how utterly amazed I was by Caroline and John; they were so poised, so prepared. It was so moving to hear them speak at the service and to watch the splendid manner in which they conducted themselves in such circumstances.

The priest provided a moment of levity during his homily. It was very evident from his remarks that this was a man who knew his parish well. A bright ray of sunshine fell across the congregation as he read the passage from John 14:2: "In my Father's house are many mansions. . . . I go to prepare a place for you." The priest then stated that he could only imagine the redecorating of those mansions that would take place in Heaven now that the great Jackie was in attendance. We were all given a moment to exhale, and to remember her as the gifted, remarkable woman who had touched the lives of so many people—even those who knew her only from a great distance.

I was honored to sing for her. I was such an admirer, particularly of the little things, the nuances: I loved the way she pronounced the nickname of the President, as though it were spelled "Jahcke," with a slight stretch on the "ahcke" part. There was limitless devotion in that pronunciation.

Surely, singing at the memorial of this much loved First Lady of our country was one of those occasions where I had to remind myself of the reason I was there; I had a job to do. Otherwise, I would not have been able to utter a single note. In those moments, you have to say to yourself, *Sing now, there will be time for a good cry later.*

That was 1994. In 2010, we would find ourselves again at St. Ignatius Loyola to say a final goodbye to the magnificent Lena Horne. Again the press was present in significant numbers, and friends from the music world and all other parts of Miss Horne's rich, fantastic life filled the church. My friend and colleague Audra McDonald sang so beautifully. It was a privilege to be invited to sit with the family and to say goodbye to this adored friend.

My first memory of the Cathedral of St. John the Divine is from my time as a student at the University of Michigan. I was in New York City, and had made my way uptown to have dinner with friends—fellow students with whom I was just becoming acquainted—and happened to find myself near the cathedral when who should bound across the street but jazz legend Duke Ellington. Although I had not seen this gorgeous man in person previously, I was certain of who he was from the moment I spotted him. It was 1968. I have since wondered if he could have been on his way to a rehearsal for the second of his three sacred music concerts—a thought that makes my heart smile. Indeed, the famed composer, pianist, and master of the big band premiered his *Second Sacred Concert* at the cathedral that year . . .

It would be years later that I would have the privilege of singing in the Cathedral of St. John the Divine, an honor offered to me on several occasions. One of the first was the memorial for Keith Haring, the graffiti and visual artist who used his artwork to advance his social activism. A friend tasked with organizing Keith's May 1990 memorial asked me if I would be available to sing at the service, and I was pleased that I had that particular date free in my schedule. I knew of Haring's work, of course, and had met him "across a crowded room" at some point, but was unaware that he had been such a supporter of my music making. So many young people and ambassadors of the arts filled that stunning space, sending a clear and powerful message about this life taken so young: Keith was loved and admired and respected. It was my honor to add to that message by lifting my voice in celebration of his life.

Three years later, I would find myself in this same sacred space for yet another memorial, one that held special significance for me: the funeral service of Supreme Court Justice Thurgood Marshall.

When my siblings and I were kids, my parents would speak of illustrious African Americans as if they knew them personally. They would relay news of these individuals from television, newspaper, or radio reports with such pride and earnestness that you would have thought them to be speaking of kin or, at the very least, members of our church or small community. It was all present and natural. We were made to feel that icons like Jackie Robinson, the Reverend Dr. Martin Luther King Jr., Miss Rosa Parks—each of them—were close to us.

Which is why the name Thurgood Marshall was as familiar to me as any of the names that made up our community, our world. He meant something to my family, to me, personally. And so of course I did not hesitate when Justice Marshall's family asked me to sing "The Battle Hymn of the Republic" at his memorial service.

Having contemplated the deep meaning of this hymn and its significance to the life work of Justice Marshall, I pondered the manner in which I should present the piece. And for the first and only time in my professional singing life, I accompanied myself with a tambourine. Considering the citizens whose plights drove the actions of this great man, simplicity was to be the order of the day, a tambourine more fitting, more suitable, more appropriate than the tremendous organ of the cathedral. I wished to serve simply as a conduit for the hymn's words. I was so honored to be there.

I was honored equally when invited to be part of the festivities surrounding Nelson Mandela's second visit to the United States after nearly three decades of imprisonment. Everyone wanted to meet and experience this man and I was no exception. I had been given the high honor of singing for him a few days prior to his visit to the cathedral, in Harvard Yard, on a tremendously vibrant early autumn day. The quadrangle was filled to the brim with thousands of people; the very air seemed tinged with joy. I had hoped privately that upon meeting Mr. Mandela I would say something sensible, that I would not be so overwhelmed by his presence that I would flub my greeting. I quickly realized that my worry was for naught. There was a calm, a quietude, a grounded strength in this man that seemed to fan out to all those in his midst. His face almost always looked as though he was about to break into a full smile. We speak often of a person's aura; Nelson Mandela's aura was one of utter peace.

Mr. Mandela was given an honorary doctorate at Harvard that day; he made the kind of remarks that one wishes to be able to recall word for word. He offered the prose of a forgiving spirit, the poetry of a heart so connected to goodness as to be free of anger, with not so much as a hint of desire for revenge. I was happy that I could offer my song without bursting into monumental tears of joy.

At the cathedral some days later, I would have the privilege again to sing for him, and this time, there was even a moment for us to speak together at more length. What luck! His wife of only three months, Graça Machel, was so very kind in her words about my singing in Harvard Yard, and Mr. Mandela asked me, breaking into that wonderful, full smile of his, "Where does all that voice come from?"

"You just stand there and out it comes!" I was thrilled that he could think my singing effortless under these most moving and thought-provoking circumstances. I was elated to have had that quiet moment with them both.

Though I have the privilege to sing in and visit some of the world's most beautiful churches, Augusta still has some of the most important sacred spaces in my life. One in particular—First Baptist Church—stands out, but for different reasons that speak intimately to my life growing up in the segregated South. Although First Baptist has long been a jewel of my hometown, it was not until I was an adult and a professional singer that I had so much as seen the inside of it—by choice of both the church's leaders and my own. I'll explain.

I had been invited to perform a Christmas concert to be telecast by Georgia Public Television, so the decision to mount this in a church in my own hometown seemed an obvious choice. For the organizers, First Baptist Church was the perfect venue, and church officials were in swift agreement. The sanctuary would provide a lovely background on which to offer the kind of visual effects so important for television, plus it was located out of the way of airline traffic patterns and other potentially disruptive urban noise. My performing there made sense to all those involved. All those except me.

First Baptist Church stood tall and majestic when I was growing up in Augusta, then an unabashedly segregated town where separation of the races was more apparent on a Sunday than almost any other day. It was a way of life that was embraced completely. And so you can imagine that there were one or two surreal moments for me in returning to the town of my birth and offering a program of joy to the world in a church in which I would not have been welcomed during the time that I actually lived there.

It was the support of family and friends that brought me to a place of comfort and calm within myself. Many of the songs on the program were those that I sang as a youngster in Augusta — "I'll Walk with God," "Bless This House," and "The Lord's Prayer." In the end, I would sing in this beautiful church with immense joy.

The energy and spirit I feel when I am communing in a sacred space, whether in the pulpit of a small church or in a vast cathedral before an audience of thousands, is a feeling very much like the energy and spirit I felt in my favorite tree oh so long ago, when I knew, for sure, that God is everywhere. This energy finds its way into so many corners of my being because I want it; indeed, I seek it. I believe in the powers of meditation and prayer.

There is a church in Berlin known as the Remembrance Church, which I attended when I lived in Germany and where, on Saturdays, services were offered in English. Although the church was bombed by the Allied forces during World War II, it remains incredibly beautiful, with the old part of the structure that survived the war complemented by a modern sanctuary. I spent many hours there, thinking about the devastation of war in that then-divided city, and about the endurance of faith.

In another country, I had one of the most beautiful spiritual experiences ever in a place that was not a church at all. It occurred while I was sitting in a magnificent garden in Marrakesh. It was my first time there and I was overwhelmed by the glory of that illustrious city and of the garden of the famous hotel there. I had arisen earlier than is normal when I am on tour, as I wished to see more of the grounds than I had been able to view from the windows of my accommodations. I walked around the garden, taking it all in, wondering what some of the fantastic flowering plants and shrubs were called. I found a beautiful place to sit and soon could hear the sound of church bells in the distance. I had noticed a Catholic church nearby. Some time later, I was in conversation in French with one of the gardeners, a young man who seemed eager to talk.

After a short while, however, chanting by a male voice could be heard somewhere off in the distance. The gardener interrupted our chat, walked over to the cart holding his gardening tools, took out his prayer mat, placed it neatly on the ground, and knelt to observe his midmorning prayers. When he was finished, he returned his prayer mat to its place on the cart and resumed our chat. What a marvelous thing I had just witnessed: the call to prayer for the Christian church and the time of prayer for those practicing Islam. I thought, why cannot the rest of the world be like this? Your prayers, my prayers, our prayers.

I told the gardener how much I was enjoying the gorgeous surrounds, and he responded so humbly by saying: "It is a pleasure to work in such a beautiful place."

For me, this is the essence of spirituality and it can be found anywhere, in any corner. Everywhere. If only we are quiet enough and take the time to appreciate our differences and celebrate our common traits.

Still, I admit that I am very much a work in progress. That is simply the nature of faith. I have a very good friend I have known since my college days who happens to be a priest, and he is truly a rock in my life. He tells me that there are times in all of our lives —even among those who are spiritual leaders—when faith is questioned and challenged. He assures me that such questions, even the occasional doubt, are a normal part of being human, fallible.

But just as easy as it is to find ourselves in a spiritual quandary, so, too, can we be full of gratitude for God's favor. This I learned from the Dalai Lama in 2012, when he was presented with the Templeton Prize at St. Paul's Cathedral in London. I had the privilege of singing "Amazing Grace" just before His Holiness delivered his stirring remarks, and "He's Got the Whole World in His Hand" directly after the speech. He insisted that he was not born "a special person"—that it would not have occurred to him as a young child that he would be the leader of a religious order or that people outside his Buddhist faith would consider him to be of any importance. He insisted, too, that he is not at all important today. Instead, the Dalai Lama said, Buddha is important, as is faith, and each of us needs to arrive at a point where we are able to extend kindness and compassion to everybody, not just people we like or those to whom we are related or people for whom we feel a kinship of some kind. "If you want to be happy, be compassionate," he stated. And because he possesses a wonderful sense of humor, he went on to say, "If you want to be really happy, then be really compassionate!"

We all are infants in that measure of faith. And I believe we need to recognize that reaching such a level of spiritual development is not an easy task, and most often—not sometimes, but most often—we will come up short. But it is the trying that's important.

It occurs to me that a performance venue could well be considered a spiritual space, depending on one's personal experience. By the time I was a student at university, the wide world seemed to present itself in tremendous new ways. For example, I found that with a student ID card, it was possible to study at the Library of Congress. You could arrive, find a free space at a table, relay to a staff member the reference book required, and have that book brought to your table. I was in Heaven!

With this same card, air travel was made possible due to the low costs offered to students. One of the places that held utter fascination was, of course, New York City and all the attractions of the place. None was regarded with more reverence by us than Carnegie Hall. On those occasions when meager funds made travel to the city possible, this hall was the destination of choice.

On one of our first visits, I became acquainted with the houseman, George. He understood immediately that we were dependent on having someone look out for us and offer us a ticket or two to a performance. He was sensitive to our circumstances and always arranged for us to come through the door and stand at the back of the hall until empty seats could be spotted. So that we would not suffer embarrassment in having to be asked to give up a seat, we could not take an unoccupied seat until after the intermission. And these were seats in the orchestra section of the house! George became our friend and superb ally, and it still warms my heart to know that there was not a single time that we, three or four of us, arrived at Carnegie without being able to witness the performance.

Time passed, and it became possible for us to purchase seats far upstairs, where the sound was just as wonderful and where we felt proud that we had actually paid our way. George was a steadfast presence in the lobby, as welcoming as ever.

Ten years would pass from my being an undergraduate at Howard hoping to gain entrance to view a performance, to my finding the great George waiting for me at the stage entrance, as he wished to show me to my dressing room. "This evening," he said, "we shall take a different entrance into the hall. Let me show you the way." It was the spring of 1975, my debut with the American Symphony Orchestra on the main stage of Carnegie Hall. My friend George was there. Oh, yes, for me, this hall will always be a spiritual space.

Die Allmacht • Franz Schubert • The Almighty

Gross ist Jehova, der Herr! Denn Himmel

Great is God, our Lord. Heaven and Earth

Und Erde verkünden seine Macht.	declare His power.
Du hörst sie im brausenden Sturm,	You hear His strength in the raging storm
In des Waldstroms laut aufrauschendem Ruf.	In the majestic call of the resounding forests.
Gross ist Jehova, der Herr!	Great is God, our Lord,
Gross ist Seine Macht!	Great is His power.
Du hörst sie im grünenden Waldes Gesäusel;	You hear Him in the green rustling leaves of
Siehst sie in wogender Saaten Gold,	the forest, and see Him in the gold of
In lieblicher Blumen glühendem Schmelz,	Waving blades of grain
Im Glanz des sternebesäten Himmels!	In the bountiful loveliness of flowers,
Furchtbar tönt sie im Donnergeroll	In the glow of a star-filled sky.
Und flammt in des Blitzes	His power is feared in the sound of thunder
Schnell hinzukendem Flug.	And the sight of flames in lightning's fast flight.
Doch kündet das pochende Herz dir fühlbarer noch	Yet, it is more deeply felt in the beating of the heart
Jehovas Macht, des ewigen Gottes.	The power of God, the eternal God.
Blickst du flehend empor	Look to God in prayer
Und hoffst auf Huld und Erbarmen.	for His protection and Grace.

5

Racism as It Lives and Breathes

"SOMETIMES I FEEL LIKE A MOTHERLESS CHILD"

Sometimes I feel like a motherless child,
A long ways from home.
Sometimes I feel like I'm almost gone,
A long ways from home.
Sometimes I feel like a motherless child, A long ways from home.

I learned about race discrimination and America's system of apartheid long before my first day of school—even before my legs stretched far enough over the side of our living room sofa for my feet to touch the floor. Jim Crow was hard to miss in Augusta in the 1950s and '60s. It was written in bold block letters above the water fountains and the phone booths and the public restrooms. It was on signs above the waiting areas at the train station and the restaurants and convenience stores, too: WHITES ONLY. COLORED ONLY. The schools were segregated, as were the churches, and the neighborhoods of Augusta were defined clearly along racial lines. There was absolutely no way the message could be ignored, especially for a curious little girl who had learned to read rather early. I understood that most white people wanted nothing to do with African Americans. The few exceptions were those whites who interacted with members of our family in the course of business or who were professors at Paine College, the historically black college in Augusta, and our family pediatrician, Dr. McGahee, who treated his white and African American children with equal care. Everyone could choose a big lollipop after a visit.

My parents, who were deeply involved in local civil rights efforts and were quite vocal about the inequities that Jim Crow wrought, never shied away from telling us children the truth about segregation. The first of the lessons I remember was delivered near Reid Memorial Presbyterian Church, on the occasions that my family gathered to see President Dwight D. Eisenhower, who worshipped at this church when he came to town to play golf at the Augusta National Golf Club, the exclusive and then-segregated home of the prestigious Masters Tournament. My father would drive to this area of Augusta, called the Hill, on Sunday mornings to give a ride to the superintendent of our Sunday school, Mrs. Paschal. My father was very fond of Mrs. Paschal and she of him. As she was a much older lady and my father had lost his mother at the tender age of six years, I believe Mrs. Paschal held a special place in his spirit.

On occasion when the President was in town, as a family we would drive near the church, and either stand on the sidewalk or, more often, remain in the car to watch him walk into Reid Memorial. There were always people gathered to catch a glimpse of the

President, but nothing like the huge crowds that a head of state would attract today. This was long before Secret Service agents began keeping onlookers at a safe distance, even though three Presidents had been assassinated and another six had survived assassination attempts. In the 1950s these sad events seemed historical, not contemporary concerns. And so it was possible that if you were outside the church at a certain time of day when the President was attending services there, you might expect that he would come close and exchange pleasantries with the children. We would be dressed for church, but my father would not hesitate on some of those occasions to turn these trips into something of a one-car political rally. He might use this time to speak about Eisenhower, about history, segregation, and Jim Crow. He wanted it understood that although it was quite a wonderful thing that in our country one could be allowed such close proximity to the President, none of us would have been allowed inside that church to worship, and any African American Augustan encountering President Eisenhower at a different place, at another hour, would more likely have been responsible for carrying his golf clubs or in some other position of subservience. Invisible. Certainly, we were made to understand that President Eisenhower and all too many other whites were not on our side. In addition, my father was opposed strongly to Vice President Richard Nixon, long before such opposition became fashionable. Many African Americans in the South in those days were Republicans—the party of Lincoln, and the party of opposition to the segregationist southern Democrats. But not us. In those early days of the civil rights movement, my parents and our community supported those who supported us, our needs, our growth, our development, our partnership in this nation—and my father believed that Richard Nixon paid lip service to civil rights but was not sincere.

And so when watching President Eisenhower or listening to social and political discussion, my parents made certain that we understood the laws of the day. Remember, the casting of a vote was not at all a sure thing for African Americans pre-1965. There were poll taxes, and literacy tests that asked ridiculous questions like how many bubbles are in a bar of soap, or how many beans in a large jar. It was not possible to know whether or not such questions would be asked; it depended entirely on the demeanor and humanity of the person working at the voting station. But my parents insisted, too, that we understood—really knew deep in our hearts—that African Americans were as good, as capable, as loved by the Almighty as anyone else on this earth. And while making sure that we understood the reality of the times, they made equally sure that we knew, without any doubt, that we were surrounded by people who cared deeply for us.

We were taught to be proud of our heritage. Our ancestors, like those of a great number of African Americans, were brought to this country mostly from West Africa on slave ships. My great-grandparents were free and owned their land, but my great-great-great-grandparents were likely slaves. (We do not have records; we can infer this from the history of the time.) We were encouraged to find strength in knowing that we came from strong stock—that my ancestors endured things that we could hardly imagine, and yet they survived. I think about this fact when I consider my own work, my profession, my desire to contribute something to this world. Thinking of the strength and faith of my ancestors keeps my backbone straight, because the timber of which my soul and spirit are made is very strong. I owe them my best.

My parents represented that strength and courage to me in many ways that are only now becoming clear. Both were fearless in their involvement in America's ever-challenging social and political landscape in the American South of the 1950s and '60s; the city in which they chose to marry and raise their family made this so. Augusta, once the state capital of Georgia, had a burgeoning black middle class, but everyone from the doctors to the maids, the lawyers to the barbers, the teachers to the janitors, was bound by a federally sanctioned set of laws that dictated strict, arbitrary, and incredibly unfair boundaries between the races—boundaries that consistently threatened the ability of African American families to live, earn a decent living, and worship and socialize wherever, whenever, and with whomever they chose. It was only natural, then, that as African American Augustans grew weary of this unfair system, they would look to the movement being forged by civil rights leaders in nearby Birmingham, in Selma, in Mississippi, and in Atlanta, and pledge to right the wrongs waged against them in the community they loved.

My father's involvement in and commitment to the betterment of our community dates to the time when, as a young family man, he worked as a master mechanic on the Georgia Railroad. This line provided a major passageway from Florida to the north and west. My father loved trains probably more than any other form of transportation in the world, and he especially loved being able to work on them. As in many other professions, making ends meet was especially challenging for him and his fellow African American mechanics, because they were paid much less than their white counterparts—a distinction that became even more stark after the railroad's master mechanics unionized, but refused to allow African American mechanics of equal or greater experience and qualifications to join them. These were men who were so attuned to how a train worked, they were able to tell from the sound of it what precisely was in need of repair. Naturally, their being shut out of the union caused a great deal of friction, tension in the workplace, and my father and his colleagues were having none of it. Deciding to find other employment, my father looked to those within our church for support, and was steered toward the North Carolina Mutual Life Insurance Company, then the largest African American–owned business in the country. The company proved a good fit for him, and he discovered that he was a born salesman. He climbed the ranks quickly to become the manager of the Augusta offices, which served the entire central Savannah River area. Members of the families of the founders and top executives of the North Carolina Mutual Life Insurance Company, the Clements, Cheniths, and Spauldings, were often guests in our home, and we took great pride in having them there—in having this connection with these true pioneering families. And while being a leader in our church and president of the PTA at the local C. T. Walker Elementary School, my father was also president of the YMCA. These positions solidified his place in helping the community to fight for rightful treatment, rightful recognition of work, and for the recognition of our humanity. He loved being involved, called upon, and needed beyond his own household. It was easy to see the pleasure that he derived from it all.

My mother, in the meantime, was actively involved in registering African Americans to vote, long before the Voting Rights Act of 1965. As a member of the local National Association for the Advancement of Colored People, she joined many others going door-to-door encouraging neighbors to register—even in the face of all the dangers that such actions could attract. I would sit by her side proudly in the annex of our church as she helped people through the voter-registration process. My job was to place the three- by five-inch index cards in alphabetical order. I recall very clearly times when she would ask me to leave the table. I did as I was told, without understanding why she made this request. Years later, when I was already finished with part of my university studies, I broached the subject. "Mama, why, when I was sitting with you during voter-registration drives, did you sometimes ask me to leave the table?"

"Because some of the people who were registering to vote belonged to our church and had never learned to read and write," she answered simply. "They would sign their cards with an *X,* and I would have to witness their signatures by writing their names for them. There was no reason for you to see that." My mother believed deeply in the dignity of people, and she passed this on to us in her humility and kindness to all with whom she came in contact. Everybody loved Mother.

Certainly, in our home there was a lot of prayer for our safety, but not a lot of fear, because of the abiding faith that was held so close. Every evening, the reporting of Walter Cronkite, Chet Huntley, and David Brinkley brought news into our homes of the latest events in the civil rights struggle, and the stories and images could be horrifying, but my parents never gave us the impression they were afraid. Concerned? Absolutely. But somehow, they were sure that this nation of ours would come to its senses and recognize the humanity of us all.

It was natural that they and other people in the community were intimately involved in the battle for civil rights to the extent that they were, because the church was our community center—where everyone would go for spiritual fulfillment and updates about what was happening in "the movement" that week, whether it was a collective effort to integrate the University of Georgia or the lunch counters at the local Woolworth's. Right there in the church pew was where we all received our information—this was where the NAACP meetings took place; we went to these meetings together.

In due time, their involvement inspired us to act. I remember very often sitting in the living room with my father and my mother as they spoke about politics. And when we were old enough, they allowed us to lift our voices on behalf of our people. My brother Silas, then an undergraduate student at Paine College, led the NAACP's local youth chapter—the same one that, in 1960, lunged headfirst into the movement in Augusta when dozens of the college's students sat in or near the front seats of the local buses, only to be arrested, jailed, and found guilty of disorderly conduct for defying Jim Crow laws. They staged sit-ins at lunch counters with the same results. The struggle was local.

Honestly, although I accepted what my parents were telling me about having to work twice as hard to overcome others' preconceived notions about my abilities, I questioned how someone could not like me when they had not even met me. It could be that we could become friends. I was full of the "whys" of the struggle. And so, with a very young child's understanding of these grown-up societal issues, I set out to make my case—a mistake.

I was almost five and we were embarking on my first big train trip, off to visit relatives who had moved from the South to the Philadelphia area. I was so very excited about this adventure. We would take our lunch and I would wear one of my Sunday dresses, because this was to be a very special train trip.

Little did I know that one of the reasons we were taking a picnic basket along with us on the train was that we would not be welcome in the dining car.

When we made it to the train station, we repaired to the side of the station marked with the large, menacing sign COLORED ONLY. It wasn't a choice, obviously; for me and my family, there would be no sitting on the WHITES ONLY side. But what would happen, I thought, if I were to wander over to the seats in the other section? Would the train not take my family and me to Philadelphia? Would we have to go back home? I was intent on knowing these things, but I also wanted to be able to sit wherever I chose. And so I did—I moved over to the WHITES ONLY section.

My mother said hurriedly, gently, "No, Jessye, you should come over here and sit."

"No, I think I'll stay here—this is fine," I said, much to my mother's distress.

And there I remained, swinging on the railing that divided the seating areas and having a grand old time. Soon someone who worked at the train station—I do not remember if this person was African American or not—came in and watched me twisting and turning on the rail. In my mind, I was proving my point. Nothing bad was happening. My innocence remained intact for the moment, and we boarded the train as planned.

Of course, as I grew older, my understanding of the issues became more sophisticated, corresponding with the level of detail my parents shared with us. I was probably around eleven years old or so when one incident in particular rocked our community. "Children, we have to talk," my father had said to us one evening, shortly after arriving home. I remember our gathering in the living room, and my mother being visibly uncomfortable, knowing what my father was about to tell us. It was a somber time, indeed. An African American man had been charged with raping a white woman, even though everybody knew that he and this woman worked at the same hospital and had been carrying on a relationship that no one seemed to talk about publicly. A policeman had discovered the couple in a car doing what people do when they care about one another and, because of the times in which we lived, rather than tell the police officer the truth, the woman claimed the African American man was holding her against her will and raping her. I did not know what rape was then, but I knew from the sound of my father's voice and the look in my mother's eyes that this was an awful thing—and it was. The NAACP, my father informed us, had sent a young lawyer to Augusta to work on the case because, surely, the man was in serious trouble; he faced the death penalty if found guilty. As it turns out, that young lawyer impressed my father. "His name is Vernon Jordan," my father said. "I don't know that he's going to be able to help the man accused of this crime, but I do know that this young man, this Vernon Jordan, is going to make a name for himself. You watch. Write down his name."

As it turns out, Vernon Jordan could not help to save the accused; the Jim Crow laws were in full force. The man was found guilty and electrocuted by the State of Georgia for a crime everyone knew he did not commit. Vernon Jordan had been hired practically the moment he completed law school to work on the legal defense team of the NAACP. As it happens, the woman who accused the African American man—in actual fact, her boyfriend—of rape lost her mind completely. She would later be found wandering around various African American churches throughout Augusta on Sunday mornings, asking for forgiveness for what she had done; she could not find peace. When she found her way to a church, she was allowed to speak, as was anyone who wanted to stand up and testify before a congregation, whether it was to give thanks for the help that a grandmother received during her illness, or for being hired for a new job. Still, when this woman finished her apology and begged for forgiveness, the church was often silent as there was no discussion.

I cannot imagine what the adults felt about all this as I was much too young to understand the nuances of the situation or the reactions of those who heard the woman's plea. I imagine that it was quite a test for those churchgoers to practice that which is a tenet of our faith: forgiveness. I have no idea what happened to this woman as the years passed.

Since that experience, at so early a time in my life, I have been against the death penalty, but firmly. And true to my father's prediction, Vernon Jordan, as we all know, went on to "make quite a name for himself." I am honored to count him and his family as among my closest friends and mentors.

Not long after this most disturbing incident, I joined the local youth chapter of the NAACP, along with my siblings and many of our friends from the community and the church. Now in middle school, we participated in sit-ins and marches, and even though we were still very young, we understood fully the necessity, the implications of what we were doing.

Of course, the reverence we felt for Dr. Martin Luther King Jr., his strength, courage, and vision in the face of extreme adversity, was at a level far beyond mere hero worship. To us he was a leader and a prophet, and even the youngest of us recognized this. We children in the family were very fond of telling the entire world that our mother's maiden name was King, and that her family was from a part of Georgia not very far from Atlanta, which naturally meant that we could have been related. Or so the tale was told. Even as those hearing the story had their sure doubts, our imaginations ran unbridled; this was too delicious a fantasy to be hampered by mere facts! No one bothered to interrupt our beginning a sentence with something like, "Well, our maternal grandparents' last name is King and they live..." It was a shared fantasy, heard and enjoyed by many. Publicly, we followed his lead, doing all we could to help change our corner of the world. The closest I ever came to Dr. King was while I was standing at the corner near the Tabernacle Baptist Church one day, only a block away from my high school in 1962. Tabernacle, one of the most beautiful of all the black churches in Georgia, was the very heartbeat of the African American community at this time. It was the site of so many mass meetings, so many discussions about civil rights, so many inspiring homilies calling the town to action against the horrors of Jim Crow laws and their more-than-willing enforcers.

Of course, everyone was excited by the prospect of the Reverend Dr. King gracing Tabernacle's pulpit. But my family's excitement reached beyond that proverbial fever pitch with the knowledge that my brother Silas, then a student at Paine College and president of the Augusta Youth Chapter of the NAACP, would actually be in the company of Dr. King on this momentous occasion. On the afternoon of the speech to be delivered that evening, the pastor of the church, Rev. C. S. Hamilton, and my brother Silas escorted Dr. King across Gwinnett Street (now Lucy Laney Boulevard) as they made their way from a visit to the church and back over to the pastor's home. Reverend Hamilton's wife, a public school teacher, had been one of my teachers in elementary school, and both she and Reverend Hamilton were prized members of the community, so it was of no surprise that they hosted Dr. King in their home. I watched from a respectful distance as these three men crossed the street in the middle of the block, not bothering to cross at the light. I remember thinking to myself that my brother and Dr. King resembled one another. Or perhaps I imagined it. I was mesmerized by the sight.

At Tabernacle Baptist on the evening of the speech, the church was packed: there was not a space on a pew to be found. White visitors were also present at this gathering, as was typical when Dr. King spoke, and all was peaceful, with an understanding of the importance of the moment.

Dr. King's voice rang out as always, challenging the status quo and exhorting one and all to go forth in the spirit of Gandhi, in the spirit of nonviolent resistance, to that promised land of equality for all. Tabernacle Church was more than its edifice that evening; the sanctuary was filled with a spirit of unity, of recommitment to the struggle. Indeed, it was a proud moment for all of Augusta.

But there were dangerous moments as well, even for us children. As a teenager, I joined other young people in my community to help integrate S. H. Kress, Woolworth's, and H. L. Green, the five-and-dime stores in our city. We seated ourselves in the areas where we knew we were not invited to sit, and we ordered food, daring the staff not to serve us. The NAACP supported us in this effort, providing the money with which to purchase the meals. It was not a matter of having lunch, of course; we were fighting for equal treatment. Much tension accompanied these protests, because many of the workers at these lunch counters were African Americans and they worried both about losing their jobs if they served us, and for our safety, the children they loved. They certainly did not want to see us suffer bodily harm as a result of our actions—a threat that was ever present. But it was a risk that we, even as children, understood and were prepared to take—one that each of us in the movement understood.

On one occasion, the prospect of physical harm almost became reality for some of us. We were marching against a supermarket that, at the time, sat squarely in the African American section of town but refused to hire African Americans for anything other than menial jobs. The demonstration was very organized: the police were present, and all the required permits had been obtained, so no one was expecting trouble. Still, as we took part in the march, a scream suddenly rang out behind us. Were it not for that scream, I am not sure I would be here today, as it alerted us to a car careening down the street. The car had jumped the curb, and the driver was heading straight for us. We were able to disperse, and no one was hurt.

This incident surely frightened every last one of us. Still, we had to keep moving, through the fear and through the danger. It was hard for us to understand the level of hatred that would bring someone to contemplate such an evil act—to run down young people marching on a sidewalk. Or in other cases, to set trained dogs on peaceful protesters, or use powerful water hoses against fellow citizens. Where was humanity in all of this?

This is a question that would resonate among my fellow students one evening toward the end of my academic years at the University of Michigan School of Music. It is the norm to find schools and conservatories offering up presentations of student accomplishment, and this was the case on this particular day, as the opera department featured several of us performing singularly and in operatic ensembles. The preparations consumed most of the day, which meant rehearsals in the morning, a break for lunch, and further preparations in the afternoon for the evening's concert in Hill Auditorium.

I was unaware of anything happening outside of that space, although I noticed my friend from the orchestra stopping into the quarters I had appropriated as my dressing room rather frequently. I assumed he thought I was nervous about my upcoming performance, and I took this solicitous behavior as in keeping with his gentle personality and his always-loyal friendship.

The concert was well received, and only after all was completed did my friend reappear in my little space to ask me to sit, as he wished to say something to me. He went on to tell me that he hoped he had made the correct decision in keeping this information from me, as the news of the day was again very sad. "They have done it again," he said. "They have taken the life of an American prophet today: Dr. Martin Luther King Jr. was assassinated." He added again: "I hope I did the right thing in not allowing anyone to tell you."

We sat together for a short while. Without either of us saying very much, we put my things together and joined the others at our usual table at a nearby student restaurant, where we all talked, finally, of this latest tragedy and all the similar acts of notorious violence that had transpired during our study years—beginning, of course, with the death of President John F. Kennedy while some at our table were yet in high school, and of Medgar Evers. We talked, too, of those horrors committed against the many unnamed and unheralded civil rights activists whose lives were taken in hate: James Chaney, Andrew Goodman, and Michael Schwerner, those our own age, killed in Philadelphia, Mississippi. I recounted how Vice President Humphrey had introduced me to the then-junior

Senator from Massachusetts, Ted Kennedy, just months prior to this, when I sang in Washington at a service dedicated to the memory of slain civil rights leaders and workers.

We talked through the night. I thanked my friend for his sensitivity to me and assured him that all was surely well in our friendship, our mutual respect and our caring.

The reaction across the country to this latest assault on the spirit of a nation would be visited upon city after city. Fire!

There were those who believed that the plight of African Americans, all we had endured, from the slave ships to the plantations and cotton fields, from the limbs of southern oaks bearing their "strange fruit" to the bloodstained roads leading to Selma, would break the spirit of our people. Yet these horrors did not accomplish their goal. And any time that I have a chance to speak on this subject, I do, because it is vitally important that those who did not live through that period of our nation's history learn about it and understand it. See it through the eyes of those who did live through it. Know that there is still work to be done. As a people, we have stood tall in faith, in determination, and in knowing that the light that guided our forefathers and foremothers is the same light that must guide this world to tolerance, to mutual acceptance, and, indeed, to the fellowship of humankind.

This is certainly what I had in mind many years later when I stood in the Capitol Rotunda to witness Miss Rosa Parks, a woman who taught the world the power of quiet resistance and self-determination, receive her due. On that day, the mother of the civil rights movement was awarded the Congressional Gold Medal from the President of the United States, President Bill Clinton. The Rotunda was filled with those whose hearts would sing out with the true meaning of democracy: justice and freedom—a celebration of the best of humankind.

As Miss Rosa Parks was honored, she honored every single one of us with her serene presence.

How does one begin to offer an appropriate degree of thanks to an American icon—a person who helped to lead this country into the light of political and social change by deciding to take a seat on a city bus and remaining there? We know now that her early work with the NAACP in and around her community had prepared her for that moment. It was nothing so prosaic as a woman taking the first seat available to her at the end of a long workday, but rather an act of true protest, motivated by the sure knowledge that the unalienable rights belonging to all American citizens, belonged to her, too. She deserved to be feted over and over again—for her bravery and for her commitment to truth.

The Rotunda was packed to the brim: the President lauded her, the Reverend Jesse Jackson spoke stirringly of her place in our nation's history, the civil rights activist Dorothy Height was present, in one of her fabulous hats—I always loved her hats—and the ceremony was made all the more moving when the choir from my undergraduate school, Howard University, sang one of the Spirituals that I, too, had sung when I was a member of that very choir: "Done Made My Vow."

> *Done made my vow to the Lord*
> *And I never will turn back.*

I will go
I shall go
To see what the end will be.
Done opened my mouth to the Lord
And I never will turn back.
I will go
I shall go
To see what the end will be.

When I was a young mourner just like you,
I prayed and prayed 'till I came through.

I was beyond thrilled to have been asked to sing for Miss Parks, and was seated on the right-hand side of the dais, facing the hundreds assembled. When we all sang "The Star-Spangled Banner," I happened to be standing directly in front of Senator Patrick Leahy, who was seated in the first row of guests. He commented to me at the conclusion of the song, "Now, that was something else," or something to that effect. I admit it: I sang with as much gusto as I have ever put into our national anthem on that day! Miss Parks, our President, the Capitol Rotunda, the nation's highest civilian award being offered to an icon I admired, making her one of a relatively small number of citizens to be honored in this way dating back to the Revolutionary War: all of it was magical.

And for me, "America, the Beautiful" had seldom been truer to its words. For a country that would recognize in this important manner the magnitude of Miss Parks, while she was living, while she, too, could marvel at the distance traveled from Montgomery forty-five years prior to this national embrace, my heart was full. Miss Parks allowed us the privilege of thanking her, and it was done in a fashion befitting a true American hero.

MY SIBLINGS AND I, except for Elaine and George, attended seg-regated schools. I would say that this experience, being taught by African American teachers who were totally devoted to the out-come that they sought, which was our success, was in many ways a blessing. We were not lost in great big schools where no one knew our names, where no one paid any attention to what was happen-ing with us, but rather had teachers who, should we have had the courage (or the poor sense) to do something against the regulations, were on the phone personally to our parents. Those teachers gave us extra work because they knew that we had to learn to handle ex-tra work. They gave us their time, even after school hours, because they wanted to—because they deemed us important and worth the effort.

There were hundreds of students in my elementary school, spanning the first to the eighth grades. Yet we were addressed by our names, because the teachers knew us. I received a first-rate education, one that made me stand out as an undergraduate stu-dent when taking those early examinations at Howard University. For example, due to the extraordinary English teachers I had all through school, I did not have to take freshman English. And it was because of one of my favorite teachers, Mrs. Viola Evans, who insisted in her eleventh-grade English class that we learn and recite a new poem every week that I had such good practice with memorization, which would serve me so well, later.

One of the people I met my second day at Howard had come from a high school in Little Rock; when she told me this, I just hugged her and we had a good cry. I knew what had happened at Little Rock; I sympathized, I empathized, and we became friends forever.

My parents expected the best from us, and this was no less true for our friends.

I knew instinctively which boys would be welcomed at home and which ones would probably not be. It was easy to see this from watching my father. He really did reveal the utmost dignity, respect, and manhood in his interactions with my mother. By watching this and many other such niceties, I learned how men of a certain generation wished to deport themselves in the presence of the women in their lives; providing such care and support seemed to come to them as naturally as breathing. On the odd occasions when the car door was opened for me as a child, I would sit up properly in the seat, feeling and looking more grown-up, since that was how I was being treated.

I learned, too, about the ways of men through fascinating conversations with my older brother's friends. I suppose I was more than a little flattered that they would sit still for a conversation with me. I was interested, genuinely, in what they were doing in high school, in the high school band, and on their travels with the band! I wished to know all, and I was so very happy that Charlie and Ronnie seemed to enjoy our little chats; it did not matter that maybe they were just being polite out of respect for their pal, my brother Silas. But those fascinating conversations, and my relationship with my father, made it so that, even to this day, I have the ability to have uncomplicated relationships with boys and men.

Of course, this knowledge did not come without its missteps when I was younger.

I knew, for instance, that a boy who was, like me, in the college prep track at school would be well received at home, and I usually adhered to those expectations. Except for when it came time for the senior prom. I worried for two weeks before telling my parents that my date was a budding basketball player who was not exactly a stellar student. I offered the news one evening over dinner, but only after my mother prompted me by asking, "Has anyone invited you to the prom?"

"Yes," I answered nervously.

"Oh, well, that's nice," she said. Understand: Mama said "that's nice" about most things. "Is it that nice boy that was over here studying with you that time?"

"Oh, no," I said. "It's not that boy."

"Oh, but I thought you liked him," she said.

"I like him fine, but he is not the one who invited me to the prom." And so I blurted out the boy's name and silently hoped for the best.

My mother gave me a quizzical look. "I don't think I know him."

I summoned my courage and out it all came—who he was, that he played basketball, that he was the cousin of my best friend, Ernestine. I had hoped that this detail would make him an acceptable date for the prom. My parents did not say much at that dinner, but I knew that I would need to coach this young man—let's call him "John," to preserve his privacy, poor darling—about how to behave when he came to my home to pick me up for the prom. He could not afford to get it wrong—not with my parents. I told him at least a thousand times: "You must bring a corsage in a little box and you will hand it to my mother so that she can pin it on my dress," I insisted. "Now, if you want to make sure we never get out of the house, just start toward my chest with that corsage in your hands. Don't even think about it."

John was fifteen minutes late picking me up, which earned a stern "Why are you late, young man?" from my mother before he could even get into the living room. He managed the matter of the corsage very well, but he missed the mark when my father asked him an extremely important question—a question my father reserved for anybody who was more than ten years old: "Young man, what are your plans?" Now, if you were going to be in Silas and Janie Norman's house, you needed to have a good answer to that question. Saying "I hope to have a job over at Kelly's filling station for the summer," as John did, was not really a plan. Not for my parents. A plan was that you would be working hard all summer because you were starting college in September and you needed to save your money for books and fees. Needless to say, John did not stand a chance. He was probably not at all distressed that our friendship did not stand the test of time, which in high school is about three weeks.

These standards, set so long ago, influence my life today: be conscious of one's choices, resolute in one's beliefs, and always maintain integrity and a work ethic that demands concentration and focus. To this day, my parents' charge inspires me to "get on with it."

This is one of the many reasons that I do not sing in a language that I do not speak or that I have not studied. Not just the pronunciation of words, but the actual language, its verbs and modifiers and subjunctive case. In preparing new compositions for my repertoire, it is important that I know how I feel about a new piece of music, and have become well acquainted with it prior to rehearsals with my piano accompanist or with the conductor. This time spent on my own facilitates a real collaboration.

I am also inspired by the community in which I grew up and from the examples of the adults in that community, including my own parents, to lend a hand in service to others, particularly children interested in the arts. When I was a youngster, arts education was simply part of public school education. In recent years, though, we have allowed this to fall out of the public education curriculum, which is unfair to children and reflects a lack of understanding of the value of the arts in the growth of our young people. Every study of the rewards of arts education shows that regardless of the socioeconomic standing of the family, a child with arts education as a part of their studies performs better in all other subjects. One of the reasons for this is that through the arts, children learn a very basic tenet, a vital thing: the benefit of repetition. Whether you are learning the capital of every state, or the C major scale on the piano, if you practice over and over again, you become better at it.

The arts also show children at an important time in their lives that they have a voice inside of them, and that the world wants to hear this voice—that they can demonstrate their individual thoughts, feelings, concerns, in a positive way through the arts: in singing, movement, painting, writing, pottery making, and all that their imaginations can conjure. The socialization that can arise from such experiences provides a foundation for interaction with others in the workplace, and in one's private relationships, for a lifetime.

It is this mission that drives the school for the arts that bears my name in my hometown. Founded by the wonderful Rachel Longstreet Foundation and its primary voices, Dr. Linda Scales and Professor Ellis Johnson, we are excited to serve talented children who would otherwise not be able to avail themselves of private arts tutelage. And while we face daunting financial challenges, I am thrilled to say that we are now in our eleventh academic year. We are supported by personal and corporate donors from all over the nation, and sometimes even from foreign countries. The county board of education provides school buses that both bring the children from their regular schools to us each afternoon and return them to their schools to be picked up by their parents and guardians.

The children are such an inspiration. They have to audition in order to be admitted, and each day they recite a creed that says in part, "I am a part of something that is greater than myself." We have agreements with the parents and guardians of all the children that state that whatever the child is studying, she or he will also practice at home. We have amazing relationships with the parents of these children, because they see the difference in their sons and daughters after just a few weeks of being with us. The children can arrive for their first days of study at the school a little nervous and a little timid, and yet, by Christmastime, they walk with assurance, their shoulders back and their heads held high.

One of our students came to us having demonstrated a wonderful gift for graphic art. He had no idea that he could dance. He happened to have passed a dance class one afternoon, thought that it looked really interesting and athletic, and decided he would give it a try. It can be difficult for a boy at age eleven to relay to his friends that he is actually interested in classical ballet. Luckily, he had the courage of his desires and now, at age fifteen, he is studying with a professional company, the Augusta Ballet, where in 2011 he performed small roles in the company's presentation of *The Nutcracker*. During the summer, he also studies with the Atlanta Ballet. He is so good, so beautiful to watch, that I can hardly see him perform without becoming misty-eyed. And to think he might have lived his life without knowing that he had this gift inside of him. When he extends his limbs, he always seems to know what his fingers are doing. The stretch is complete. Any choreographer will tell you how important it is to dance with every millimeter of one's body, and Justin does exactly that. And it is hard not to be overwhelmed by his dedication and confidence and that of the other children. You will not hear them say "I want to be a dancer." But rather "I *am* a dancer." If that coming out of the mouth of an eleven-year-old does not bring joy to the heart I do not know what will. There is such talent, but also purity of thought, kindness to one another, determination to succeed, and enjoyment that one sees on every face.

We are blessed with a dedicated staff and marvelous teachers. They are with us because of their love for the children; it is easy to see as they extend themselves so beautifully in all that they offer to their students. We are not trying to form little Marian Andersons or a new Ossie Davis; most will doubtless go on to careers outside the arts. Our hope is to assist these children in becoming complete people. Creativity equals self-knowledge. This knowledge can lead to wisdom, and wisdom to the understanding of others, which undoubtedly leads to tolerance. The guiding principle of the school is that if children are able and encouraged to engage in artistic expression, they will be better qualified to lead and heal the world. They will see the light in themselves and deduce that this light must also exist in everyone else. I express a simplistic view of the world—because love and loving are simple acts.

ALTHOUGH WE HAVE made great strides since the 1950s, we cannot pretend that racism is no longer a huge problem in the United States and in the world. Just two weeks or so before graduation ceremonies at Howard University in 1967, the centenary year of this lauded institution, I would learn that racism could be so ingrained in our society as be present in the mind of practically anyone at all. There, in the pulpit of Andrew Rankin Chapel, a sacred place at that school where all manner of religious, political, and academic leaders have offered speeches, calls to action, and homilies over many decades, the National Teacher of the Year arrived to give a speech.

The problem arose when he made mention of having "an Afro-American friend," a friend who enjoyed a drink once in a while, he said. He carried on to show us how his friend would "entertain" when intoxicated, complete with a bit of "soft-shoe," with head swinging and arms flailing about in the air. All this in the pulpit of Rankin Chapel!

I was beside myself with frustration and shock, and it showed. I felt that I could not just leave the choir stall, as I wished to do nothing to compromise my own impending graduation. The concert choir, as always, was seated in our normal place in the chapel, behind the speaker. I stood with the rest of the choir when it was time for our presentation, but could not utter a note. The thoughtlessness and disrespect displayed by this man had been more than my spirit could manage.

A faculty member who noticed my difficulty came to my aid after the event and suggested that I not attend afternoon classes, but take a walk around the reservoir to clear my mind and my heart of my extreme distress. Dr. Doris McGinty, the first American to have received a doctorate in Musicology at Oxford University, was that faculty member. We remained friends and in touch until her passing in 2005.

WE HAVE OUR FIRST African American President, but racism exists all over this planet. Discrimination due to the color of one's skin, religious affiliation, belief, creed, or sexual orientation — all the reasons that we use to separate ourselves one from another — pervades our world. Although I travel all over the world and count presidents, prime ministers, other heads of state, and some of the most fascinating, accomplished, intelligent people of this great earth among my audiences, I am not immune to racism's sting.

Take, for instance, a few short years ago, when I had an encounter with a security guard while exercising in the swimming pool at the Casa Del Mar Hotel in Santa Monica, California. It was about 7:00 p.m.; I had waited until well after the sunbathers had left the area so that I could work out in peace and quiet, minus the less-than-interesting conversation that inevitably comes when a group of people are relaxing around a swimming pool. About forty minutes into my water aerobics routine, just as I was telling myself, *You have fifteen more minutes—keep going, kid,* I noticed a pair of shoes at the pool's edge; I looked up, and filling those shoes was a young-looking man who appeared to be addressing me. I had earplugs in my ears so I couldn't hear him, and since the last thing I wanted to do was stop my routine, I kept exercising in the hopes that he would simply leave. He did not. Exasperated, I took out one earplug. "Can I help you?" I asked.

"Are you a guest of the hotel?" he asked confrontationally.

By that time, I'd been a guest of the hotel for five days. "Who are you?" I asked.

"Security."

"Well," I said with as little emotion as I could muster. "How do you think I would have gotten through the lobby dressed in a wet suit and wearing plastic and foam exercise boots, not to mention holding these handheld weights, if I were not a guest of the hotel? Obviously, I am a guest of the hotel."

Think of this: a first-generation American, as demonstrated by his manner of speech, was comfortable in confronting and questioning a fourteenth-generation American as to her right to be in a hotel's swimming pool!

In the end, I asked his name, completed my workout, and returned to my accommodations before engaging the general manager of the hotel in conversation by phone. I explained that I had not been pleased with that security guard's questioning, and suggested that in order that the matter not escalate into something that would be even further distressing, perhaps he would consider making a contribution to a charitable organization of my choice. The contribution was made; the Casa Del Mar and I parted company forever.

Maybe there is just something about the nature of hotels, because that was not my only experience with racism in one. Such was the case when I was invited, sometime in the mid-1990s, to leave the cold, dark-too-soon-in-the-day February climes of the Northeast to give a series of recitals in Florida. One visit was to Naples, a city that, at the time, had a thriving chamber music series. As is always the case, I allowed time in my schedule for the adjustment to a change in climate, arriving three days prior to my first performance date. I checked in to the Ritz-Carlton Hotel and did my usual ritual of unpacking: always the performance clothing first, so that any creases from the travel might fall away without any further attention required, and then the rest of my things. I do not tend to rush such matters, but it was the middle of the afternoon and I could hardly wait to take a walk on the beach. My gym shoes were at the ready, as was my Miyake two-piece outfit. And off we went.

The interior garden of the hotel was quite large, so it was a bit of a walk to find an exit that would take me to the beach. I came upon an open-air restaurant—"pretend rustic," I call such places

—and spotted a table at which a group of people sat, dressed for a winter conference in New York rather than a walk on a Florida beach. They were the sole table of guests there. I smiled to myself, thinking that I was the only one dressed for the premises.

No sooner had I begun to make my way around this restaurant and out toward a boardwalk to the beach than the skies changed suddenly. Rain looked imminent. Five or six others were standing in the same place, probably reconsidering their own beach-walking plans. I had been waiting only a few minutes when I noticed one of the wait staff pointing in our direction as she spoke with a man dressed in some sort of uniform. I did not pay close attention to this, as I was far more concerned with the rapid changes taking place in the sky. Moments later, this uniformed man came over to me, past the other people standing in the same place, and asked if I were a guest of the hotel. My response, apparently, was not good enough for him; he demanded that I show him my room key.

This was more than I was prepared to accept.

I asked to speak with the hotel manager, and soon found myself in the office of a Mr. Conway (or something similar), to whom I related my story. He insisted that there were no bad intentions on the part of the staff and that he was "sorry for the inconvenience."

Inconvenience!

Seeking to make other accommodations in Naples for the remainder of my stay, I contacted the performance organizer. "You would not be happy with the other hotels in the area," she insisted, adding that "hearing such things" had made her "sad." And that seemed to be that, from her point of view.

Later that afternoon, an African American employee of the hotel was dispatched to my accommodations in an effort to "soothe things." She wished me to understand that she "enjoyed" her job in the press office of the hotel and that there was surely no racism at the Ritz-Carlton. I thanked her for her visit and, as I really felt uncomfortable on her behalf, gave her permission to leave. I did not care to discuss the matter further, and surely not to hear explanations of the goodness of her employers.

I performed my recital in Naples that week. But I have never stayed in another Ritz-Carlton Hotel, other than the Hotel Arts Barcelona, which joined the Ritz-Carlton chain long after I had been staying there for years. I have a long relationship with that particular hotel, not to mention a long-standing love affair with Barcelona.

Racism is so pervasive in this country and in the world at large that it has, in many instances, become unconscious. It can slip into the daily discourse and go unrecognized, even by people who clearly ought to know better. Consider that in February 2013, a public school teacher in the South was so insensitive to racism and its painful past, she assigned her students "slave mathematics" questions: "A slave was whipped five times per day. How many times was the slave whipped in a month?" It is hard to believe that someone could be so oblivious to the effect of such misguided thinking, but such was the case. I have faced it myself in the course of my professional life.

Early in my performing life, I found myself in a situation that to this day astounds me on those rare occasions when it is recalled. In a piano rehearsal for an opera with a conductor and several other singers, the conductor complimented me on my Italian pronunciation. I responded that I had enjoyed performing in Italy that year at the Maggio Musicale in Florence, and took pleasure in listening to the Italian spoken around me, so much so that, while there, I had joined into conversation with much more confidence in my skill in the language. I had studied Italian, of course, but the visit to Florence had been only my fourth trip to Italy.

"Is your family from somewhere other than the United States?" the conductor went on to ask.

I told him that we were descendants of Africans, with, as is very often the case, some Native American blood. Without missing a beat, he responded: "I was sure you were no ordinary Negro."

I excused myself from the rehearsal, citing its proximity to the orchestral rehearsal slot and reasoning that perhaps it would be wiser for me to rest my voice for an hour or two. My voice needed no rest, but my spirit most assuredly did. Pervasive racism sears.

Still another conductor would have a similarly inappropriate thing to say to me, this time during a discussion about the efficiency of the stagehands who were working on the very quick scene changes needed during one particular act of the opera in which I was performing. The conductor stated with glee: "Oh, those boys are working like blacks!"

On neither occasion did either of these supposedly educated, experienced "men of the world" apologize for their remarks. The racism was indeed unconscious.

Yet another example of this came a few years ago when I was invited to sing for the Queen's birthday in England. Those respon-

sible for planning the festivities programmed some of the music of
Scott Joplin, the African American composer who helped create
ragtime—a decision that surprised me. I was to lead the chorus of
the Royal Opera House in singing "God Save the Queen," as well
as a rarer melody, "I Dreamt I Dwelt in Marble Halls." I recognized that the Queen Mother's birth (the mother of Queen Elizabeth II) would have overlapped with the musical career of Scott
Joplin and that perhaps the organizers were making that connection, along with the obvious upbeat quality and spirit of the piece.
Joplin's "Marching Onward" from his opera *Treemonisha* would be
performed. The evening would be guided by a well-known English conductor.

Our piano rehearsal went well until we happened upon the Joplin. The piece is composed in what is called a slow drag, a style with
two beats to the bar. The conductor had obviously not spent much
time reviewing this score, and was conducting it in four, while the
rehearsal pianist struggled to accompany his beat and my singing. I
could see how he could make the mistake. So after we rehearsed it
in the wrong meter and after people cleared for their break and so
as not to embarrass him—because there is never a reason, ever, to
do that—I went up to the podium and, in confidence and with the
utmost respect, said, "Excuse me, but a slow drag is in two."

Instead of saying, "Oh my goodness, thank you very much," he
snapped: "Well, it's *your* music. You *must* know."

The insult was clear. I wasted no time stating, "I can also talk to
you about the second movement of Schubert's C Major Symphony,
when you have time. Because I always prefer the second movement
a little bit slower than conductors are doing it these days."

For the rehearsal with the orchestra, the conductor found the correct meter for the Joplin and we proceeded in the performance as professionals should.

Certainly, this kind of insulting behavior is not reserved for the stage. I face a fair share of bad behavior, too, in just the normal course of business—behavior that reminds me that racism, more than anything, is about ignorance and misunderstanding. Consider that a major network thought it a fine idea to invite me to play a role in a sitcom pilot about three maids who take the bus to work in the suburbs of Chicago. It is important to note that at that moment, my stage work consisted of roles where the lead was that of a queen of a country, as Alceste, Dido, Jocasta, and so forth. The person who sent me this prospect surmised that "the hook that would spark my interest" would be that my character had a love interest, and that this "unusual relationship" would be the center of the story from time to time. Utter foolishness! And it's the kind that never seems to end. More recently, I was asked to consider playing a maid in a Civil War–era stage play written for Broadway. I made it very clear that this would be a consideration only if the play would depict the Civil War from the point of view of the maid. This, as it turned out, was not the plan. Pervasive racism.

Some years ago I attended a holiday party only to find that the hostess, a record-company executive at the time, had invited music critics to the same gathering. I have never thought it sensible to fraternize with those whose jobs require them to judge the work of others, and I have therefore endeavored always to avoid such situations. One does not wish to give the impression of favoritism by social interaction with critics, or to present one's self as being open to their ideas or influence. In any case, I was in the midst of a busy season and so my stay at this party was going to be relatively brief. After discovering that these particular guests were in attendance, I decided to take my leave even sooner than planned.

Before I could make my exit, however, I was confronted by one of these critics, who asked to speak with me about something. My curiosity got the better of me, so I assented. But the moment he broached his subject, I knew our conversation would not end well.

A colleague of mine had been in the news recently, not for artistic matters, but rather for what was described as behavior unbefitting that of a prized performer. Unable to stop himself, the critic blurted out, "The story going around is that you stated that someone needs to tell her she is black." The story was bogus, of course, but the critic, in presenting himself this way, had revealed a mean-spiritedness that left no doubt in my mind as to his inability to witness a performance by an African American and present a measured, nonbiased assessment—not with this kind of foolishness floating around in his being. Was he implying that such behavior was acceptable for anyone *except* those of African descent? Would my having confirmed this story legitimized the implication in his mind?

Yes, there is a lot of prejudice and intolerance of all kinds in all disciplines, and if people think this is not the case in classical music, they are mistaken. Sadly mistaken. Remember, it was within my young life that the great Marian Anderson was invited, finally, in 1955, to perform with the Metropolitan Opera, after more than a quarter century of performing for kings and queens and dignitaries around the world.

At one point, I started keeping a journal of what I termed "racialism as she is spoke," to document the language of racism that I encountered not only in the United States, but worldwide. I was paying particular attention to newspapers and television in England and Australia, countries in which I was performing over an extended period. In the case of Australia, the pervasiveness and normalization of racist language was evident during my first visit to that continent. In conversation with my "new friends" about their country and its amazing natural beauty, one of them actually referred to Native Australians as "jungle bunnies." I had never heard this term before, but it took only a nanosecond for me to comprehend its meaning. The person who used the term did so flippantly, oblivious to any social breach.

Another "friend" in England complained that there were "only three white children, real English children," in her child's school class. "Oh, what should I do?" she worried.

"Do?" I stammered. Why not help her child understand that the majority of people on the planet on which she resides are not of her skin color? Would that be a starting point?

I abandoned the journal after a few months, as it soon became thick with examples of such thoughtless, mindless discourse, and I thought I was doing a disservice to myself in rereading and rethinking them.

As we continue the search to find ways of helping our fellow humans to a place of respect and comfort for all, I am reminded of the words of Anna Julia Cooper. There are several quotations to be found in the pages of a U.S. passport, and one of these quotes is hers, this luminous African American scholar of the nineteenth century: "Freedom is not the cause of a race or sect, a party or class. It is the cause of humankind; the very birthright of humanity."

For me, freedom is clothed in the understanding and recognition of the worth of every soul on this earth. Every soul is as full of value as one's own.

I take great solace in knowing that even as race continues to divide us, innocence abounds. I am reminded of this when I think of a little friend of mine, a French girl I shall call Yvonne, who was no more than eight years old when I came to know her through her parents, who taught French, English, and Spanish in an international school in the South of France. Yvonne had a lot of different-looking friends because of the nature of her environment, and so she tended to focus on traits and qualities such as kindness or laughter in describing them. The way children do. One Sunday afternoon after a lovely, leisurely lunch, she and I went for a walk in the fields of her parents' property, having a fine visit, when she told me about a new friend she had made. "He is from a country called Africa," she said proudly. "That is a place very much south of here, but they have some of the most beautiful people I have ever seen. My new friend is wonderful. He is just such a very nice person and I am so glad he's in my class at school."

"He's from Africa?" I inquired.

"Yes," she said excitedly. "We know where Africa is because we saw it on the globe in school."

That child went on and on, talking about her new friend and

the continent from where he came and how nice he was, and never once did she mention his skin color. So I asked her about it: "Yvonne, what color is his skin? Does it look like mine or does it look like yours?"

Her answer was so simple. "Je vais aller jeter un coup d'oeil demain," she said: "I will have a look tomorrow."

What is more beautiful than this? She just saw *him*. Nothing more. Nothing less. Just a beautiful new friend who came from a continent called Africa. This helps confirm what I grasped instinctively as a child: that society will, inevitably, come to the understanding that racism is mindless, lacking in all the light that is within us. And despite all evidence to the contrary, I still hold to that belief today. I am an eternal optimist and thus believe that one day all of humankind will embrace the fact that we started from the same basin and share a common origin. Our migrations around this planet determined our manner of speaking and the way we look, but that's about as far as the true differences go. It is wonderful to see us evolve on the issue of race. Laws have been changed, and although there are still people wedded to their thoughts and feelings in bigotry and prejudice, many more are coming to understand the emptiness of such thoughts. And the times have, in many important ways, changed. I do wish, like so many others, that my parents had lived to see President Barack Obama take the oath of office. Not once, but twice! I feel that both my mother and father, along with countless others, were disappointed that their hard work, particularly of the 1950s and '60s, did not yield more tangible fruit in their lifetimes. But I remain steadfast in my belief—the belief planted in my heart by Janie and Silas Norman Sr., that some fine day, the world will right itself and say, collectively, "Well, yes, that person looks different from me, has a different belief system, a different creed, but what does it matter? We are all one gargantuan family: human."

INTERLUDE:
MARIAN ANDERSON

"MY LORD, WHAT A MORNING"

My Lord, what a morning,
When the stars begin to fall.
Done quit all my worldly ways, join that Heavenly band,
My Lord, what a morning,
When the stars begin to fall.

*O*ne of the neighbors who lived next to my childhood home in Augusta was Miss Daisy. She did not have children of her own, but she had us, the Norman kids, and we loved her as she loved us. She was really Mrs. McCluskey, the wife of a well-known minister, but we children all referred to the female grownups in our lives by employing "Miss" and their first names.

I have many fond memories of Miss Daisy, and in particular the two huge, beautiful pear trees in her backyard and the phonograph that adorned her living room—both of which she allowed us to use practically at will. But, I promise you, by the time I left home for university, I had had my fill of pears. It seemed that every piece of fruit those trees bore ended up in our house one way or the other—

as pear purée, pear preserves, canned pears, baked pears, pear pies and tarts. Everything you could do with fruit, we did with Miss Daisy's pears. I was pear-free at Howard University. The season for the cherry tree in our own yard was much shorter, and one had to be quick to beat the birds to the harvest, so I never tired of cherries.

In our house, we did not have a phonograph that played seventy-eights, but Miss Daisy did, along with a wonderful collection of recordings, many of which had been given to her as gifts. Miss Daisy loved music, and as a nurse at University Hospital, she understood its healing power and was one of the first persons I knew to have played music for her patients. Miss Daisy never once hesitated to allow free access to her living room and to her phonograph. I could visit whenever she was at home and enjoy listening to her recordings.

One of the recordings to which I listened at Miss Daisy's house has never left my mind: it was a 1937 disk of Marian Anderson performing Brahms's "Alto Rhapsody"—a wonderfully extended song for male chorus and orchestra, set to the text of Johann Wolfgang von Goethe's poem "Harzreise im Winter" ("A Winter Journey in the Harz"). I am still as inspired by the text and this music as I was all those years ago when it was not absolutely clear to me what all the German words meant. But somehow I felt that the words were important. I wondered how a female voice could sound so deep, so rich, so beautiful. At the time, I was more accustomed to what I now know to have been soprano voices. Of course, Marian Anderson was a famed contralto. I listened again and again to the recording, mesmerized by that voice and somewhat amused that Miss Daisy's phonograph bore no resemblance to the one we had at home, which played LPs and which had the little disk that held our thirty-threes in place and allowed them to drop down to be played one by one. This machine at Miss Daisy's house seemed a far more serious piece of equipment.

The name Marian Anderson was already a part of my consciousness. For several years, in the celebration of Negro History Week—which later became Black History Month—I had been encouraged by my mother to go to the library, to read as much as I could find about this great lady, and to make her story my assignment for this single week of celebration of our unique history. Our parents and teachers made certain that we knew the stories of renowned African Americans past and present, and so I was aware of Marian Anderson's importance in the world, along with performers like Mattiwilda Dobbs, a fellow Georgian, and Roland Hayes, both internationally known opera singers, as well as other luminaries like Ralph Bunche, Jackie Robinson, and, later, Hank Aaron. The list became longer as my knowledge and experience increased.

One day, a year or two after my wonderment at hearing "The Alto Rhapsody," I was playing in the yard with pals when my mother called to me to say, "There's something on television I want you to see." It was summertime and early evening, with the promise of several more hours of daylight. I was having a good time outside and did not welcome the idea of going inside to watch television.

This, of course, was at a time when television was not the vehicle for trivial entertainment it is today. We did not so much as have a set in our home until I was about nine years old. We had our favorite shows: *The Firestone Hour,* a classical music presentation sponsored by the Firestone Tire Company, which featured live

American symphony-orchestra performances. Then on Sunday afternoons, *Leonard Bernstein's Young People's Concerts,* with the New York Philharmonic, was a must-see. This was followed by a program that my brothers and I also loved, which had nothing at all to do with music: *Wild Kingdom.* We would all sit together early on Friday evenings to watch *The Goodyear Television Playhouse,* which offered live theater on television—imagine that! This is where I first saw a young Julie Harris and the heralded Geraldine Fitzgerald along with such famous English actors as Laurence Olivier. Television certainly had its merits.

Still, playing happily in the yard, just beyond the garden of corn and cucumbers and beets and greens and okra we tended and prepared for our family meals, was much more fun, and I wanted to stay outside.

"No, this is very important," my mother insisted.

I dusted myself off and went inside to watch this important television program. And right there, on our console black-and-white television set with the rabbit ears on top, was the story of the woman whose singing had entranced me a year or two earlier: Marian Anderson, in a documentary of her life, *The Lady from Philadelphia.*

I sat there, totally transfixed by the narrative of this beautiful, stately, majestic African American woman singing all over the world, in several languages. I was completely engrossed by the images of her being presented at court in Norway, England, and Austria. And though I was beginning to process the separate and unequal treatment we faced in the South, I nevertheless had a hard time understanding how a woman as magical as Marian Anderson could face the same discrimination, the same obstacles, as all other African Americans. Seeing her image in our living room that afternoon, I am sure, ignited a passion in me—gave me insight into what could be. I was singing at the time at all different types of events in our community, and singing was as natural as breathing. I had no thought of singing as a possible profession. A path to such a goal was not apparent.

Around the same time, I found and read Miss Anderson's biography, *My Lord, What a Morning.* By now, I was a total devotee. I could hardly bear to read about the trials she'd faced, the hardships placed in her path in her own country.

A WORLD-RESPECTED AND ADMIRED ARTIST, Marian Anderson's voice was described by none other than Arturo Toscanini as being "a voice that comes around once in a century." She sang the world over, at a time when an African American classical singer was an anomaly; there were so few. The reverence she garnered around the world was clouded by the separate and absolutely unequal laws of the day. Despite her talent and extraordinary ability, Miss Anderson was barred from studying at the colleges, conservatories, and universities that would have given her the opportunity to work with those able to support such an enormous gift. At this time, historically black colleges and universities offered wonderful choirs and courses that prepared students for teaching positions in music, but not solo-performance studies.

Even though Miss Anderson saw her professional life truly soar in the years leading up to her debut at the Metropolitan Opera in 1955, this grand lady of the world was relegated to segregated train cars, saw doors to hotels and restaurants closed to her, and was even banned from performing before integrated audiences. Yet on the stages of the smallest church halls and high school auditoriums, she offered that much-revered voice with a majesty that was hers uniquely. And when she lifted her beautiful voice for the masses on the steps of the Lincoln Memorial in the 1939 concert organized by First Lady Eleanor Roosevelt, a fitting response to the Daughters of the American Revolution's refusal to allow the great Miss Anderson to perform on its stage at Constitution Hall, Marian Anderson forever solidified her place in America's consciousness — in America's history. She demonstrated the full meaning of her faith and her humility when she offered as her first song that Easter Sunday morning "My Country, 'Tis of Thee."

> *My country, 'tis of thee,*
> *Sweet land of liberty,*
> *Of thee I sing.*

It was the actor Ossie Davis, a friend of Anderson's who had been a student at Howard University at the time, who recounted to me the details of that groundbreaking concert and who spoke so movingly of just how subtly, powerfully, she used her voice that day in what is widely recognized as the first-ever public protest concert in America.

"There was a chill in the air," he said. "Spring had not quite settled in on the Potomac, but the sun was shining, and once we all packed together it was fine. And when she came out, there were all those microphones and television cameras waiting to capture the moment. Miss Anderson was wrapped in a coat, not showing the least amount of worry, just opening her mouth to sing her spirit and soul."

Miss Anderson had never considered herself to be an activist, but in fact, on that Sunday morning, she was. When I think about how, despite the pervasive prejudice she experienced, she did not allow hatred to dampen the song within, I can only be grateful. Just by lifting her voice, she opened doors and turned on the lights so that the rest of us would be able to see our way more clearly. I am grateful to her. With my whole self, I honor her.

This is, indeed, what I had in mind when we celebrated the beginning of the new millennium at a New Year's Eve celebration in Washington, a magnificent soiree that would have as its centerpiece a concert on the steps of the Lincoln Memorial. I thought it fitting and proper that Marian Anderson, who died in 1993, be honored at this celebration. My colleague Kathleen Battle agreed readily to join me in singing "My Country, 'Tis of Thee" with a live orchestra and, on a large screen behind us, the film of Marian Anderson's 1939 performance of the same song. Blessing us. It was a remarkable visual.

Miss Anderson was famous for speaking of herself and her performances in the third person plural. She would say something like, "We sang for the king of Sweden," not in reference to herself and her accompanist, Franz Rupp, but herself and her God. Her faith did not allow for time to dwell on those things that were meant to cause her pain. She felt that doing so would cater to that part of the human spirit that she did not wish to feed. Her spirit was not different, in many ways, from what we understand of the expansive hearts of Gandhi and Dr. Martin Luther King Jr., and of the Dalai Lama; open-hearted embrace of all.

Each understood that they were placed on this earth for a purpose, and that nothing should inhibit their missions from the Divine. Even in our quiet, intimate moments when I was blessed to be in her presence and I dared to ask her how she felt about the spectacle created by the Daughters of the American Revolution, she did not wish to elaborate on it other than to say, "All of Washington came. I was so glad to be in good voice. The morning was cool and we sang for the people." That was all.

THE FIRST TIME I had the pleasure of being in the audience with Miss Anderson on the stage was during my second year at Howard University.

For her performance in Washington on her farewell tour that year, Miss Anderson would sing on the symbolically charged stage of Constitution Hall. The poignancy of this, the history of it all, surely was not lost on us. We students, from all of the colleges and universities in the Washington area, could attend an entire series of concerts sponsored by the Washington Performing Arts Society under the leadership of one fabulous impresario, Patrick Hayes. The charge for the tickets for the entire series was twelve dollars. Naturally, our seats were practically in Heaven, but we cared not a bit, as we were in the hall and the offerings from the stage transfixed us. On this particular evening, there were so many people wishing to greet Miss Anderson after the performance, I worried that Patrick Hayes would have to forgo his practice of allowing the students to step in first to say a quick thank-you ahead of the other audience members. But this was not the case; we were able to be in the very same room. I have no recollection of the words that fell from my mouth upon meeting her, but I hope that at the very least I mumbled "Thank you," as one of many in the sea of admirers happy to be in her presence.

Only seven years later, in 1972, just two years into my own professional life, I had the wonderful surprise of being present for a performance of *Les Troyens* at the Metropolitan Opera House, on an evening when the great Marian Anderson was in attendance as well. I do not know which made me happier: seeing this production or knowing that Miss Anderson was in the house. Coincidentally, this would be the opera in which I would make my Metropolitan Opera debut in 1983, though such a thought was far from my mind on this particular evening. Meeting Miss Anderson by chance in the lobby of the opera house was more than one could even dream. I was introduced to her. She was as gracious as one could imagine she would be.

"Where were you born?" she asked simply.

"Augusta, Georgia," I responded, probably too quickly, being rather excited.

"Oh, yes," she said. "I sang there, I think sometime at the end of the forties or the beginning of the fifties, at Paine College, in your hometown."

"Yes, ma'am," I said. "And everybody still remembers it, I promise you."

Of course, I was barely a gleam in the eyes of my parents at the time Marian Anderson graced the stage at Paine College in Augusta, but to this day, a highwater mark in that city and for the college is the memory of "that time that Marian Anderson came to town!"

At the Met, now, a crowd began to form around her and the whole place seemed to be abuzz. In our short, personal time together, I felt an aura—an energy that was unmistakable. There was a kindness and joy there. Surely, there were lots of reasons why she could have displayed quite a different character, but she showed only patience, the patience that comes from knowing oneself fully. I watched from the sidelines as she greeted her admirers with a humility and warmth that were unmatched. I learned a great deal that evening: kindness is its own reward.

Over the years, we forged a friendship and bond that I shall cherish forever. She lived not too far from my home in New York, about forty-five minutes due northeast, in Danbury, Connecticut. I was always struck during our visits by the fact that she was much more interested in what I had been singing and where, than in recounting her remarkable life. I would say something like, "Oh, please, just talk about any of your experiences—I do not mind what. Tell me about any trip or program," and she would answer, so gently, "No, no, let's not talk about that. What did you sing in your last performance? Where did you sing this? How did you feel?" That simply amazed me. It still does.

Because life can sometimes offer blessings beyond anything you might hope for, I had the opportunity to sing for Marian Anderson at a matinee performance at the Met in *Ariadne auf Naxos,* of Richard Strauss, conducted by James Levine, with Kathleen Battle in the role of Zerbinetta. The entire cast had been told that she would be present. Miss Anderson was seated in the center box of the parterre, so we could sing the entire performance to her. There was neither nervousness nor worry, even though that performance was being videotaped for an international audience, for the purpose of turning the recording into a DVD. The thought of her presence had a distinctly calming effect on me. I wished only to do the very best that I could, because one of my mothers—one of the people who helped to form me—was sitting in the audience. Miss Anderson served as a wonderful inspiration for that performance, and I was so grateful that she was there. She came backstage afterward, as did the music producer Quincy Jones, also in attendance that day. We took loads and loads of photographs and had a perfectly wonderful afternoon together.

Erlkönig • Franz Schubert • Erl-King

Wer reitet so spät durch Nacht und Wind?	Who is riding so late in the windy night?
Es ist der Vater mit seinem Kind.	It is a father with his child.
Er hat den Knaben wohl in dem Arm,	He holds the child close in his arm
Er fasst ihn sicher, er hält ihn warm.	He holds him securely and keeps him warm.
Mein Sohn, was birgst du so bang dein Gesicht?	My son, why such fright in your face?
Siehst, Vater, du den Erlkönig nicht?	Father, do you not see the Erl-king?
Den Erlenkönig mit Kron und Schweif?	The Erl-king with a crown and tail?
Mein Sohn, es ist ein Nebelstreif.	It is the play of the fog, my son.
Du liebes Kind, komm geh mit mir!	You beautiful child, come with me
Gar schöne Spiele spiel ich mit dir.	I will play wonderful games with you.

Manch bunte Blumen sind an dem Strand,	There are magnificent flowers on the beach
Meine Mutter hat manche gülden Gewand.	My mother has costumes made of gold.
Mein Vater, mein Vater, und hörest du nicht,	Father, my father, do you not hear
Was Erlenkönig mir leise verspricht?	What the Erl-king says to me so quietly?
Sei ruhig, bleibe ruhig, mein Kind:	Be calm, rest easily, my son
In dürren Blättern säuselt der Wind.	It is only the rustling of dry leaves in the wind.
Willst, feiner Knabe, dur mit mir gehn?	Lovely child, won't you come with me?
Meine Töchter sollen dich warten schön,	My daughters are waiting for you already
Meine Töchter führen den nächtlichen Reihn	My daughters make their dance of the night
Und wiegen und tanzen und singen dich ein.	And will rock, dance, and sing you to sleep.
Mein Vater, mein Vater, und siehst du nicht dort	Father, my father, do you not see there
Erlkönigs Töchter am düstern Ort?	The daughters of the Erl-king in that dark place?
Mein Sohn, mein Sohn, ich seh es genau:	My son, I see it clearly
Es scheinen die alten Weiden so grau.	The gray of the willow trees shines in the night.
Ich liebe dich, mich reizt deine schöne Gestalt;	I love you, I am enraptured by your body
Und bist du nicht willig, so brauch ich Gewalt.	And if you are not willing, I'll take you by force.
Mein Vater, mein Vater, jetzt fasst er mich an,	Father, my father, he's taking me
Erlköning hat mir ein Leids getan!	The Erl-king has done me harm.

Dem Vater grauset's er reitet geschwind,	The father in horror rides quickly
Er hält in Armen das ächzende Kind.	while holding his moaning child.
Erreicht den Hof mit Müh und Not:	He reaches the farmyard exhausted and fearful
In seinen Armen das Kind war tot.	The child in his arms is dead.

6

Growing Up in Germany

"ON MY JOURNEY, NOW"

On my journey now, Mount Zion,
And I wouldn't take nothin' for my journey, now.
One day, one day, I was walking along
When the elements opened, and the love come down,
Well, I went to the valley, but I didn't go to stay,
Well, my soul got happy and I stayed all day.
You can talk about me just as much as you please,
But the more you talk, I'm gonna bend my knees,
On my journey now, Mount Zion,
And I wouldn't take nothin' for my journey, now.

I say often that I grew up in Berlin. It was where I came to understand more fully that the world was made up of so very much more than I had imagined or studied. The Berlin Wall was erected in 1961, and of course this historical event was discussed in our high school history classes. Yet it was quite another matter to arrive in this city and experience the starkness of the wall firsthand, and to find that "Checkpoint Charlie" was nothing more than a series of temporary metal-and-glass sheds, and that crossing from

West Berlin into East Berlin with an American passport was a matter of walking across a street. No bridge, no overpass—just a short walk to the other side of a city street. The distance was not very far, but the divide—economically, politically, socially, and yes, culturally—for a people with a common heritage could hardly have been wider.

My mind expanded there. I learned a great deal in a relatively short time. For instance, I was introduced to the great works of German expressionism—something that I do not recall having studied in my art history courses. I was fascinated by the German romantic painter Caspar David Friedrich. East Berlin served as a major part of my world university. And I was a sponge absorbing it all. I was engaged to sing at the opera house in West Berlin, yet I would spend a great deal of time on the other side of that menacing wall.

I came to know students and their families, and to find that the wall prevented travel for anyone under the age of sixty-five who wanted to leave the Eastern bloc, beyond what one referred to as the Iron Curtain. I was asked by adults not that much older than myself to describe Paris—to talk of the city lights, the River Seine, and the Eiffel Tower—or even something closer, such as the grand concert hall in West Berlin, the Philharmonie. "What does it all really look like?" they would ask.

Until then, I considered my education to have been well rounded, while understanding at the same time that one never really stops learning. But this experience of East Berlin and its sister countries across such an awesome political divide was profound. The warning to never take anything for granted was driven into my consciousness in a new way.

Having been raised in the United States, with the blessing of fresh fruits and vegetables from my grandparents' farm and the variety of foods available at the neighborhood grocery stores, it was surprising to visit a part of the world where you could go for two years without coming across oranges for sale, or where you would have to be up at 4:00 a.m. in order to have a chance at purchasing a loaf of fresh bread.

Yet despite such deprivation, or more likely because of it, the arts thrived. The concert halls and opera houses were always full in Eastern Europe. People arrived at arts performances early, long before the scheduled starting times, to take their seats. I experienced a deeper understanding of the power of music, the transformation that can come from gazing upon a great work of art. In Eastern Europe, the arts provided a source of strength and spiritual nourishment that could not be taken away by the building of a concrete wall or the denial of civil rights—of human rights. The human spirit would not succumb even in the midst of such politically inspired cruelty.

ON MY VERY first visit to Germany for the Bayerischer Rundfunk Internationaler Musikwettbewerb competition, two years before I moved there, I'd found it illuminating to meet so many other young musicians at about the same stage of preparation and study as I. The competition was not limited to singing; many other disciplines were included, such as piano, wind instruments, string ensembles, and solo orchestral instruments. It was such a delight to meet a singer from the Netherlands named Marco, who was already a television star in his native country, with his own Saturday-evening variety show, in addition to the members of the then newly formed Tokyo String Quartet, and the American clarinetist Richard Stoltzman.

After my disturbing exchanges with the judges in the first two rounds of the competition, I'd found the third round by far the most challenging in every way. All of the finalists performed with orchestra and all of us required rehearsal time. The conductor was charged with preparing a good deal of music within a rather short time period. Hercules Hall was full that evening; the sense of anticipation and excitement was palpable. It was all I could do to maintain concentration. After all the finalists had presented the required two or three compositions, we could do nothing but wait for the adjudicators' decision. We were taken to a room backstage; the audience waited in the hall. Trying to relax in such a situation is fruitless; I sat with a book, pretending to read.

For hours the jury deliberated. One of the things that made these hours almost bearable to me was the knowledge that the following day would be my twenty-third birthday. Only my friend Julius knew this—not another contestant, and surely no one waiting in the hall for the announcement of the winners.

Sometime late in the evening the door to our backstage quarters opened. Hermann Reuter, the designated head of the jury, entered the room with various papers in hand. I sat up in my chair and, as did everyone else in the room, waited for his remarks. He began by thanking us all for being a part of the vocal competition, and wishing us success in our professional lives. We waited. Eventually, Mr. Reuter read the names of the singers who were to receive honorable mention prizes. Then, as is customary, he announced the fourth prize and upward. The first prize for the men's section of the vocal competition was read: Michael Schoepper took that honor. Mr. Reuter seemed quite emotional in reading this name, as a German singer had won first prize on his native ground. Finally, the first prize for the women's vocal competition was announced.

I do not recall my own reaction to hearing my name, but I do remember the kindness of every one of my fellow contestants as they rushed over to congratulate me and give me a hug. Soon we were all on the stage of the hall again, with the patient remaining audience members in their seats, and the announcement of the prizes was offered in precisely the same manner as had been done backstage. The audience erupted when my name was read. I was overwhelmed by the response. It was after midnight. Only then did I say to one of the other contestants that it was my birthday. I was too shy to allow her to make a general announcement, so we kept that bit of news to ourselves.

I had no way of making phone calls that evening, as my youth hostel had no private telephone and the concierge was by then long asleep, making any plea to use his phone impossible. The next day, however, I had two calls to make: the first, to the United States Information Agency to announce my news and ask, "What now?" Most of the contestants who had been sent to Europe by the USIA had been entered in more than one competition. We had all been advised that should we be recognized in the first contest, awarded an honorable mention or whatever, rather than continuing on to the next competition we should instead take advantage of a Eurail pass and travel to a European city of our choice for our further education and a round of sightseeing, before returning to the States waving whatever level of recognition we had received in the first competition. However, there had been no instruction as to what the protocol was if one happened to *win* the first competition. My second competition was to take place in Geneva, and all my plans for traveling there were set.

Having had to wait until a reasonable hour to make the call to USIA that day, given the six-hour time difference, I had had a moment to absorb the events of the previous night. It was with no small amount of cheekiness that I spoke with the appropriate person at USIA, first with the news of my win, which he insisted I repeat, thinking he had perhaps misheard me, and then to ask, "Well, what about Geneva now?" We both relaxed and laughed as it became clear that I would not be continuing on to Switzerland for the next competition. I was overjoyed, over the moon.

The next phone call was of course to my parents. In my mother's absence my youngest brother, George, then about nine years old, answered the phone. He was happy to find me on the other end of the line and insisted on having a conversation. I asked where Mother was, and he informed me that she was in the backyard. My entreaties to him to go and get her fell on ears not hearing a word. George had begun piano lessons a few months prior to this time, and he took tremendous joy in his progress. Rather than go find my mother, George insisted that he now play something for me. It happened that in our house the piano and the telephone were in the same room. As I stood in the post office at the train station in Munich, the pile of coins that I'd brought with me for the pay phone became smaller and smaller as I listened to my brother's piano solo. After his performance, George returned to the phone to tell me that not only was the piece, "The Little Red Hen," new, but that he had just played it with both hands! I did not wish to seem unenthusiastic, but I am sure a bit of desperation must have begun to creep into my voice. Finally, my mother came to the phone and I was able to tell her my news. She said she could not wait to call my father and everybody else. Then, with a tone in her voice that identified her as a mother, she asked, "But you are still coming home for Thanksgiving, yes?"

"Of course," I responded.

We talked until the coins ran out completely, with her last words ringing in my ears: "Happy birthday, honey."

I learned two important lessons then and there: Coming in first in an international competition would be significant from a professional point of view. But only with my family, the supporting characters in my life, my mentors, my teachers, my friends, was it possible to "win" anything.

In Munich there were several promoters and agents who traveled to the big international competitions, on the lookout for emerging talent. I was lucky to be offered some engagements that were to begin in a matter of months. I would have to take a deep breath and plan the next steps with advice, clarity of mind, and the full knowledge that I was only twenty-three years old. I was, for all intents and purposes, still in my "babyhood" for a singer, with a voice that could not be characterized as "coloratura" or "light lyric soprano," or one that, over the course of time, would most likely remain in the same repertoire. I understood that my voice was changing, and I was willing to allow that to happen and simply looking forward to the experience. Yet in singing, as in so much in life, people are more comfortable in their interactions with you if they are able to place you in a category that is supposed to reveal to them all that you are able to do, the music that "suits your voice," the roles that you will sing onstage, and indeed the roles that you will play in life.

Soon after winning the Munich competition, I had the dubious distinction of being the subject of a print interview where the journalist, perplexed at the few performance notices I had by then received, in which my selections had ranged from music typically performed by altos, mezzo-sopranos, and "young dramatic sopranos," did not hide his frustration at deciding where I "fit" in all of this, stating something like, "Well, what kind of soprano are you, anyway?"

My response, which I credit as being the only really clever thing I had said to date, arose out of my twenty-three-year-old consciousness: "Excuse me, but I think that pigeonholes are only comfortable for pigeons." The journalist was not greatly amused by this statement.

I returned to the States after Munich and joined Elizabeth Mannion, with whom I had been studying at the University of Michigan. She had now taken a position in the voice department at Indiana University, in Bloomington. I had no means of support, so being invited to stay with Mrs. M.'s family and enjoy the extremely good cooking presented daily by her mother was simply magnificent. One does not forget such kindness—such openness of hearts and hearth. Her daughters, Grace and Elizabeth, became close pals of mine. As for Mrs. M., I am so grateful that our work together continued over the years. She has always been there to say something like "No, you are not giving yourself time for the preparation of that very low note; the vocal chords need a moment. They must articulate very slowly indeed, to give you a sound at such a low pitch. After all, yours is a female voice. Take your time." She has absolute passion for maintaining agility in the voice, no matter the type of voice. The aria "Una voce poco fa," from Rossini's opera *The Barber of Seville,* is one of her favorites for this task. I must say I have been met with amusement from time to time when, in preparing to sing the music of Berlioz, Strauss, or Wagner, for example, and I am warming up my voice with this particular aria, some of my colleagues have come to my dressing room door to say something like "You're surely full of surprises." I find this very endearing. Most people do not normally associate fioritura/coloratura singing with all types of voices. Nor do we always understand that the ability to maintain agility in the voice is as necessary to long-term singing goals as learning to breathe properly.

One of the reasons a runner is able to manage a marathon is because of having mastered the shorter distances — having learned at what point, if the body is not allowed to relax into the best position for such a long run, it will tire. Pacing is learned in the shorter distances, making it possible to understand the adjustments that need to be made in the change from a thousand meters to eighteen kilometers. Marathon running and lengthy operatic roles have a great deal in common in the manner in which pacing and breath control contribute to the best result. The physical support that is given by the breath is very much the same.

I RETURNED TO GERMANY in late January of 1969. Due to my good fortune in Munich and my association with the United States

Information Agency, recitals were arranged for me in what were then called Amerika Häuser. These centers were established directly after World War II as places for the general public to gather for artistic evenings, lectures, and so forth, to learn about all things American. At these gatherings, even American food was served. I have to say that some of the best hamburgers I have eaten, in the days when I still ate meat, were served at these wonderful receptions following the recitals. I would offer programs of European music except for the last group on the program. Encores were always songs from America, and mostly Spirituals. During this time I visited Munich, Frankfurt, Berlin, Cologne, and Hamburg. I would remain in Germany for about three weeks.

Because I look at my life as something that happens "while I've been making other plans," it transpired that in May of that year, an American industrialist from Cincinnati, Ohio, J. Walter Corbett, arranged for directors from some twenty different opera houses in Europe to spend about two weeks in New York at his invitation, to listen to American singers. Mrs. Corbett, I understood, had herself wished to pursue a singing career, and had endured the rigors of traveling from opera house to opera house in Europe for auditions. Several people involved in classical music in the States agreed with Mrs. Corbett that there had to be a more reasonable way for opera directors from Europe to hear American singers. Her very willing husband possessed the means to make this happen. Avid philanthropists, they were supporters of the arts and a number of cultural institutions in Cincinnati, and were prepared to take on this challenge. And they did.

Opera house general managers mostly from Germany, Swit-

zerland, and Austria came to New York to be feted by the Corbetts
and to listen for several days to singer after singer. They were there
to offer advice, surely, but also to evaluate the singers, all of whom
arrived in New York at different stages in their performance lives,
for employment opportunities afforded by more than fifty opera
houses with full seasons.

Through some miracle, I was among the singers chosen to travel
to New York and perform before this august group of opera house
managers. Arriving in the city, I was accommodated in a hotel on
West Fifty-Seventh Street. The day of my audition was rainy. I was
not prepared for inclement weather, the hotel did not offer umbrel-
las, and it was difficult to find a taxi. A bit damp and my hair and
makeup now somewhat the worse for wear, I finally hailed a cab
and asked the driver to take me to Town Hall. "Where?" he asked.
I restated the name of the venue. He claimed not to know where it
was. Eventually I arrived at the hall, where the directors were just
about to take a break for lunch. Talk about luck. I would have time
to dry off, retouch my makeup, and even warm up quietly. I had
begun my preparations, of course, in my hotel room, but by now,
that felt like it had happened in another century. I was able to calm
myself, to find the pianist, with whom I would have no rehearsal,
and to offer copies of the two arias that I would perform: from the
opera *Samson et Dalila* by Saint-Saëns, the aria "Mon coeur s'ouvre
à ta voix," and the composition that was by then my standard audition piece, Elisabeth's second aria from Wagner's *Tannhäuser*.

I offered my performance and returned to the holding area
backstage, where by now a few other singers had gathered. We
exchanged pleasantries and I began gathering my things to leave.

I was not certain what to do, since no one had greeted us back-stage or given us any information as to what we should expect once our performance was completed. As I was about to take my leave, a very tall gentleman with a distinct German accent called out to me in perfect English and introduced himself as Professor Egon Seefehlner, the general director of the largest opera house in Germany, the Deutsche Oper Berlin, in West Berlin. He complimented me on my audition and asked almost nonchalantly if I happened to know the rest of the opera—*Tannhäuser.* Too quickly, and full of excitement, I said, "No I do not, but I could learn it in about a week." And I meant it. He gave a wry smile and stated just as quickly, "No, it need not be quite so fast, but I do have an evening in December when I would be able to offer you your debut in my opera house in the role of Elisabeth in *Tannhäuser.*" I must have taken a breath or something to gain a modicum of composure before saying something along the lines of "Thank you. I'll start working now."

Before this unimaginable day I had spent three months in Durham, North Carolina, living on something now deemed to be unhealthy—the rice diet—and studying conversational German, which I audited at Duke University with a visiting professor from Berlin. Now, with this invitation to have my debut in Berlin in six months, both the rice diet and my conversational German studies took on totally new meaning. I worked hard—very hard—on both. In no time at all I had memorized not only the role that I would sing in Berlin, but the rest of the opera as well. This was long before countless CDs of the opera would be available, long before even the invention of the CD, so after a wide search at various record stores,

I was able to find a long-playing disk recording of *Tannhäuser,* with the wonderful Wolfgang Windgassen in the title role.

Eight years prior to this, my esteemed colleague, the legendary Grace Bumbry, had created nothing short of an international sensation in the role of Venus in a 1961 production of *Tannhäuser* in Bayreuth. She was magnificent in the part. The rest of that year's casting received far less attention for their strong contributions to the production. Venus, the goddess of love, the erotic seductress in *Tannhäuser,* is the polar opposite of Elisabeth, who embodies the quintessential, mythological, highest purity of German womanhood. The choice on the part of Professor Seefehlner to have me sing the part of the "pure as the driven snow" Elisabeth, rather than the temptress Venus, showed remarkable comfort in his role as intendant of his opera house.

The thought of arriving in Berlin unable to speak German never came into my mind. I would work at this and happily so. I wished to reward Professor Seefehlner's confidence in me from the start by being able to address my colleagues at work in rehearsals in the language of the country in which I would sing.

The role of Elisabeth in *Tannhäuser* is a beautiful one, complete with one of the most glorious opening arias of any opera that I know: "Dich, teure Halle" ("You, dear treasured hall"). This happens to be the very same aria that the adjudicators in Munich had "requested" me to sing during the Bayerischer competition. It was curious indeed to think that this competition had taken place only one year and two months prior to my standing in a rehearsal room in Berlin.

Elisabeth enters the opera in the second act. In the production in Berlin, while singing this powerful music I was required to walk down a nearly forty-five-degree incline that began far up-stage and ended downstage, on the flat part of the set. I rehearsed on a mock-up stage in a rehearsal room, but not on the real stage with a real set. As this was not a new production, I had not been offered an "on the stage" rehearsal. I was much too naive to know that I should have asked for one, or at least for rehearsal onstage with the piano. Thanks to the Windgassen recording, the orchestral sounds were in my head.

Fortunately for me, the singer for whom the production had been created four years earlier, the wonderful Elisabeth Grümmer, made it her business to seek me out on a rehearsal day, even as she was preparing to sing another of her signature roles that evening, the Marschallin in *Der Rosenkavalier,* by Richard Strauss. The generosity of this gesture, of this thought, of this kindness, still touches me. She wished to relay that in managing the incline, I should walk with my head erect but with my eyes fixed firmly on my feet, something no one in the audience can notice, she assured me, because they cannot see the position of your eyes from the height at which you begin the aria. She went on to say, "I do this all the time, and have never had to be concerned at all with tripping over my own feet." She gave me an embrace and I thanked her repeatedly for this advice, and shall do forever, as it has saved and served me in many an opera production.

While I came to understand rather quickly the physical perils accompanying this particular opera production, it perhaps took a little longer to fully grasp the social, political, and even cultural daring on the part of Professor Seefehlner in casting me in the role of Elisabeth. He trusted that I could arrive on a professional operatic stage for the very first time, sing a quintessential female German operatic role, in German, in an opera of Richard Wagner, in his opera house, where even the street on the side entrance for artists is called Richard Wagner Strasse. For his faith in me as well as his innumerable kindnesses, I will be grateful forever. After all, Elisabeth is the lead female role, the character who through the very goodness of her heart and spirit wins the devotion of the hero, Tannhäuser. She wins his heart in spite of Venus and all her sensual enticements. Venus demonstrates in the extreme the adage that "Hell hath not fury of a woman scorned," and immediately sets in motion the destruction of Tannhäuser, his fall from grace, his banishment from the presence of the woman of his heart, Elisabeth. Elisabeth and Tannhäuser end their lives seeking his pardon and the hope of their being reunited.

German twelfth-century mythology is filled to the brim with stories of saintly women and their opposites. Elisabeth, the sainted one in *Tannhäuser,* had never up to that time been performed by an African American, and it is indeed bittersweet to state today that this role, which I have sung in Berlin, the Royal Opera House at Covent Garden, London, as well as the Metropolitan Opera, has not to date been filled by another African American.

History has proven Europe to be more receptive of diversity in artistic presentation than America, and, indeed, of the artists themselves. During those long periods in American history when the stage doors, the theaters, the concert halls, the opera houses were shut firmly against its own citizens, artists of color found places for their art to call home. The stories are legion. One thinks particularly of the period after World War II when Langston Hughes,

James Baldwin, and others created their own artist colony in Paris. Paul Robeson found success as a matinee idol in Europe for his great acting ability, most particularly in his portrayal of Othello, and for his deep well of a singing voice. The Soviet Union gave him respect and a stage; he would pay dearly in America for accepting these gifts to his spirit and soul. The story of the great Marian Anderson is well known.

Robert McFerrin Sr. would soon follow Miss Anderson's 1955 debut at the Metropolitan Opera, as would Mattiwilda Dobbs.

Sissieretta Jones, the first of us all, found a home on the stage of Carnegie Hall in 1892, a scant year after it opened. They were few, but there were promoters and organizers who had the humanity and courage to insist that the performing arts had no room or patience for prejudice and its dangerous and limiting influence.

THAT OPENING NIGHT in Berlin would prove to have more surprises in store for me than for the audience! The second act, in which Elisabeth makes her first appearance, went very well. I was grateful to have the support of my more experienced colleagues, in particular the "always in voice and ready to perform" Hans Beirer, in the leading role, and Martti Talvela, with his rich bass-baritone voice, in the role of the Landgraf. Martti and I became lifelong friends, and I will always cherish the kindness he and his entire family have shown me over the decades.

I was in my dressing room preparing the costume change for the third act, with all the staff assistants from the opera house carrying out their various duties, when who should tap on the door but the general intendant himself, Professor Seefehlner. Of course I was delighted that he had been happy with my performance in the second act, but I was not at all prepared for him to state, then and there, that he wanted me to become a member of the opera house, and that he had brought the contract with him.

I responded by reminding him that we had not yet completed the opera. I still had act three to do.

He smiled and stated that he had heard me sing the aria from the third act in New York, and that he had been in the rehearsals and was confident that this act, too, would go well. I was nonplussed.

I stumbled over my words, saying something like "Well, Herr Professor, legalese is for all intents and purposes unreadable in English; I cannot imagine what it must be like in German."

I added that my father had always impressed on me that I must never sign my name to anything before reading it thoroughly. Another smile came from Professor Seefehlner when I suggested that perhaps the folks at Amerika Haus would be able to help me with the translation. Professor Seefehlner asked if I would perhaps prefer to have an agent assist in the matter. Would an agent be absolutely necessary? I asked. And since it was not, I declined such assistance.

Before parting, Professor Seefehlner said that he wished me to have a wonderful time in the third act. "Something tells me you are going to be all right in this profession. No agent? Hmmm."

I SHALL ALWAYS be grateful for Berlin, artistically, socially, and politically. For broadening my view of the world through everyday experiences and what I am sure was a subliminal absorption of rituals and practices. For me, Berlin allowed for a very personal cultural revolution.

I made a habit of being in the company of those new friends of mine who spoke only German, to train my ear to colloquialisms and to understand and incorporate phrases that are to this day peculiar to Berlin.

The singers that I joined in Berlin understood the feeling of being the new person in town. They went out of their way to invite me to sit with them in the canteen of the opera house, or to share a beer following a rehearsal (I enjoyed the camaraderie more than the beer).

Everyone had been an *Anfänger* (a beginner) at some point in their lives. Since a performance life is a very demanding one, the support that we offer one another behind the stage can mean the difference between success and the lack of it.

My Berlin education was not just musical and cultural, it was also political, as I made many visits to East Berlin with a day visa, requiring a return to West Berlin by midnight. I was always on time.

I was on time the evening when one of the East German or Russian soldiers in East Berlin demanded my passport, escorted me into a room with no lights on, left me there, and locked the door behind him as he left. Midnight passed. I was on the wrong side of the Wall. There was no lavatory, no water, no manner in which to advise anyone in West Berlin as to what was happening to me.

Finally, well past 2 a.m., the door was opened, my passport was handed to me, and a soldier stated in German, "you can go now." I received no explanation and surely no apology.

I crossed the street at Checkpoint Charlie, wondering how I could explain my now very late arrival at the barrier. As I began to speak, the soldier there stopped me, gently, and asked if I had enough money to take a taxi home (rather than the subway). He stated, "You have had quite a night; get home safely." I was grateful for this extraordinary kindness.

I allowed time to pass before crossing over into East Berlin again, but indeed, I did return. On one occasion, when our new student pals from the east accompanied those of us who had visited as far as they were allowed to go, we talked for a moment through the chain-link fence that held them on that side of the divide. I suppose I must have been a bit teary-eyed by the time we reached the crossing. One of the West Berlin soldiers looked at me and said, "Sie Konnen nichts dafur," meaning, "you cannot do anything about this"!

I remained in Berlin for three years, always with the freedom to pursue my recital performances as well as those with orchestra all over Europe, and after a short while in the States, as well.

The opera house had more than eighty operas in its repertoire, providing me the opportunity to see performances that I could not have seen in the States. My first acquaintance with the operas of Leoš Janáček, for example, came in Berlin. It would take another decade for these operas to be presented in England and in America.

I was still a relative neophyte, however, and I was being offered roles that were not suited to my still-developing vocal apparatus and artistic acumen. After a time, it became clear to me that in order to preserve my chances of singing for the long haul, I had to gather the courage of youth and take matters into my own hands. I presented myself in the office of Professor Seefehlner one autumn morning.

I thanked him for the trust he had placed in me in bringing me to Berlin and allowing me the experience of a lifetime: to learn, to hear music of the highest level, both at the opera house and over at the Philharmonie, with Herbert von Karajan and that rather fabulous band of his, as well as being able to go across the road to the Schiller Theater and listen to German that was so beautifully spoken, it was hard to imagine that the plays of Shakespeare had not been written in that language.

The great opera director Walter Felsenstein was at the time working magic on the opera stage in East Berlin. All of this was there for me, providing an unrivaled arts education.

But then, because I had no one to do this on my behalf, I stated that I thought it wise for me, best for me, to leave the opera house for a few years and seek further vocal development, in order to return to the opera stage when in my thirties.

In my mind, it seemed a reasonable plan. Professor Seefehlner was not unkind—but he was not as taken with the idea as I, and did not hesitate to say as much.

He wished me well; I took my leave.

One of the things that gave me great comfort in this fairly major career decision was something that a very famous colleague of mine had said to me only a few months prior. I will not embarrass her by mentioning her name, but the advice is unforgettable. I had the great pleasure of working with her on a recording. In the various breaks, we had time for conversation; I treasured these moments. One day she said, "I wish to say something to you that I trust you will remember always." Looking me straight in the eyes, out of earshot of all our other colleagues, she continued. "Remember always, you are the only person in the world who will look after your voice. I want you to promise me that this is what you are going to do. You are the only one who does not have an agenda for your voice that has nothing to do with your vocal preparedness at this time in your young life. You are the only one who will care for your voice in the way that it needs. You are the only one who can say no. No, my dear, is a complete sentence."

Whenever possible, I pass these words on to the many young singers who wait so very impatiently in the wings for their chance to shine.

I HAD NO GRAND PLAN as to what I would do next after leaving Berlin; only a bit of work in England. I sent my possessions into storage, packed the necessary things for my new obligations, and off I went.

This professional decision made sense, it seemed, to no one but me. The thought of leaving colleagues who had become good friends, of forgoing a steady paycheck and such benefits offered by the Deutsche Oper Berlin as a month's vacation and two weeks annually at a health farm in order to preserve one's fitness for the work, might have seemed ill considered. Yet I gave all of this up to, in my mind, preserve my professional life, my voice; to save myself.

It was not until I was comfortably tucked away in a rented flat in London that I shared my decision with my parents. My father's reaction was a long silence on the other end of the line. My mother, on the other extension, said something like "Well, I am sure you must know what you are doing. What are you singing in London and do you have a place to stay?"

Thank Heaven for my parents.

Let me say here quickly that only a few years later I was assured that Herr Professor did not hold a grudge. When he was named director of the Vienna State Opera, he was kind enough to offer me the opportunity to sing the very last role he had offered me as a twenty-seven-year old in Berlin, the leading role in *Ariadne auf Naxos*. Then well past thirty, I was more than happy to accept.

I WAS VERY FORTUNATE during this beginning stage of my professional life to work with great conductors, and to witness the work of other magnificent artists with whom it would be my pleasure to make music later. It was my privilege and honor to perform the songs of Gustav Mahler with the wonderful conductor Rudolf Kempe, who encouraged me to remember the teachings of Carolyn B. Grant: that singing should be a natural and enjoyable expression. When singing words full of sadness and longing, it is our responsibility to bring those emotions and thoughts to the minds of our audience. The dramatic content is important for informing our own performances, he would point out, but it is our duty to "bring the audience to this depth of emotion." This we do through our musical expression: the cord of empathy from the stage to the audience and back again.

This idea of words and meaning was made ever clear to me one day in a master class at the University of Michigan with the wondrous baritone Pierre Bernac. His book on French singing technique remains a classic, especially for those whose native tongue is English, and should be in the hands of anyone wishing to understand and perform this literature with assurance. His vast experience made it possible for him to offer advice in other languages as well.

A fellow student in the class was attempting the Schubert song "An die Musik" ("To Music"), which is a tribute, a celebration of all that music is. The singer, like the rest of us young and inexperienced, was having trouble understanding Bernac's instructions about engaging his soul and spirit in the singing of the song.

Bernac then asked the piano accompanist to change the key of the song so that he himself could sing it comfortably, and thereby demonstrate vocally what he had tried to convey in words.

Bernac, a renowned interpreter of the French song now well into his seventies, not having sung in public in many years, showed us all in that moment the importance of every single word. We heard his joy in the very existence of language, of song, of art. The sun suddenly shone, the light enveloped the classroom. No one who witnessed his impromptu performance that day will ever forget it: we understood what it meant to be called a singer. Singers have another level of responsibility beyond that of our instrumental colleagues: we have words, and they must be given their due.

In the early years of my professional life, it was Pierre Boulez who convinced me, very easily, that I would find great artistic joy in the music of the composers of the second Viennese school: Arnold Schoenberg, Alban Berg, and Anton Webern. I relished exploring what to me was rather uncharted territory. These compositions and their particular technical challenges and rewards demand still more attention to our musical offerings, so that audiences that might not have thought themselves ready for a dose of twelve-tone music might just as well go away from a concert refreshed and renewed in their love for the arts in general, having come across something unexpected yet very satisfying.

Indeed, it was most interesting to be told several years later regarding the recording of Schoenberg's *Erwartung* that was my privilege to make with James Levine and the Met Orchestra, that one writer found "the vocal line to be eminently singable, sensuous and expressive."

Being in Paris and having the joy of watching the great Karl Böhm in rehearsals for *Die Frau ohne Schatten* of Richard Strauss was pure pleasure along with a good deal of education. The cast included Birgit Nilsson, Leonie Rysanek, Ruth Hesse, and James King—a dream team! Böhm was always positive in his critiques, and his wry humor made for some interesting exchanges between himself and his very experienced cast. Böhm's conducting was always at the service of the music in allowing the brilliance of Strauss's orchestration to shine, but never at the expense of the singers. I watched him work as often as I could, which turned out to be many, many rehearsals and performances. Much later I had the joy of recording Beethoven's Ninth Symphony with him, and we recalled those wonderful days when I first watched him in the mid-1970s in Paris.

Leaving the Deutsche Oper Berlin and finding my way in the world was one of the best decisions I ever made. And when I returned to the operatic stage in 1980, I was vocally fit, prepared, and ready to take on new challenges.

I performed many recitals and orchestral concerts in the United States in the 1970s, having made my debut with orchestra in 1970 at the Temple University Music Festival in Philadelphia, with Dean

Dixon conducting the Pittsburgh Symphony. There were many occasions when I would perform operas in the '70s in concert version. This included *Aida* as well as Mozart's *Don Giovanni,* both at the Hollywood Bowl. In the mid-1970s, I sang Aida with the Orlando Opera. Yet my actual operatic stage debut in the States came with the Philadelphia Opera in 1982, where we mounted Stravinsky's *Oedipus Rex* and Henry Purcell's *Dido and Aeneas.* During the summer of that year, I also had a wonderful experience in the role of Phèdre in Rameau's *Hippolyte et Aricie* at the Festival of Aix-en-Provence. The words of Racine in this opera filled my heart with joy, as they are exactly the same words as in the play. Racine's Phèdre just happens to be the one nonsinging role that I have always dreamed of performing onstage, so the opportunity to perform Rameau's version of Phèdre was a great pleasure.

A year after this, after about a decade of having been considered for various roles by the Metropolitan Opera, I made my debut at the Met singing the role of Cassandra in Berlioz's *Les Troyens,* for the opening night of the house's one hundredth anniversary season. It seemed a good time to say, "Yes, I would be happy to join you; thank you." And it was truly a memorable night in every way. Later, when the occasions arose for me to sing not only the role of Cassandra in what is the first part of *Les Troyens,* but also Dido, in the second part of the opera, I was thankful for the vocal health and physical stamina available to me so as to be able to manage these two roles in the same performance.

PERFORMING AROUND THE WORLD can provide some very interesting experiences offstage. For example, while making a recording

The author at age thirteen.

With other finalists of the Bavarian Radio International Music Competition, Munich, September 1968. I was honored to be awarded first prize.

All photos from the author's personal collection, except where otherwise noted.

LEFT: The front page of the *The Augusta Chronicle,* reporting that local philanthropist Peter Knox IV had donated the building that would house the Jessye Norman School of the Arts in Augusta, Georgia, my hometown. *The Augusta Chronicle*

BELOW: With President Barack Obama and Ben Vereen at Ford's Theatre in Washington D.C., 2009, for a concert commemorating the 200th anniversary of the birth of Abraham Lincoln.

Performing the role of Sélika in Giacomo Meyerbeer's opera
L'Africaine at the Maggio Musicale in Florence, 1971.
Maggio Musicale Fiorentino

Aida at La Scala, Milan, 1972.
Archivio la Scala

In the recording studio with British
mezzo-soprano Dame Janet Baker.

As Phèdre in Jean-Philippe Rameau's *Hippolyte et Aricie* at the Aix-en-Provence Festival, 1982. *Aix-en-Provence Festival*

With pianist Dalton Baldwin, a longtime collaborator.

As Cassandra in *Les Troyens* by Hector Berlioz, 1983, my Metropolitan Opera debut.
The Metropolitan Opera Archives

With conductor/violinist Vladimir Spivakov.
The Metropolitan Opera Archives

As Dido in *Dido and Aeneas* by Henry Purcell at the Opéra-Comique in Paris, 1984.
Opéra-Comique de Paris

With accompanist Phillip Moll, with whom I worked for many years.

With conductor Claudio Abbado at the Edinburgh Festival.

With conductor Seiji Ozawa during a recording session.

With conductor James Levine.

With James Levine in recital.

As Elisabeth in Richard Wagner's *Tannhäuser* at the Metropolitan Opera. Some years before, I had made my operatic debut in this role at the Deutsche Oper Berlin.
The Metropolitan Opera Archives

As Ariadne in Richard Strauss's *Ariadne auf Naxos* at the Metropolitan Opera.
The Metropolitan Opera Archives

With Yves Montand.

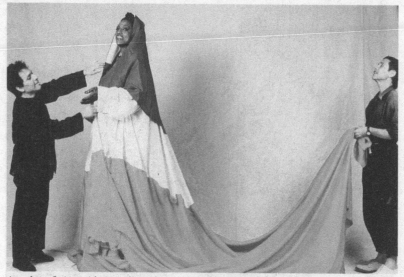

At a dress fitting with Azzedine Alaïa and Jean-Paul Goude, for the bicentennial of the French Revolution.

As Judith in the Metropolitan Opera production of *Bluebeard's Castle* by Béla Bartók, with Samuel Ramey in the role of Bluebeard. *The Metropolitan Opera Archives*

As Alceste in Christoph Willibald Gluck's *Alceste* at Lyric Opera of Chicago. *Lyric Opera of Chicago Archives*

Being awarded the French Légion d'Honneur at the Palais Royale in Paris.

As Sieglinde in Wagner's *Die Walküre* at the Metropolitan Opera, with Gary Lakes as Siegmund.
The Metropolitan Opera Archives

As Kundry in the Metropolitan Opera production of Wagner's *Parsifal,* with Plácido Domingo in the title role.
The Metropolitan Opera Archives

Shaking hands with Hillary Rodham Clinton at a White House state dinner for the Prime Minister of South Korea, November 1993.
White House Photo Office

With Girl Scouts and students from LaGuardia High School for Take Our Daughters to Work Day at the Metropolitan Opera.

As Jocasta in *Oedipus Rex* by Igor Stravinsky, in a production by Julie Taymor in Matsumoto, Japan. *Saito Kinen Festival*

As Emilia Marty in the Metropolitan Opera's first-ever production of Leoš Janáček's *The Makropulos Case.*
The Metropolitan Opera Archives

Performing Arnold Schoenberg's monodrama *Erwartung* at the Salzburg Festival, in a production by Robert Wilson.
Salzburg Festival

With President Bill Clinton following his second inaugural address.
White House Photo Office

Presentation of the Kennedy Center Honors at the White House with President Clinton,
December 1997. *White House Photo Office*

With the Norman family at the White House reception for the Kennedy Center Honors.
White House Photo Office

Singing atop Masada for the fiftieth anniversary of the State of Israel.

With Anna Deveare Smith.

Jenny Warburg

With Gloria Steinem and Sonia Sanchez.

Jenny Warburg

With my present piano accompanist, Mark Markham, at a gala benefit for Robert Wilson's Watermill Center.

With flutist Alain Marion.

Performing in the Statuary Hall of the United States Capitol Building in July 2013 for the congressional commemoration of the fiftieth anniversary of the March on Washington.

in Dresden, and as is my habit, I started speaking the texts of the recording that I was to make the following day. There was a clock on the wall, and it caught my attention that whenever I started speaking, the second hand on the clock would begin to move. When I stopped speaking, the second hand would stop. It was then that I realized my room was under surveillance. To make absolutely certain that I wasn't imagining this, I tested the theory, stopping and starting my speech. Again, every time I began to speak, the second hand would move; it would stop when I stopped. Once I was sure of this action and the resulting reaction, I moved to the corner of the room away from the clock and continued reading through my texts. I cannot say that I experienced any real fear, or believed that the surveillance was targeted specifically for me, but it was nonetheless unsettling.

I had a similar experience much later, in St. Petersburg. I was invited there with a group of other Americans in 1990, to celebrate the 150th birthday of the great Tchaikovsky. Yo-Yo Ma and Itzhak Perlman were participants in this event as well. We were having a grand time. One afternoon I was in my hotel room and found that the temperature was either too hot or too cold, the perfect conditions for catching a cold. I said to my friends who were traveling with me at the time, "I think I will open the window, put something in front of it, so that the air doesn't rush in and make the room too cold again." I thought perhaps this would result in a room temperature that was comfortable and safe.

Soon after I had made this remark a hotel staffer arrived at my door with a stack of blankets. I asked her, "How did you know that I needed blankets?" She responded simply and in English,

"Someone told me to bring them." Again, my reaction was more of bemusement rather than fear. Although I found the Cold War and its ramifications often cumbersome, I understood that the world was made up of many thoughts, ideas, and practices, and that one had to take the best parts of life on this planet and treasure them, celebrate them, live them. And that one of the very best, most necessary things in life is freedom.

And when the opportunity arose to help a fellow singer find this for herself, I was willing to assist. Anxious, yes, but very willing.

Mind you, this was prior to 1989. There was no reason to think the Berlin Wall might one day come down. I had become acquainted with a singer from East Germany while making a recording there. She happened to have had a small role in this particular recording.

A short time later, her East German opera company made a guest appearance at the Edinburgh Festival, where I was performing as well. I had rented a small apartment in one of those very grand places outside Edinburgh, with beautiful grounds, flowers, and grass that seemed to go on forever. I was delighted to invite her —let's call her Claudia—to tea in this splendid house. We enjoyed the views and walked the grounds, and after a time I felt comfortable enough to present my idea.

I began tentatively with something like, "Claudia, you have a marvelous voice, and you're so very comfortable onstage. You would have a very different kind of professional life were you to simply remain in the West."

For a few moments, she didn't respond, but instead stared

straight ahead. And then she said, simply, "I have not allowed myself to dream about such a thing."

She went on to explain that she had job security in East Germany, that the director of her opera company was supportive of her work. And aside from that, her mother had not yet turned sixty-five, which was the age that would make it possible for her to travel freely in and out of East Germany—and therefore she would not be able to join her should Claudia defect. She and her mother were the very best of friends. Her father had long since passed, and she was an only child.

I was not ready to let the subject drop. "Do you think your mother would want you to miss the opportunity of having a more expanded artistic life?"

Claudia remained silent, and we continued our walk. She performed wonderfully with her company at the festival, and left Edinburgh. We remained in touch by occasional phone calls and the odd letter.

Fate, though, is a miraculous thing.

We would meet again in Vienna, and it quickly became clear that by then she was beginning to realize the professional possibilities for her in the West. We took courage in hand, and in quiet conversations, when we were sure that we would not be overheard, we began to think through a possible escape for Claudia from her homeland. She would begin by leaving some of her precious belongings in the West when she was a guest performer at various opera houses. She was becoming quite well known. Together with a friend of ours in Munich, we talked about the subject whenever we thought it was safe—never, ever on the phone—as we arranged to secure everything that would be needed to make this daring plan a success. It took about a year for the three of us to get everything organized.

The whole matter came to a head in, of all places, Vienna, where we would again sing in the same city at the same time. One of the things that had us the most energized was that on that last night, nearly ten years after our conversation in Edinburgh, Claudia would remain in the West. I was present for that performance, and I am not sure that Claudia ever sang better. It was wonderful to hear the expansiveness in her voice—to witness the freedom in her movements onstage—for, surely, freedom waited for her in the wings.

WHEN THE PERFORMANCE was done, instead of traveling back to East Germany, Claudia changed out of her costume, put her things together, and with the help of our friend, was driven by car to West Germany. Her defection had begun. A friend had arranged a place for her to stay. She was able to obtain all necessary documents required for anyone defecting from East Germany to the West. After a few days she had the courage to advise the director of her opera house of what she had done.

Of course, her mother was distraught, but on Claudia's side in all of this. And it was truly a time in our lives that was altogether amazing and frightening, because Claudia was free and my pal and I understood well that we could find ourselves in serious trouble. I remained in Vienna for other work while Claudia, in effect, was hiding out in Germany. During that time we did not dare speak by telephone. But in a situation such as this, you go forward. You try to manage each day as well as you can, because it is the only thing to do. We had followed through with a courageous plan and it seemed to have worked. Claudia became a member of one of Europe's leading opera houses and remained with this company, performing in all of the wonderful roles that she had prepared and portrayed many times with her opera company in East Germany. She blossomed into the complete artist that she knew—that we all knew deep down—she could become. We are still close friends. She always makes a point of calling me at Christmastime and on my birthday. Our meetings these days in the new, undivided city of Berlin are filled with joy, memories of that anxious time, and pure delight.

As it happened, in just three short years after her defection, Claudia would be reunited with her mother—a reunion that came not from any clandestine arrangements, but from a much greater miracle: the collapse of the Berlin Wall. I happened to be performing in Taiwan when suddenly, seemingly without fanfare, it was announced that after years of being trapped within the borders of East Berlin, people could now "cross the street" freely. At the time, the Chinese government in Beijing (or Peking, as we called it then) was inviting people from the West to observe innovative surgical procedures that were reportedly being performed without anesthesia, utilizing only acupuncture and the music of Mozart to control pain. The science fascinated me, and I was doing everything I could to get there to witness one of these operations. But the United States was having its usual troubles with the Chinese government at the time, which made it very difficult for Americans to get to

Beijing. Due to the political stalemate between China and Taiwan, there were not (and still are not) any direct flights from Taiwan to Beijing. It would have been necessary to fly through Hong Kong. And even if I *could* have secured a flight, the all-important visa for entering mainland China remained elusive. Still, though, the procedure was very much on my mind.

The person who arrived to escort me to the concert that evening called my hotel room to say that I was to be ready in thirty minutes. Then, minutes later, the phone rang again and I, thinking it was the same person, answered, "No, no, I know—I'll be down in thirty minutes." To my surprise, the call was from a friend of mine in Germany. I became concerned immediately, fearing that it was bad news or yet another story of injustice in this divided nation. Instead, he declared simply: "The wall is coming down." Honestly, at first I thought he was talking about the Great Wall of China! He said, "No, no, the *Berlin* Wall."

I turned on CNN and saw a crowd of people tearing down the wall, some, it seemed, with their bare hands, others with hatchets. I was so excited that I went downstairs, telling everyone I saw, "Do you know what is happening in the world? Do you know what is happening in Germany?"

Singing that night was a great relief, while the extraordinary was happening in a city where my performance life had had its birth. My accompanist on this tour was Phillip Moll, who lived in Berlin. When I told him what was happening, he was incredulous and asked me to repeat what I had said. That night, the music poured through us and from us. The excitement, the music, the knowledge, the fact that the two of us—two Americans—had this connection with Berlin was amazing in every way.

I traveled to Berlin soon after and went to Potsdamer Platz, where I was able to find a small piece of what had been the Berlin Wall. I took it and held it in my hands, and then thought, *I'll take this back to the States with me.* I often say that I grew up in Berlin, because I went to live in this country at such an early age, thinking at the time that I knew something about the world. But it was here that I came to understand something of the vastness of this planet, the gulfs that exist among us. There were people who lived behind a wall that had been erected in their lifetime. A person living in Berlin in 1960 could move about the city without a great deal of difficulty. And then, an international political decision divided this city in 1961. Now, some of these same people lived to see the Wall and the political stance that had created it collapse. Germany would be reunited. At least that one gulf had been bridged.

I was in Germany in November of that wonderful year, 1989, to make a recording. The Wall had begun to crumble just two weeks earlier. By chance, a recording had been scheduled to take place in this period two years prior to this monumental happening, and it would take place in Dresden, which was suddenly no longer behind a wall! The recording was of Beethoven's only opera, *Fidelio,* the theme of which is political persecution.

The timing was impeccable. The streets were full of people simply meeting and hugging one another. Some, from the former West Berlin, carried crates of fresh fruit that they offered to all whom they passed, as they knew all too well that months and even years could pass with their East German families and friends not having sight of fresh grapes, for example.

I witnessed a young boy on the street showing an adult man how to first peel and then eat a kiwi. As simple as that; as momentous as that.

In complete contrast to my many other visits to the eastern part of this country, there were copies of newspapers from the West left lying around on tabletops. Freedom has many faces, many expressions. There were copies of the *Economist, Time,* and *Der Spiegel* sitting nonchalantly on a table. Such publications were seeing the light of day legally for the first time in this part of the country. Just a few weeks earlier, one could have been fined or even jailed for subversion for spreading ideas contrary to the communist system that had long since failed, but which had refused to lie down and die.

THE RECORDING SESSIONS produced some wonderful results, especially from the marvelously trained men's chorus. At one point in the opera, the male chorus sings of the glory of release from imprisonment. In the Dresden recording session one day, the singing of just one word—*Freiheit*—freedom, was done with such power by this chorus as to have almost shattered the walls of the hall. Imagine singing this word and meaning it, truly, for the first time in your life! Of course the sound would originate in the deepest part of you and ring out like no other in such a moment in time.

People were joyful and open and smiling from a real place in their spirits, not a pretense, not to cover extreme distress, but genuine happiness. It was truly something to witness, and it was easy to feel like a bit player in the tremendous drama of those days: a country reunited and a world observing the stunning shattering of an old order.

Dr. Martin Luther King Jr. once stated, "Freedom is never voluntarily given by the oppressor; it must be demanded by the oppressed."

And so with whatever hammering and cutting tools they could find, quickly and with their bare hands, the symbol, the enshrinement of this horror, was beaten to the ground.

O namenlose Freude, Fidelio · LUDWIG VAN BEETHOVEN · Oh, Joy Beyond Naming

O, namenlose Freude!	Oh, joy beyond naming
An Leonorens Brust!	The comfort of Leonore's breast
Nach unnennbarer Leiden	After unspeakable suffering
So übergrosse Lust.	This larger than life pleasure.
O Gott, wie gross ist dein Erbarmen!	Oh God, how great is Your Grace.
O Dank dir, Gott, für diese Lust!	Oh thanks to God for this delight
Mein Weib, mein Weib	My wife, my bride
An meiner Brust! Du bist's!	On my breast; you, Leonore, you are!
O himmliches Entzücken!	Oh, the Goodness of Heaven
Ich bin's Leonore!	I am your Leonore
Leonore!	Leonore

7

The Singing Craft as Art Form

"OH, GLORY!"

> *Oh, Glory; there is room enough in Paradise*
> *To have a home in Glory.*
> *Jesus my Lord to Heaven is gone,*
> *To have a home in glory,*
> *He, whom I've fixed my hopes upon,*
> *To have a home in glory.*

Singing gives me many rewards and many blessings for all the hard work it requires and on which it depends. Only through hard work can such a craft rise to the level of art.

Singing, for me, is actually life itself. It is communication, person to person and soul to soul, a physical, emotional, spiritual, and intellectual expression carried by the breath. Life!

WE CAN APPROXIMATE and thereby appreciate the physical act of oxygen rushing in great waves throughout the body, as it does in singing, by distance running or a vigorous bicycle ride. Oxygen flow is deeply satisfying to me, as is my ability to communicate through poems and prose, often in centuries-old texts that can illuminate our thoughts and lives today. Songs that revel in the beauty of taking time to enjoy nature's splendor, or to fall in love. There are a million songs about love—unrequited love, secret love, the love of a father for a son, or a mother for a daughter, or perverted, inappropriate love, like that which Jocasta holds for her son in Stravinsky's *Oedipus Rex,* or Phèdre for Hippolyte. Conveying each of these ideas to an audience with words and music can be physically and mentally invigorating.

I love the discipline involved in bringing the breath out of my lungs and past my vocal chords with a specific control that gives me a certain quality of sound: singing! Music gives wings to words—makes it possible to say "I love you" to a person in the most moving, touching, personal way. So much so that the one who hears these words can walk away with a melody that lingers. The words have a tune to accompany the beautiful sentiment. This does not mean that the words are less meaningful if offered without music; it is simply that the music adds yet another dimension to their meaning. I am thankful that I can employ my voice to convey these meanings. Of course, a lot of music we listen to and adore has no words at all. Sometimes you can think of words that might fit an instrumental melody just because of the way that it touches you: the haunting sounds that come through the instrument, the depth of color or the beautiful length of the phrases. Each of these things can cause you to think, *Oh, wouldn't it be lovely to have words to that!* Some composers, particularly of that grand period of European songwriting in the eighteenth and nineteenth centuries, would begin their compositions with the text and then compose the music. But there were composers like Johannes Brahms who would sometimes compose the melody first, and then look for a suitable text. Either approach could yield a song deeply satisfying for its ability to touch, to speak, to inspire.

I do tend to gravitate toward operatic characters that are multidimensional, complex. I love to sing the stories of women for whom I am capable of empathy. For me, it is both interesting and challenging to delve into a complicated character and role, such as Virgil's Dido, who, after losing her husband and taking on the responsibility of seeing to the full economic resurgence of Carthage and its return to its place of honor and proper reverence in the eyes of the world, allows herself to fall in love again, against her better judgment — only to have Aeneas, the man whom she allows herself to love thoroughly, leave her. He considers his call to duty more significant than the love he feels for her. And what a duty it was: he would go on to found Rome!

Dido's reaction to this tragic turn of events, as taken from the fourth book of Virgil's *Aeneid* and translated into beautiful French, set to the meltingly romantic music of Berlioz, is, I feel, one of opera's greatest treasures. I feel the same way about *Erwartung* of Schoenberg, the one-woman opera in which the character surges and suffers through a wide range of emotion as she searches frantically in the darkness for her lover, only to find that he has been murdered. She is at once frightened, angry, apprehensive, unsure, insecure. Alone. It is possible for me to sing this particular opera, which spans little more than half an hour, in three different characterizations: as the person who has committed the murder, as the person who has observed the murder, and as the person who is imagining these dire events in her head. This type of complexity is the kind of challenge that I grab with both hands! I am sure when I say such things that Sigmund Freud, who was Schoenberg's contemporary, would have his own interesting interpretation of what goes on inside my head.

Our responsibility as singers is to find a level of reality in the sometimes complex characters that we portray. I enjoy becoming deeply conversant with that hurt, that aching, that yearning, that joy, to truly understand the role, and use all of this to reveal the character as fully as I can onstage. It truly is not necessary that the audience should speak and understand every word that I sing in a foreign language, but I must convey the very essence of the texts I am singing. If the audience is not able to glean that I am extremely distressed, or that something wonderful has just happened, or that I am anticipating something that could be a challenge to life and limb, then I am not doing my job. To be able to communicate these everyday emotions is the basis, the thrust, of acting. Acting must support a singer's onstage work.

There is a thrill that comes with opening a score for the first time, and the entire learning process is immensely rewarding, but it also takes devotion and a great deal of work. I say this very often to young musicians who feel that they want to make singing their life's profession: "You must be committed to this, and even if it brings you more joy, pleasure, and fulfillment than any other thing you might be able to do in your life, you still have to be willing to do the hard work." The work is very detailed and demanding. Enjoyment of this process is key.

I love the searching, the exploring, the whole process of becoming truly one with the work. This is as true for the preparation of operatic roles as for the singing of songs.

Putting a recital program together can be an endless process: choosing the songs, the order, and, these days, a theme. But there is so much joy as well.

For opera, one of my most memorable research expeditions occurred the first time I was to sing Schoenberg's *Erwartung*. I had the privilege of visiting the University of Southern California's Arnold Schoenberg Institute, which has archival responsibility for the composer's music and personal papers, as well as dissertations from the world over about him and his music. Normally, only those working on their doctorates—musicologists and the like—would be invited to review the archives. But I was afforded the same access to Schoenberg's work as that received by experts of his music. I felt very scholarly in being escorted into those rooms to view the original copies of this music and the correspondence between Schoenberg and Marie Pappenheim, the Viennese physician who wrote the libretto of *Erwartung*. The air in the room was cool, carefully climate-controlled to preserve the delicate documents, and I was provided a pair of gloves so that the oils from my fingers would not harm the documents while I handled them. It was splendid to sit and to take into my hands the correspondence that was sent between the composer and the writer of the libretto. Very often, documents of this kind would be available to view only through glass. But I held those papers in my hands—saw up close the notes and suggestions that Pappenheim wrote in the margins of her text and the responses of Schoenberg, who acknowledged her suggestions and followed them to the letter. I found this astounding, considering his stature at the time and the fact that Pappenheim was an unknown librettist. It was clear they had a very strong and mutual admiration, one that manifested itself in their complete trust in one another. Pappenheim even wrote what she thought the mood of the music should be at particular points and how much time there should be to transition between these moods. Schoenberg composed in a white heat—a matter of weeks, rather than months or years—and this was a testament to their amazing collaboration, as Pappenheim, too, created the text in a very short period. I felt very privileged to see all of this, and I was in awe at having not only a deep insight into their intentions for the work, but a physical contact with it that was unmatched by any other research I had done previously. I left that room feeling as though I had actually been in their presence, as the energy that seemed to run between them, practically jumping off the pages, was evident and powerful.

I will say, though, that there is nothing quite like working with living composers: it is an amazing joy. I had the privilege of this kind of live collaboration early in my performance life while working on a recording of the oratorio *A Child of Our Time,* by the British composer Michael Tippett. It was the mid-1970s and Tippett's composition was already thirty years old, but how marvelous it was to be able to talk with him about his creative process, the various ideas he'd poured into the piece. It was inspired by the 1938 assassination of the German diplomat Ernst vom Rath by Herschel Grynszpan, a German-born Polish Jew distressed that his family had been unceremoniously expelled from their homeland by the Nazis and left destitute at the border of Poland. The assassination was the impetus for Kristallnacht, the vicious outburst of violence against

German Jews that flung wide the door to their economic and political persecution and signaled the beginning of the Holocaust. Michael Tippett, an unyielding, unapologetic pacifist, penned *A Child of Our Time* as a magnificent cry against the destruction war wreaks on our world: the cruelty and brutality of evil. I was able to question him about his use of Spirituals in the composition, which he employed much as Johann Sebastian Bach presented chorales within such works as the *St. Matthew Passion*.

Bach's chorales and Tippett's Spirituals are used as interconnections within the compositions. With Bach, the chorales fall between Scripture verses; with Tippett, the Spirituals are interspersed throughout a libretto that concerns the senselessness of inhumanity. Tippett stated in one of our conversations that he had come across recordings of the Wings over Jordan Choir, one of the first choirs to make recordings of choral versions of Spirituals, and that he had taken this music to heart and to his manuscript paper. I was happy to hear of his acquaintance with this choir and the wonderful recordings they made. Our recording sessions would turn into completely joy-filled moments of music making and learning.

Another opportunity to learn and work with a living, breathing composer came in the 1980s with Olivier Messiaen's *Poèmes pour Mi,* a song cycle that Messiaen wrote in homage to his wife. I had the joy and honor of working with Messiaen at his apartment in Paris, where the woman for whom he had written this particular set of songs—his nickname for her was Mi—made tea for us. It was absolute madness—but wonderful madness! Was this really happening? It was tremendous to be invited to their home and to discover this music with the composer at my side. He could not have been more gracious and complimentary of my spoken French and pronunciation in singing. We spent hours together. Indeed, at one point Messiaen asked me if I wanted to stop. I answered quickly, "No," and told him that I would stay and rehearse throughout the night if he wanted. And during our entire time together, his wife said not a word. She focused on making sure that her husband was comfortable, that he had the proper lighting to read his music as the day wore on, and that he was sitting properly at the piano. Her dedication to him, and his to her, was beautiful to see. To hear him talk about the poems and the music—and then to sing with him and for him, with the love of his life nearby—was something out of a rather fanciful storybook.

Of course, it is a very special kind of collaboration, too, when you can work with a composer as the composition is being written. Performing a work of Mozart composed hundreds of years ago is surely a blessing every time, but it is what it is—and making changes or adaptations to it can result in a few raised eyebrows. But sitting side by side with someone writing something specifically for you is an inspiring collaborative process that many musicians crave. One can say to the composer, for example, "This passage is beautiful, but can you give me a few more bars of instrumental music prior to the part where we launch into singing about the thrills of the prime of life, perhaps?" And the composer can respond with, "Why, yes, I can extend that and I can also change this word or that phrase to make the passage more comfortable for you." Such easy collaboration is a joy to the spirit. But we understand, too, that writers and composers can become very attached to what they create and resistant to making any changes at all. Such is a time for the most diplomatic and considerate of conversations in order to foster the best possible outcome. Tact, mutual respect: all good and useful tools.

No such tools were necessary when I had the grand pleasure of working with Judith Weir on woman.life.song, an extended song cycle that I was able to commission at the invitation of the late Judith Arron, then the executive director of Carnegie Hall.

We had the most wonderful of experiences.

The song cycle traces a woman's life from infancy to advanced age through the poetry of three writers for whom I have the greatest of admiration, respect, and love: Maya Angelou, Clarissa Pinkola Estés, and Toni Morrison. Creating the music for their narratives was left in Weir's capable hands—a process that took about two years as we worked together to produce this wonderful piece. Part of what was deeply satisfying about the process was our ability to work together to find solutions to create the best composition possible. For instance, I could say to Judith, "It is difficult to pronounce a word like that so high above the scale," and we would put our minds together and derive a mutually satisfactory solution.

It was extraordinary, too, to arrive in a hotel somewhere in the world and find a message from Toni, Maya, or Clarissa, which included their latest part of the text. It was like Christmas every week or so. I had thought long and hard about the kind of composition I wanted this to be, and a piece about the life of a woman, written by women, and with music composed by a woman seemed a Heaven-sent idea. And it was.

The year prior to the commission, I had met Judith Weir when we were both presented with honorary degrees at the University

of Aberdeen in Scotland. In speaking with her and shortly there-
after becoming acquainted with her music, I knew that I wished
to work with her in some way. And when Carnegie provided the
opportunity, it was easy to call upon these three great friends to
compose texts for the different stages of womanhood. We were a
happy group. The results of this collaboration uplift and inspire me
every day.

Another such opportunity came with *Ask Your Mama!,* based
on Langston Hughes's 1961 collection *Ask Your Mama: 12 Moods for
Jazz.* This multimedia production was a part of *Honor! A Celebration of the African American Cultural Legacy,* which it was indeed
my honor to direct and curate for Carnegie Hall in 2009. It was
such pure pleasure to work so closely with the composer Laura
Karpman in creating this production. Laura was the first to fully
realize the performance potential of the Hughes text, and orches-
trate the entire set of poems. The artistic and executive director of
Carnegie Hall, the wonderful Clive Gillinson, was born to lead this
iconic performance space. His intelligence and energy go hand in
hand with an abiding understanding and deep, deep love for music
and for all that music makes possible in our world. Even when the
production of *Ask Your Mama!* and the fifty-one other events of the
festival threatened to send us straight to the poorhouse, Clive stood
as our foremost cheerleader.

Laura and I corresponded practically daily in this process.
Langston Hughes, one of my mother's most favorite writers,
worked his magic on all of us, and the musical results are truly
soul-satisfying.

I find it particularly delicious when many art forms come together, as in the presentation of *Ask Your Mama!* and surely in opera productions—when the conducting, singing, choreography, and stage effects all work together to produce a living, breathing, magical series of moments onstage.

Such was the case when the conductor Seiji Ozawa, determined to bring the best of the arts to the Japanese Alps, founded a music festival at Matsumoto, in 1993.

This was my first opportunity to work with the marvelous Julie Taymor onstage, a treat in and of itself. The entire cast of Stravinsky's *Oedipus Rex,* already enthused about working with Julie and Seiji in this new festival, became all the more excited upon seeing sketches and drawings of costumes and sets that made it clear that this presentation was going to be an artistic experience on an exceptional level.

Preparing for the festival had its challenges: getting to Matsumoto was made easy by Japan's intercity train service, but finding a place to stay over a period of several weeks was no easy feat. The only place that seemed able to fulfill my simple requirements happened to be a spa for men, located not too far away from the festival site. This, in itself, turned out to be quite the experience. The men were as startled to see me as I them. They were not used to having even Japanese women at their spa, and I was truly an exotic find for them as they strode the corridors in vintage dressing gowns and sandals. Some actually would dart back into their hotel rooms if they spotted me before I spotted them. The best approach was a quiet one: I let them be, and passed them without looking up or acknowledging their presence in any way. I had no way of knowing if my employing the standard greeting of *Konnichiwa* would cause some sort of uprising or bring a cordial response. I chose simply to "let it be."

Rehearsals were exceptional experiences. Inspiring. Julie was having her first outing with opera singers and it was something else to see the care and mutual respect that flowed from the orchestra pit up to the director, over to the performers, and back again. We were having a kind of artistic love-fest, getting to know one another while working on a Greek legend of the ages, set in Latin, in a twentieth-century orchestral rendering from Stravinsky. It seemed a very appropriate venue for this piece, in this country that is thousands of years old, yet one of the most modern in the world.

I remember saying to Julie early in our rehearsals that I would probably be unable to sing with my hands covered in the large, sculpted "puppet hands" that were part of the innovative staging. My hands, after all, were half of my voice, I explained. Julie listened patiently, probably wondering what I was going on and on about so passionately. I learned to use her hand extensions easily and to enjoy doing so, thoroughly. And when all was said and done, it was Julie, too, who convinced me to lie down on a platform on the floor of the stage and to have that platform raised three stories into the air, up out of the sight of the spectators, to signify the death of Jocasta. I do believe she is the only person in the world who could have convinced me that this was a fine idea. I found that as long as I kept my eyes closed, I felt no discomfort or worry. They could not have been shut more tightly, I am sure!

To this day, I find the film of this production of *Oedipus Rex* to be one of the few truly fine opera films available. The young musicians of the orchestra were honored to adhere to Seiji's every musical suggestion and the collaboration amongst all of us was a wonder: rare and inspired beyond ourselves.

OF COURSE, THOSE who work with singers must understand and respect that we are musicians who carry the musical instrument inside the body. I have found that far too often, stage directors for the opera envision what they wish the stage to resemble, with no understanding of or willingness to explore how their vision melds with reality or how it will affect the musicians with whom they are working. Such was the case during one production when a young colleague of mine was having a moment with our director, who was demanding that the singer run up a series of stairs while singing. Now, their discussion had nothing at all to do with my own role, but I was in busybody mode and things were reaching an unpleasant level, even though only slight changes were needed. With the hope of calming the waters, I took a moment during one of our rehearsal breaks to make a suggestion to the director in a cheery "Let's talk about this" manner. I relayed that it was simple physics, and the physiological use of the breath made it possible to run *down* a flight of stairs and sing, but that running *up* the same flight of stairs while singing was not something that one could manage easily. A singer with empty lungs from having run up a flight of stairs against gravity would need a few seconds for physical recovery: only then could there be singing. I understood the dramatic intentions here, but there were real physical limitations to realizing these intentions.

And yes, against his will, I made a friend of this director. And my young colleague performed fantastically.

One must consider, too, the equally fascinating art of dance as it relates to the body as instrument. Some invaluable lessons were gleaned in working with dance great Rudolf Nureyev, whom I had long admired. We had come to know one another in the 1980s, and found ourselves together in Paris in the mid-'80s while I was performing Purcell's *Dido and Aeneas* at the Opéra-Comique. He was present at practically every performance, giving me helpful hints and notes after each one. Once, he stated that a performer's back "has something to say as well," and that even if one's back is toward the audience for a time during a performance, the stance of the dancer, the tension in the body, must make it clear that the performer is in full attention—never at rest, even if one is not actually singing or dancing at that very moment. This one statement from him has traveled with me to many productions. And this energy is visible in practically any film of Nureyev's work. You can hardly take your eyes away from him, even when he is not moving at all and has his back to the camera. Wonderful.

The lessons continued when I sang from the orchestral pit while he danced on the stage of the Metropolitan Opera House. It was during these performances that I learned to establish a tempo in complete collaboration with the dancer. Keeping that tempo, even in the highly romantic and soul-stirring music of Gustav Mahler's *The Songs of a Wayfarer,* was essential. There is no room for improvisation or flights of fancy on the part of the music makers. A certain number of steps bring the dancer to a certain place both in the choreography and on the stage. He might wish to improvise one evening, but the support, the music, must remain the "magic carpet" on which all of this can take place.

Nureyev was a fine musician in his own right. I was once present when he conducted the complex Prokofiev *Romeo and Juliet* orchestral score, and, by Jove, he knew what he was doing. Admittedly, he had danced Romeo many times, but one could see that conducting this score gave him immense pleasure. I have to say that I was thrilled to witness this. It was doubly thrilling that the illustrious Margot Fonteyn was onstage—not in her signature role at this point, but the circle of life was completing itself: the two of them were making art again, together.

Of course, it is equally powerful when the art exposes not only your heart but the very things in your wide world that make it sing. The brilliant dancer and choreographer Bill T. Jones is truly one of a kind in this regard. In the days when performing artists were not at all reluctant or hesitant to use their public platforms for advancing their ideas on social and political issues, Bill T. would have been amongst like-minded peers. As it happened, he found himself often on the frontlines of such discussions and actions without a lot of company. I admire this fearlessness in him. His artistic achievements leave me rather amazed at the number of his "firsts," and the altogether stunning work that has emerged from his mind and his body. Bill T. is unique, too, in that he is not one who places physical standards on the body type of a dancer. No one is too tall or too short, too wide or too thin to be taught to move gracefully. He believes with all his being that it is the soul that is on display in dance, and that the physical self is but a conduit. A vessel.

Working with Bill T. on *How! Do! We! Do!,* which premiered at New York's City Center in 1999, was a revelation: I witnessed the depths to which he was prepared to reach in order to find that thing that would satisfy his idea of a movement, a gesture, the lighting, the appropriate apparel. I learned, too, after some resistance, to do something that dancers do all the time, and that is to count dance steps in uneven numbers. It may sound simple, but believe me, it is not, if you are also working hard not to seem as though you have no coordination at all. I managed to relax and take in many new thoughts and to simply allow Bill's brilliance to speak.

The result was an evening of sheer joy in movement, talk, and music, all of which seemed totally and completely improvised, even though we had worked together for months. One of a kind, indeed. In our show, we offered some of the stories of our lives in poetry, movement, and song. Bill sang a little; I moved in tandem with him (I would not be so bold as to say that I danced!). We shared our love and deep admiration for our own art forms, as well as those beyond our individual disciplines—because love is easy to share, love is easy to demonstrate, love is easy to accept when the whole heart is involved.

Long live art, long live friendship, long live the love of life!

L'île inconnue, Les nuits d'été · HECTOR BERLIOZ
Island of the Unknown

Dites, la jeune belle, où voulez-vous aller?	Tell me, young girl, where do you wish to go?
La voile enfle son aile, la brise va souffler.	The sails swell in the breeze,
L'aviron est d'ivoire,	The oar is of ivory
Le pavillon de moire,	The flag of silk

Le gouvernail d'or fin;	The helm of finest gold
J'ai pour lest une orange,	For ballast, I have an orange
Pour voile une aile d'ange,	I have the wing of an angel for the sail
Pour mousse un séraphin.	For a deck hand, a seraphim.
Est-ce dans la Baltique,	Shall we go to the Baltic Sea?
Dans la mer Pacifique?	To the Pacific Ocean?
Dans l'île de Java?	To the island of Java?
Où bien est-ce en Norwége,	Or perhaps to Norway
Cueillir la fleur de neige,	To take a flower of snow
Où la fleur d'Angsoka?	Or the flower of Angsoka?
Dites, la jeune belle,	Tell me, young girl,
Dites, où voulez-vous aller?	Where would you like to go?
Menez-moi, dit la belle,	The young girl said, "Take me
À la rive fidèle	To the shore of faithfulness
Où l'on aime toujours.	Where love knows no end."
Cette rive, ma chère,	My dear, this shore
On ne la connaît guère	One hardly knows at all
Au pays des amours.	In the universe of love.

8

The Song, the Craft, the Spirit, and the Joy!

"THE LORD'S PRAYER"

Our Father, which art in Heaven,
Hallowed be Thy name,
Thy kingdom come,
Thy will be done on earth as it is in Heaven.
Give us this day, our daily bread,
And forgive us our trespasses
As we forgive those who trespass against us
And lead us not into temptation,
But deliver us from evil.
For Thine is the kingdom, the power and the glory forever,
A-men

I am asked often who my favorite composers are—which of the songs I sing in recital or the roles I perform on the stage are my most beloved. This, I find, is unusually simple to answer: all of them! I could not possibly say that I prefer Wagner or Strauss or Berlioz over Schubert or Mozart or Brahms. Ellington over Gershwin or Cole Porter. I sing the music—and this is really true—that I love. There is so much music in this world, I cannot think of a single reason to perform anything that does not give me pleasure and that fails to give something back to me. All of this giving out, this grateful sharing with the audience, is replenished. I am refilled by the music, by the very act of singing!

Many different factors are at play in my choosing repertoire: chief among these is whether or not the music will expand my thoughts and my horizons, and increase my knowledge and understanding of my craft. I am certainly drawn to beautiful melodies, or perhaps it is that the text is so beautiful and I am so grateful that someone has set those particular words to music, that I add that song to my "to do" list immediately. Sometimes, I might find myself wanting to sing a particular piece in order to perform with a particular ensemble. The ways of finding repertoire are endless and great fun.

I am surely open to suggestions. It was my pal Michael Tilson Thomas who said in about 2007 that I should think about the music of John Cage, whose centenary would arrive in 2012. He was sure I would find this music challenging and enjoyable.

And it happens that he was absolutely correct. We have been having the best time performing this music in various places with members of the San Francisco Symphony. We performed at Ann Arbor, at my former school there, the University of Michigan, and at Carnegie Hall. Plus, I have realized a great fantasy in working with Joan La Barbara and Meredith Monk, both of whom had the opportunity of working directly with John Cage. What a group!

I find it difficult to respond to the question of my creative process, as I work, I would think, in unconventional ways. I work first alone at the piano, and delay working with my piano accompanist or with the conductor until my own ideas about the composition have come together, at least to a degree.

Language is of course extremely important to me. The only language in which I sing that I do not speak or that I have not studied as a language is Hebrew.

Long ago I purchased a book with the wonderful title *Hebrew in Ten Minutes a Day.* The publisher neglected to mention how many *decades* of ten-minute sessions this might require. When I received the joyous invitation to perform and record Bartók's *Bluebeard's Castle* with Pierre Boulez, I learned to read Hungarian. I had to do this! It was an utterly different preparation process than rehearsing an opera written in French, for instance. I had tutors on both sides of the Atlantic working with me from the same textbook so that each would know where I was in my studies when our turn to work together came. It was marvelous, like being in school again.

I ONCE GAVE serious consideration to taking a year off and preparing Racine's *Phèdre,* the play, to perform onstage, as I was so enamored of the words. And then, as mentioned earlier, when the opportunity arose to sing the role of Phèdre in Rameau's opera *Hippolyte et Aricie,* and I discovered that the libretto used the precise wording of Racine, I did not hesitate to accept. The production in Aix-en-Provence gave me the added opportunity of working with two new opera directors at the time, Patrice Caurier and Moshe Leiser. We worked diligently together on the three scenes of Phèdre, and I am thrilled that there is video documentation of the results, as to date I have performed this role only at that festival.

The actual director for the production, Pier Luigi Pizzi, was happy to have the three of us working away on the stage during the height of the afternoon sun, when no one else wished to do anything other than have a good lunch and a siesta. In hot sun and all, we mapped out (or, in theater jargon, blocked) the scenes and went forward from there. Pizzi left us to our own devices. It was a pleasure to work unhurried and in music and words that provided their own cooling, calming atmosphere to that very warm stage.

I am ever grateful to Richard Strauss for having produced so much beautiful music that is particularly suited to the female voice. From the moment I heard Strauss's *Vier letzte Lieder* (*Four Last Songs*), I wished to sing them. They remain such an integral part of my repertoire that I cannot imagine my singing life without them. In fact, some years ago, representatives from Strauss's family presented me with a large portrait of the composer during the Salzburg summer festival. It is one of my most treasured possessions, but I keep only a small photo of the portrait on display in my bookroom, as the portrait really needs a bigger space than my home can provide.

I admire the critical acclaim that Strauss enjoyed during his lifetime as well as the financial success that came with his being a celebrated composer. Strauss is believed to be the first composer to have received royalty payments from the publication and performance of his compositions. Think of all the composers who preceded him who could not so much as have dreamed of such good fortune.

Sometimes I think what a beautiful thing it would be to go back in time and invite Franz Schubert to dinner. A composer with music in his every pore, who gave us nearly a thousand works of art in his short lifetime, Schubert was barely able to sustain himself financially. I fantasize about planning the grandest of dinner parties for him and then sending him on his way after a fine supper, to return again soon, for another.

Even in the last years of his bountiful life, Strauss was evolving, creating, and learning—and composing what I feel to be some of his most enduring works. The poems he employed in *Four Last Songs*—"Im Abendrot" ("Glow of the Evening"), by Joseph von Eichendorff, and "Frühling" ("Spring"), "September," and "Beim Schlafengehen" ("On the Sleep Eternal"), by Hermann Hesse —are quite simply magnificent. "Beim Schlafengehen" embodies the calm, peace, and expectations that should come with the end of one's physical life: the wonders of the afterlife—"You will fly on wings of light and glory into a life anew." What a wonderful thought: the afterlife as something beautiful that beckons us and that we should not fear. It is a thought that other cultures have embraced as well. The Chinese, for example, have held this idea for thousands of years, believing that we spend our lives on earth preparing for the next experience. Then there is the celebration of spring in "Frühling," welcoming new growth out of the somber mood of winter. For me, this song is spiritual in a profound way. Trust in the newness, the certainty that the bare trees will fill with green, and flowers, long asleep, will awaken with such glorious colors to gladden any spirit. The cycle of life.

I find particular enjoyment in "September," since September happens to be my birth month, and the beauty of the change of seasons at this time of year has always been special to me. Remember the thrill of falling into a pile of colorful autumn leaves that were green just weeks prior? Think of the scent of autumn, the coolness that greets the morning dew and comes again with the early setting of the sun.

"Im Abendrot" is for me a grand celebration of the fullness of life: the joys and the sadness, lived hand in hand with another; a connection of the heart and the soul until the end.

"The time for rest from this life is near as all becomes quiet and calm in this stillness, in this waiting."

Who would not feel blessed to be able to share the experience of these songs with an audience?

Speaking of the Chinese philosophy of the afterlife, I must also mention Mahler's *Das Lied von der Erde,* the text of which is translated from Chinese into German. This wonderful composition for two voices is a full-length symphonic work that never ceases to inspire in its celebration of the peace and joy of life on earth expanding into eternal life: the philosophy of spiritual continuance as a never-ending phenomenon. My gratitude in being able to perform these two spectacular compositions, the Strauss and the Mahler, is without bounds.

JOINING THE WORLD of Italian opera on a stage served already by a truly stunning array of singers, masters of this repertoire, did not hold my interest. Other than *Tosca,* I cannot really claim personal interest in the stirring and ever popular operatic roles of Puccini. I did perform *Aida* in the beginning years of my singing life, and made recordings of some of Verdi's first operas. Lady Macbeth is, for me, probably the most fully captivating of the Verdi roles. This grabs and holds fast my attention.

I live so happily in my wide mélange of periods of composition, composers, styles, and genres. Bach, Handel, Purcell, the music of *la belle France,* the German romanticism that is at the center of my "to sing" list, along with endless choices from the first and second Viennese schools, keep me up late at night in preparation and as happy as can be onstage. Not to mention music composed here and now, and my boundless devotion to the songs of the American musical theater and all that jazz!

Richard Wagner's operas provide me with truly tremendous performance experiences. Yet I doubt that he and I would have been friends, given his well-documented, limited embrace of humankind. But there his music sits in the virtual center of my operatic repertoire.

I think one has to separate the character of the composer from the art. If we were to judge art according to the character of those who created it, we would dismiss a lot of artists, and miss some truly magnificent art. We would be bereft of a great deal of glorious music. I do not welcome those occasions when one is expected to "justify" a love of Wagner's music and a desire to perform it: I am happy to leave that debate to those who prefer not to view the operas of Richard Wagner simply as a gift. That this inspiration landed in the mind and heart of a person whose character might not be compatible with ours is one of those accidents, one of those purposeful accidents of nature.

Music has great power and can have meaning attached to it far beyond a composer's intentions and purpose. Such is the music not only of Wagner, but also of Richard Strauss: Wagner because of reasons that are well known, but also Strauss, whose work during the period of the Nazi regime calls into question his actual political beliefs. I was therefore somewhat surprised when, while planning for the 1994 concert season of the Israel Philharmonic, Zubin Mehta suggested that we program songs by Strauss. He stated that he and the orchestra had performed Strauss's tone poem *Till Eulenspiegel* the previous season and that the music had been accepted. Still, I had my concerns.

I agreed to go forward with this plan of offering our program of the songs with the proviso that I would make clear publicly that I remained in complete and utter sympathy with anyone who might be offended by our programming. I also wanted to assure the Israel Philharmonic's thousands of subscribers that I would be returning to Israel with other music in the not too distant future. The print interviews took place and were completed even prior to the first rehearsals with the orchestra; I was more settled and ready for the work ahead, once they were done.

When rehearsing for the first time with an orchestra, I always sing while facing the musicians, so that we all can get to know one another a bit better, and such was the case with the Israel Philharmonic. My heart skipped a beat or two when I noticed the intense joy in some of the faces of the orchestral members as they played —many for the very first time—Strauss's song "Zueignung," a song about devotion in its strongest, most sincere of terms. After rehearsing others of the five songs I would perform, I could see the orchestra members relax into allowing themselves to participate with their hearts, too, in their always splendid playing. It was such a special moment. Richard Strauss was not given absolution, perhaps, but his music was allowed to find a place in some new spirits and minds.

In order to accommodate the thousands of subscribers to the orchestral concerts in Israel, the performances are offered several times, and this was our plan here, as well.

Meanwhile, friends who could not be with me were keeping close tabs on things, as they knew that there was the possibility for unpleasantness. So I was not surprised to hear the fax machine churning in my room on the early morning of the first performance. I did not get up to read the transmission immediately, thinking that it was wiser to get a bit more rest on a performance day. There seemed to be a bit more commotion outside my window than on previous days, too, but I allowed this to happen without being too concerned.

It was only after rising and reading the fax that my heart sank. A friend had seen on television that for the first time in Tel Aviv, a bomb had gone off on a city bus. I was advised to turn on the television news, which I did. Upon discovering rather quickly that my hotel was a short walk from the scene of the bombing, I wondered what would happen as a result of this attack. Soon after, the orchestral manager called to inform me that the evening's concert would go forward and that I should not worry.

At Mann Auditorium that evening, concert preparations seemed to be moving at a normal pace. It helped that Zubin Mehta was very supportive and assured me by saying something like, "Music will help at such a moment." I did not doubt the premise, but really, I was concerned about our choice of repertoire on this particular day, in this particular city.

The concert went very well, and at the end, the maestro asked if I might sing an unaccompanied Spiritual. As this was an unusual request following a performance with orchestra, where in normal circumstances an encore would have been prepared with the orchestra accompanying, I was at first surprised. Yet I agreed readily to sing; I understood that these were not normal circumstances. At the very moment that I began to say, "I wish to sing in memory of those who lost—" someone from the audience yelled out, "Don't mix politics and music. Just sing!" And I obeyed.

Without music, life would be a mistake.

—Nietzsche

Music is a moral law. It gives soul to the universe, wings to the mind, flight to the imagination, and charm and gaiety to life and to everything.

—Plato

Music doesn't lie. If there is something to be changed in this world, then it can only happen through music.

—Jimi Hendrix

Another opportunity to perform in Israel came in the celebration of the fiftieth anniversary of the founding of this great nation. I was so honored to be invited to sing. It was high summer and the performance would take place in a momentous location. Standing atop Masada on that very warm July day, I thought repeatedly of the history of this mountain and of how that history, so many, many years ago, mirrored that of my own ancestors, and I was moved to tears more than once during the course of the experience. I would sing in Hebrew. I had rehearsed and rehearsed, and I was prepared. I was to sing "Jerusalem" live, but to a soundtrack the orchestra had recorded two days prior to the filming. This was a very special difficulty, as no matter the number of takes needed in order to achieve the preferred camera shots, I would be obligated to sing the song the same way each time, for each rehearsal on the site.

I soon fell into the habit of doing this, and was helped magnificently by the very special television crew from Tel Aviv as well as the representatives from CBS, the network that would broadcast the telecast in the States. Everyone was professional and extraordinarily kind and attentive. I promise you that the dressing room that had been created for my use on the side of this mountain would rival any of the very best that it has been my privilege to have available to me closer to the ground!

My one and only concern throughout the filming rehearsals was for the safety of the head cameraman, who was positioned in a helicopter, attached along with his shoulder camera by a harness to the inside of the helicopter. He sat on the floor of this flying machine with the door open and his legs dangling over the edge. Of course I understood that he would be able to take some wonderful shots from that angle, but I still worried, and wondered who in the world would do such a thing!

While camera angles were rehearsed, I worked with the makeup artists, as such considerations are very different in outdoor lighting settings, as opposed to controlled indoor-lighting setups. The assistance here of a person who became a wonderful friend, Ruta, provided a natural calming agent in this unusual situation, and I still thank her for the care and concern during the long periods of standing in the sun, the redo more than once of hair and makeup, all the while going through every word of the song in my mind . . . waiting.

We wished to wait for the setting of the sun for the "real" filming, so all had to be prepared since, when the time arrived, we would have but one chance to get the shot. In the end there were a lot of rehearsals for a song that would take only about three minutes to perform. We were ready.

The hour arrived: the words in Hebrew were now welded in my brain, the helicopter cameraman, Ilan, was in place, and we went forward with all our might.

Those wonderful crew members and I are still fast friends. This was an important moment in time for us all.

OTHER THAN IN the midst of such unusual events as singing atop Masada, I am not flustered when it comes time to go onstage. The one thing that can cause anxiety, though, is a lack of rehearsal. I am not one to arrive the night before an opera performance to be introduced to the person playing the role of my beloved, or to be given a day's notice as to who will be standing where on the stage. This manner of working is just the thing for some of my colleagues, but I resisted such habits even as a beginning singer in Europe, where it is easier to hop from one opera house to another due to the shorter distances. My spirit is not in an ideal state in this kind of situation. I enjoy the time spent in getting ready, with everyone involved.

I find enormous pleasure in singing Schoenberg's *Erwartung* and Poulenc's *La voix humaine,* both monodramas. To my knowledge, I am the only singer to perform these two operas on the same evening. Naturally, even for the performances of these monodramas and in song recitals, there are many other people involved in a presentation. It is marvelous to have the opportunity, for example, of working so closely with a lighting designer who has to light only the set and my persona. We can choose whatever gels we prefer; no one else will be disturbed. What is more, in these situations I can rehearse until I drop from exhaustion, having caused no other singer to suffer long rehearsal sessions. These one-person operas pose high levels of vocal, musical, and physical challenges, and I find the same level of satisfaction in bringing them to the stage.

Song recitals can be inspirational, refreshing, glorious. The chance to work with a pianist and to present a whole list of songs, each one different from the other, to an audience waiting to be taken on about twenty different little journeys in one presentation, is something very special. This type of performance is not for every singer or listener. Without the benefit of sets and spectacle, it does not please everyone. But for those of us who thrive in this genre, it is the life's blood, indeed, to all else that we do. I am so very, very lucky in the piano accompanists that travel this journey with me. Irwin Gage walked with me through all the newness of my profession and for several years was my steady musical partner. Then I worked with Geoffrey Parsons, who accompanied so many singers that he could play any song that I brought to him in many different keys. We used to have wonderful fun with this. I really put him through his paces in a rehearsal in North London, in the reception room where so many of my esteemed colleagues had also rehearsed.

Dalton Baldwin's knowledge and experience, most particularly in the French song repertoire, is unparalleled. I have also had the benefit of the vast experience of his longtime musical partner, Gérard Souzay. I hear Duparc's "Phidylé" in my ears, as coached by Gérard and Dalton, to this day.

Phillip Moll's readiness to perform is always a wonder. He enjoys instrumental ensemble playing as much as working with singers, and his energy never flags. It is very special to us both that we met in those first days in Berlin. Finally, Mark Markham and I have performed together since the mid-1990s and see no reason to pull back now. Whether we are deep into the soul of a song of Hugo Wolf, or in flight in Richard Strauss, or in a virtual smoky cabaret with Duke Ellington's "I've Got It Bad (and That Ain't Good)," his total musicianship is stunning. We are in ecstasy, too, with our jazz combo. The journey continues.

I do not tend to subscribe to rituals before going onstage. Indeed, I learned early in my performance life that these things need to be kept to a minimum if I am to get the job done well. Surely, as a very young singer in Berlin's Deutsche Oper, I did take notice of how the more experienced singers looked after themselves and their voices, and I even tried to incorporate some of their customary pre-performance rites into my own preparation. I remember one singer intimating that a raw egg mixed into a cup of tea was just the elixir she needed prior to a performance. That concoction held no magic for me. I did, however, try the "tea and honey" ritual that is the habit of many singers, and I used to prepare this mixture in a thermos and take it with me to performances. Once, while

I was rushing out of a hotel in Vienna to sing a recital, my old-fashioned thermos, with its glass interior, fell out of my bag and crashed onto the floor. The noise of the shattered glass astonished me. What would I do? My tea was ruined! Would I be able to sing? How could I go onstage now? Right then and there, I halted that "ritual," which had become simply a mental crutch. From that moment on, my only drinks have been water and certain fruit juices, which have the benefit of releasing sugar slowly into the bloodstream. Hydration; this is all that is needed.

To harness the energy and the adrenaline coursing through the body at a performance takes thought and determination. I consider performance nerves to be healthy anxiety, when managed. What I require is to be centered, to be quiet. I always arrive at a venue hours before the performance is to take place. For performances outside of an opera house, I take care of my own needs: my hair, my makeup, and my clothing, all because I need that quiet time to prepare, to think. I find it inspiring to acknowledge in my body that beautiful feeling that comes from knowing there are three thousand people out there waiting for me to come out and sing!

Knowledge, in order to embody completely the wholeness of my craft, is essential. For instance, with the Kaddish, as arranged by Maurice Ravel, I have to thank Rabbi Friedlander in London for being so patient in working with me on the transliteration of this great Hebrew prayer. Many people can say these words by heart and know exactly what they mean and on what occasion the words are used. I do not speak Hebrew and therefore for me to presume to sing these words, a great deal of homework is done. But once a performance begins, my sole concern is to offer the music fully and thoroughly, and to enjoy the process.

I will say once again that in every good performance there is energy that makes its circle from the stage to the audience and back again. Even when there is complete silence, this energy is present and alive! It is wonderful to receive the applause that indicates a certain amount of recognition for a performance, but it is also possible to experience a silence that is so full of energy and support that you think to yourself, *I can do anything tonight. I am feeling well, I am feeling healthy, my shoes are comfortable, I think my dress is looking really good. We can go on all night.* What joy!

A great deal of a different kind of work is done offstage in order for me to be able to accomplish this energy release, its reception, and then its return. The practice of hatha yoga came into my life as I found myself in stressful situations, particularly during summer festivals where there would be so much going on at once that I found little space for the peace and quiet preferred in order for me to prepare for a performance. The meditative aspect of this particular yoga practice is spirit-sustaining. I simply had to find a method that would allow me to center myself even on a crowded bus, on a train or a plane or in a dressing room too near a busy stage. It took a lot of practice, as it is not easy to sit and clear your mind, center yourself, concentrate on your breathing and your posture and your chosen "ohm" chants. You have to work out for yourself what it is in your mind that you need to discard in order to center your thoughts. By now, I can practice hatha yoga anywhere. I had to be gentle with myself and give myself the time to become a real practitioner, and today I can speak very strongly to its rewards.

Any fitness expert will speak of the necessity of remaining as physically flexible as possible throughout one's life. I tend to stay in hotels that have swimming pools so that I may carry out an aerobic routine in the pool. I have long ago given up thinking about how it looks to those who stop their conversations near the pools to watch! The swimming pool's chlorine is not the best for health, especially hair and skin, and it is not good for me to be in a place where I cannot open a door or window and allow some of that chlorine to escape. So I must be aware of this and limit my time as necessary. But as many a traveler knows, exercise bands can go a long way to "getting the job done."

Of course, there is what one might consider the glamorous side to the life of a performer. It is a privilege to meet people from all walks of life, to meet heads of state, or to have a kindergarten class in Florida draw, color, and then send twenty different versions of your performance dress that they have seen on television, and to see my own face and hair sometimes in the most amazing color combinations. Or to meet a kind young woman in the Midwest who arrives to turn the pages for a recital and who announces, almost nonchalantly, that at her birth seventeen years ago, her parents decided to give her the same first name as mine, spelled the same way. "Yes," she said, "my parents named me after you!"

It doesn't get much more glamorous than that.

I HAVE ON more than one occasion had the honor of appearing before statesmen—sometimes on short notice. In the autumn of 2002, I was having a grand time in Seoul at the city's Arts Center. I was so happy to have the opportunity to present a song recital on one of the evenings, straight from the classical canon: Schubert, Brahms, Ravel, and Wagner. All great music, offered to a most welcoming public.

Later in the week, with my jazz group, we presented an evening of the music of Duke Ellington. It was just the kind of performance experience I so cherish: the music of the great Europeans on one evening, swiftly followed by the music of a great American that same week. It was total delight to offer these different genres of the world's music, and of myself!

We were preparing for our final performance in Seoul when I received a message from Atlanta that President Carter wished me to sing at the ceremony in which he would be awarded the Nobel Peace Prize, in only a few days' time. I was happy that the date was free and, looking at the map, thought it would be an easy trip from the Far East to northern Europe. I could not have been more wrong. The trip would necessitate flying back to the middle of Europe, or thereabouts, and then flying north to Norway, as there were no direct flights from Seoul. And so we made the long flight to Norway via London.

The awarding of the Nobel Peace Prize attracts worldwide attention and recognition, of course, and it was a pleasure indeed to sing on this occasion and for a fellow Georgian: the peanut farmer and Sunday school teacher who had risen to become our President. The hallowed halls of the Oslo venue are so beautiful in shades of blue, with marble and gold leaf everywhere. It was such a glorious feeling to be included in the ceremony.

I chose music that would befit the occasion and the man, I felt. From Handel's *Messiah*, I sang "He Shall Feed His Flock."

He shall feed his flock like a shepherd,
And carry them in His bosom,
And gently lead those that are with young.

This was followed by one of President Carter's favorites, "Amazing Grace." Inspiring words about President Carter were spoken, and his acceptance remarks were beautiful, humble, and uplifting. It was a wonderful morning.

One of the guests who spoke to me afterward stated that as a youngster, she had attended a concert by Marian Anderson and had remembered the experience all her life. She was no longer young. The photograph that had been taken that evening showed a young girl standing next to the great Anderson, a photo that was kept, I was told, close by at all times. I found this very moving, and even more so when this woman asked if, now, she might have a photograph taken with me. We took our photograph. President Carter, having been so gracious in thanking Mark Markham and me for the performance, was now on the other side of the room as he waved and mouthed the words *Thank you.*

The trip to Norway was complete.

A SIMILARLY WONDERFUL message led me to a memorable visit to the White House and with President Obama. I learned that I was to receive the National Medal of Arts through the National Endowment for the Arts. When I discovered that two very good friends, John Williams and Michael Tilson Thomas, would be honored at the same time, it gave an extra lift to the spirit. Tremendous joy and equally wondrous gratitude, arriving in the same package!

Our new President would present the medals, and there would be a reception at the White House. This was all scheduled to take place in November of 2009, only months after President Obama had taken the oath of office, but had to be rescheduled when Washington, D.C., experienced a "nonpolitical" shutdown of the government due to a storm, a hurricane, and an earthquake, all in short order. The date was changed to February 2010 and just happened to fall on the date that President Obama would have to spend hours and hours, prior to this White House ceremony, with those of the opposing party in discussions of the Affordable Care Act. But, true to form, the President rushed into the East Room, where we all waited patiently, and began his remarks with a lightness of heart that was nothing short of amazing. He apologized for being a few minutes late because, as he stated, he "had this other thing" that he "had to do."

The room erupted in laughter, and happiness threaded the rest of the day. It was the most wonderful thing to have the President place the medal attached by lovely grosgrain ribbon around our necks, and all of us accepted the President's invitation to enjoy the tremendous ambiance of the White House along with the deliciousness of the spectacular buffet.

With our invited guests, the twenty honorees for the arts and the same number for the humanities visited the rooms of "the People's House" and enjoyed most thoroughly this unique opportunity, this most special occasion with our President.

THE CHALLENGES OF this profession are too great if one is not committed fully. A difficult, demanding profession can feel easier when you are doing something that you love. Little things can take on far more importance than they deserve: the hotel fails in its service or your performance dress comes back from a pressing looking much as it did when it left your hands. I try hard at such times to abide by what my aunts always told me all those years ago: "Get on with it." Whenever I have the opportunity to speak to budding professional musicians, I tell them the same thing: "You really need to be committed to doing this and understand what you are asking of yourself. Rehearsing is endless, continuous discovery is vital, enjoyment is crucial. This profession will often take you away from your family and friends, familiar and comfortable surroundings, not to mention the difficulties of travel itself." Be certain that you are willing to offer this much of yourself to your craft, as only then will you have all that is inside you to offer for those occasions when your craft might well be realized fully.

I am continually amused and bemused that those who are outside of the arts world often think that those of us who make a living in these professions—and they are our professions, not our hobbies—are willing and ready to perform at the drop of a hat. More times than I can count I have found myself as a guest at a gathering where more than one person will approach to ask if I'll be performing. I have, on occasion, rather cheekily responded by asking, "What, may I ask, is your profession?" When I hear the person's response, I ask if he or she intends to "perform dentistry that evening," or "teach a class on Chaucer?" People are always surprised when they are reminded that we performers are really working on those stages. We work hard to make the offerings seem as light and joy-filled as is appropriate to the piece in question, but these are indeed professions. Let us look to and celebrate these demanding, wonderful, challenging opportunities for communication through music, dance, the spoken word on a stage, works by master photographers as well as those haunting photos taken by children given cameras in order to document their own neighborhoods, designs by the greatest of graphic artists as well as those who cannot stop themselves from expressing their life story with a spray can on the side of a building. All of this conspires to make up our world!

Still, even though I consider it my craft, my love of singing comes from my understanding that if we are given a talent, it is our duty to explore and cultivate that gift. And I love the depth of meaning, the very soul of the music that I sing. There is this soul in all of it—every note of Schubert's and every work by Duke Ellington or Thelonious Monk. The list is very long and we are very blessed! ... A soul, after all, is touched by things that are familiar to it, even when those things are new. Surely, you can feel as overjoyed walking into a Buddhist temple in Japan as sitting in the pews of a Baptist Church in Harlem. They are both places of spirit and worship, and though they touch your heart and mind in different ways, you are still being moved. The same is true if you are listening to a song of Leonard Bernstein or an aria of Mozart. Depending on your own life experience you will be touched in very specific ways. This is why it was possible for me as a youngster to listen to Nat "King" Cole singing "Stardust" and love it, even though I had not lived long enough to understand the twilight of life and love and all those deeper meanings that eventually become clearer with living. I was attracted to the sound, the beauty of his voice, the music, his art.

The same can be said of music from the classical canon, particularly for people who have never given it a serious try. The sheer depth and breadth of the musical offerings make it possible for anyone to choose that which speaks to them. It need not necessarily be opera; it could be the piano music of Chopin or the string quartets of Beethoven or the symphonies of Mahler. But exposure to these beautiful works makes choice possible. I spend a certain amount of time in helping to make adults who are coming to classical music a bit later in life comfortable and happy. Some who are new to the genre express concern that they will not be able to appreciate songs or opera arias sung in a foreign language or, perhaps more typically, that they need special training in order to understand classical music in general, or they worry about something as unimportant as applauding at the wrong moment. To which I say: Fear no music! Fear no art!

Growth in one's craft is essential. Life can be a marvelous teacher—it can tell you so much more about what it is that you, as a singer, are charged with truly offering to your audience. While we can lose the youthful energy and the natural ability to make those twenty turns as a ballerina or sing a very long phrase in one breath, if we are lucky, we gain more courage to take a little bit more time or try a different interpretation of something familiar. These are new ideas that come from living. For me, it is possible to spend a lot of time rehearsing in the studio, but true learning comes from performing—seeing how I need to pace myself now and be at my very best when I reach the most challenging part of a presentation. I have said that I want to keep getting better, and this is certainly my aim. I want to be as good as I can be, always. I want to see and experience the new. I perform a great number of recital programs, for example ... and I have no idea how many, but it is not and never has been my idea to perform the same programs continually. I enjoy development, growth.

I am pleased, too, to know that my audiences grow with me. There are music lovers who come to my performances, particularly in France and Germany, who were students, the same age as I, when they first became audience members. Later they came to the performances with their children. And now they come with their grandchildren. For this, and so much, much more, I am grateful.

Sanctus, St. Cecilia Mass · CHARLES GOUNOD · Holy

Sanctus, Sanctus	Holy, Holy
Dominus Deus Sabaoth	Lord God of hosts
Pleni sunt coeli et terra eterna	Heaven and Earth are full of
Gloria tua.	Thy Glory.
Hosanna in excelsis.	Hosanna in the highest.

9

Woman, Life, Singer

"RIDE ON, KING JESUS"

Ride on, King Jesus,
No man can hinder me.
For He is King of Kings
He is Lord of Lords,
Jesus Christ, the First and Last
No man works like Him.
I was but young when I begun,
But now, the race is almost won.
King Jesus rides a milk-white horse,
The river of Jordan He did cross.
Ride on, King Jesus,
No man can hinder me.

In modern usage, the terms *diva* and *prima donna* are used interchangeably, and not always as compliments or acknowledgments of special accomplishments. In former times, the labels were unabashedly positive and applied most often to female opera performers. Divas were adored and showered with adulation. Being labeled a prima donna or diva meant something very special: goddess, deity, divine.

Early patrons of the opera considered the female voice to be something very special, particularly as the era of the castrati, the male singers whose vocal registers were so high as to make them able to sing female roles, was coming to a close. The castrati were the matinee idols of their day, when it was not well thought of to have women in performance onstage.

I resisted employing the terms *diva* and *prima donna* in any way for many years. I agreed finally to focus on their historical meanings when I entitled a series of programs with the music of Edward Kennedy "Duke" Ellington *The Duke and the Diva* (and again, later, *The Duke, the Diva, and the Dance,* when I had the grand pleasure of working with the Trey McIntyre Project at the Vail International Dance Festival in the summer of 2007). I thought that assuming the label would confound those who had so happily assigned it to so many women, surely including myself. A few stories, full of dramatic content, intrigue, and extreme inaccuracies, have served to confuse music fans as well as the general public about the connotations of these terms in my own case.

I AM HAPPY that it is easy to count the comparatively small number of occasions when, in my decades of performance life, I have had to cancel an appearance. However, I am reminded of one occasion on which a postponement was called for: a series of concerts scheduled to take place in Brazil in 2001, just three weeks after the terrorist attacks of September 11 in the United States. Anxiety soared as the world braced for further attacks, and frankly, I was much more amenable to being with my family and friends at such a worrisome period than I was to traveling far away from both home and the people I loved. I therefore published an open letter to concertgoers in Brazil explaining the necessity of postponing the performances. I could not have been clearer as to my state of mind and promised to reschedule as soon as could be arranged. The message ended with the sentence "I ask your meditations and prayers."

It was therefore surprising, to put it mildly, when my brother called just a few days after I had forwarded my letter to Brazil, to tell me of an article that had run in the *Detroit Free Press* claiming that the reason I would not appear as planned in Brazil was that the hotel in which I was to stay had refused to honor my request that seventeenth-century Japanese prints be placed in my accommodations. Truth to tell, I have to tip my hat to the person who came up with such a creative tale!

Aside from the fact that no hotel accommodations had even been finalized at the time, a request of this kind would be so "un-Jessye" as to be utterly ridiculous. Still, this story was carried by none other than the Associated Press, and to this day, I have no idea as to its origin.

The same is true of a fantastic tale surrounding one of my many performances at the Salzburg Festival. It's a wonderful summer festival and I have probably offered more solo recitals and orchestral and opera presentations there than I have almost anywhere else, over the twenty-five-year period that it has been my joy to perform there. My recitals are very often on Sundays, and I prefer this, so that my most ardent audience members, many of whom are only free from their work on the weekends and can purchase only the tickets with seating far from the stage, or watch the performances outdoors on the large screen at the cathedral square, can actually be present. Performing there for the whole public is my heart's joy.

As is my professional habit, I arrived at the hall hours prior to the performance. I prefer to be in place in good time for my routine: the warming up of my voice, then makeup, hair, and performance dress, all managed without assistance. The performance was scheduled to begin as usual at 8:00 p.m. After I was settled in the dressing room and had begun my vocal warm-up exercises, there was a knock at the door. "Come in, please," I responded, in a rather high, singsongy voice, as I always do when I am warming up for a performance. The person who entered informed me that, due to the rain in the afternoon, the summer's stunning production of *The Passion Play,* which is normally performed outdoors, was in fact still in progress on the stage of the Großes Festspielhaus, the stage for my recital. Because the stage sets would have to be broken down following the conclusion of the play, the recital would need to begin at 9:00 p.m. "Thank you very much," I replied, adding that with the air being heavy with moisture and a little cool, it was good to have the extra time to warm up slowly and carefully. I asked that my piano accompanist, Geoffrey Parsons, should please be advised of the change once he had arrived. Any string player will tell you how much more difficult it is to tune an instrument in preparation for a performance when there is excess moisture in the air, particularly cool air. For singers, very much the same is true.

I thought nothing more of the conversation. Geoffrey and I rehearsed on the stage at the appointed time and further readied ourselves for the performance. We had a wonderful time that evening; the audience was marvelous and we were happy. We presented a program of Brahms and Hugo Wolf, some of the core works of the long catalog of German lieder. Afterward, the director of the festival came backstage as he always did, but he looked somewhat uneasy. "I was so pleased that you were able to give us such a performance after having been so very upset," he said. I asked, "Hans, what do you mean?"

"I was just so surprised that you were so upset," he said, "because you, of course, understand *The Passion Play* and the need to present this indoors when the weather is unfavorable. I remember another occasion when you had to do this."

I was now completely confused.

It turned out that the person who had given me the message about the delay (a personal assistant to one of the conductors) had invented a tale that he passed on to the festival staff. He had relayed that I had "exploded" when he advised me of the delay, that I was absolutely furious and practically "bit his head off." This of course meant that the whole festival staff had sat in the audience wondering whether my performance would be affected by my reported anger. They could not have known that there was absolutely no reason for concern, as I was completely at ease, oblivious to the tension this storyteller had invented, and had been grateful for the extra time to prepare.

Who knows why the tale was told. Perhaps it was a case of

what psychologists label "projection." Perhaps this person thought that an outburst, as he chose to describe it, would somehow have been expected, or maybe even acceptable.

Sold-out performances are practically the norm in Salzburg, as many music enthusiasts from all over the world make a point of visiting this festival every year. It can be great fun just to observe the audience's attire, which competes most favorably with any Hollywood red carpet.

A person who might take these habits of the audience members, the full houses, and the enthusiasm for the performances, as having to do only with them, could well assume a degree of unhealthy self-regard.

We all know that there is no real substitute for honesty and good manners.

These lessons were not only drummed into my consciousness during my growing-up years, but also demonstrated so very beautifully one fine day in the beginning years of my professional life. I observed my more experienced colleagues arriving early for rehearsals and performances and taking most seriously the obligations of the profession: preparedness, courtesy, respect, and enjoyment of the work.

The great Dietrich Fischer-Dieskau offered a lesson in amity and professionalism to me on a memorable day in Berlin. It was 1973, and we were to rehearse Mozart's *The Marriage of Figaro*. I was to sing the role of the Countess and he would be my onstage husband, Count Almaviva. Fischer-Dieskau, one of the greatest singers who ever lived—a generous artist, universally admired—walked into the rehearsal room and proceeded to introduce himself, shaking hands with everyone and announcing the role he was to sing, as if we did not know who he was or how thrilled we all were with the opportunity of performing with him. It was, however, the professional and courteous thing to do, and I never forgot it. This is not something that we do as often in the United States, but any musician who has spent time working in Europe knows this to be the habit. To this day, when I arrive at a rehearsal, I walk into the room, say hello, and shake hands with everyone, paying particular attention to those I may not have met previously. It is a fine way to begin a rehearsal and shows we are all colleagues, and that working together, we are more likely to achieve the happy results that we all want.

This is not easy for everyone. Performers, after all, are a microcosm of society at large. Not everyone shares this desire to create an atmosphere of comfort. And let us not pretend that there is anything "regular" about going onto a stage in a house with hundreds and sometimes thousands of seats, to offer up your craft while interacting with colleagues, the conductor, and the orchestra without so much as a microphone! Oh yes, it is thrilling, this wonderful phenomenon of live performance. The challenges to body and soul are real. I recognize that in certain situations, a degree of anxiety can develop that can cause us to deport ourselves in unusual ways. We all work hard to keep difficult behavior to a minimum.

On the other hand, there are often honors and distinct recognitions that remind me of how extraordinary a performer's life can be. This life, precious life.

Just such a moment arrived for me in the summer of 1988. I was in Paris, only a few days into the recording of *Carmen* with

Seiji Ozawa, when an emissary from the office of President François Mitterrand, Mr. De Pavillion, asked to meet with me. I was, of course, more than a little curious. A time was set aside, the press manager for Philips Records introduced me to Mr. De Pavillion, and we sat for our meeting.

Mr. De Pavillion and I spoke for a moment or two about my artistic ties to France and how often I perform there, and then he stated his mission: on behalf of President Mitterrand, he was asking me to perform the French national anthem, "La Marseillaise," the following summer, on July 14, 1989, for the celebration of the bicentennial of the French Revolution. I was stunned—and a bit confused. After listening a while further to De Pavillion's plans, I could not wait a second longer before asking, "Is the president of the thought that I come from one of the former French colonies in Africa, or from Martinique, Haiti, or Guadeloupe, perhaps?"

Mr. De Pavillion broke into a slight smile and said, "I assure you, the president knows that you are American."

Still wanting verification, I said something along the lines of, "And I am to sing the anthem alone or with a choir?" to which he responded, "No, you are being asked to sing alone, please. We are considering that this will be performed at the Place de la Concorde, for historical reasons."

I stated that it would be my high honor to accept the invitation and that I looked forward to further news of the arrangements as they progressed. Needless to say, I went back to my recording session that day full of beans!

The following year, the Place de la Concorde was, indeed, chosen as the performance place. The French American Jean-Paul

Goude was asked to organize the entire *défilé* (parade) and I was informed that I would sing live.

No prerecorded anything; live! Excitement does not begin to describe this moment in time, which was bolstered even further by the news that the great designer Azzedine Alaïa would create the gown that I would wear.

Working with Azzedine was an experience unto itself. In his atelier, an assistant placed me in muslin from neck to feet, which provided the canvas on which Azzedine would create the gown. He arrived in the fitting room with forty meters of quadruple-weight silk in each of the three colors of the *tricolore drapeau*—the French national flag—which he announced he would pin to the muslin and thereby actually cut the fabric for the gown on me. We had a laugh about this, as Azzedine is not very tall and, in order to accomplish this complicated cutting of the fabric as I stood, he had to use a ladder. What he managed was miraculous: he cut each portion of the three colors asymmetrically so that the fabric of the gown would fall away from my body. I stood there watching this magic in several mirrors, in total wonder. Azzedine joked that he had made sure he would have enough fabric on hand in case the plan that he had in his head did not work and we would be obliged to come up with another idea. Indeed, he cut the three portions of the gown and created the design at the same time. He did this only once. Perfection.

Further, Azzedine cut the bottom part of the dress, the red part, in such a manner that if there should suddenly be a breeze at the Place de la Concorde while I was singing live with estimated billions watching worldwide, the dress would not be taken up easily by the wind in an unflattering manner. I was amazed that he had even thought of such a thing. He also designed blue see-through gloves for my hands to match the blue of the top part of the gown.

We agreed that I would wear my own red silk shoes — comfortable feet being an extremely important part of this enterprise. The entire bicentennial experience was, of course, something to remember — always. The gown, the flag, the anthem, the history.

Fifty-five heads of state were in attendance in Paris the week of the celebration, and it happened that a dinner had been organized in their honor the night prior to the big event. President Mitterrand sent word that evening that at the end of our rehearsal, those of us working on the national anthem part of the celebration should join him and the heads of state for dinner at the Musée d'Orsay. We were in summer clothing for rehearsal. No one was dressed for such a dinner invitation. But we were assured our presence was wanted, and after rehearsals were completed, off we went.

We arrived at the Musée d'Orsay well after the other dinner guests had been seated, of course, but were thrilled to be there. My beautiful young brother George and my close friend from Germany were with me. As it turned out, my brother was not seated at the same table as I, and this resulted in a bit of confusion when word spread that he was an African head of state. The organizers were especially sensitive to this issue, as earlier in the week had been an unfortunate mix-up of the names of two African heads of state, and a mild incident had ensued. Nothing serious, just a small matter that, given the circumstances, grew into something much larger — the confusion of two gentlemen from former French colonies. Feelings were bruised. There was much relief all around when I said, "Oh please do not worry, this is my brother George!" George ended up being seated next to the brother of President Mitterrand, who stated to him, "Yes, I know what it is like to be someone's brother." As is always the case with my brother, he had a beautiful evening and was practically on a first-name basis with his fellow table guests by the end of the evening.

The dinner was the stuff of dreams, in one of Paris's glorious museums. Wonderful.

As it was getting a bit late, I asked to return to my hotel, the performance to come looming in my mind. We made it back safely, but even with the help and direction of the people whose job it was to escort us from place to place, we had difficulty making our way through the crowds—a million or more tourists flooded the streets of Paris for the week's festivities. A very large crowd had gathered in front of our hotel to catch a glimpse of certain heads of state who were being accommodated there.

All security and police had, I would learn afterward, been instructed to use minimal action in dispersing crowds, wishing to make the entire experience in Paris that week a wonderful one for everyone. I was on the verge of becoming a little desperate when an idea came to me. I looked at my brother George and, in a rather loud voice, stated, "Par ici, Monsieur le Président," which means, "Come this way, Mr. President." I promise you, the crowd parted as if by magic to allow George through; they applauded this VIP, having no idea who he was. I followed close behind and we made it inside the hotel.

For years afterward, when George visited me in France, everyone who knew this story called my young brother Monsieur le Président. He loved it.

That glorious day, July 14, 1989, came in no time. I was to sing at what would be the close of the défilé, the parade. I needed to be in place at the Place de la Concorde from the beginning of the evening—around 7:00 p.m.—even though I was not expected to sing live until after 11:00 p.m. or so. My accommodations were stellar: a wonderful space, with electricity and water, mirrors, a makeup table, comfortable chairs, and television monitors, was created for me to serve as a dressing room, all under the stage, which had been built in front of the Luxor Obelisk at the Place de la Concorde. I was charged with singing the first stanza directly in front of the obelisk, descending the few stairs and walking on to what would be a moving platform that would take me into what was actually the middle of this great crossing of the various streets at the Place de la Concorde—with me singing all the while. The conclusion of the song, and therefore the conclusion of the défilé, would take place in the middle of this great crossing.

Mr. De Pavillion was with me in the dressing room, as was Azzedine and a couple of friends. Meanwhile, my brother George and friend from Germany were out there somewhere in the throng. At one point, after we'd watched about an hour or so of this marvelous event via the television monitor, Mr. De Pavillion came to me and very privately asked if I were nervous.

"Mr. De Pavillion," I replied, "I have gone over the text for this hymn more times than I have seen the sun rise. I promise you, all will be well. I can hardly wait." I'm not certain that this little bit of cockiness put his mind to rest. But, all was well.

I was thrilled to work with France's then Minister of Culture, Jack Lang, who, along with his wife, Monique, remains a good friend to this day. It was some years later, when Jack became Minister of Education, that I was asked to allow my performance of "La Marseillaise" to be used in the schools to teach the students their national anthem. It is still used today. I glow with this thought!

A year after the French Bicentennial celebration, with the wonderful events of the evening still ringing in my spirit, I was awarded the Légion d'Honneur at a ceremony held at Paris's Palais Royal, with all the accoutrements that such an award would dictate. President Mitterrand was again offering me an unimagined gift.

Members of the Orchestre de Paris presented a most cherished concert, and the Minister of Culture, Jack Lang, offered the stunning red ribbons known the world over as the symbol of this privileged recognition. I presented my response in French and thought that I would be able to sing the great Cole Porter song "I Love Paris," but mostly, I wept; I had been crowned with far too much beauty and emotion to sing properly.

But no one seemed to care at all. The room was filled with friends of long standing who understood my intention and excused readily the results.

These beautiful red ribbons reside next to the green and white ribbons of the Ordre des Arts et des Lettres, which was presented to me upon my tenth year singing in France. (My first performance there had come two and a half years into my professional life.)

Oh, yes, France and I have been together a long time. In 2012, when President Sarkozy elevated my rank in the Légion d'Honneur, I took a deep breath of gratitude and thought of my time with the great Pierre Bernac, who said to me during my days as a student in his master series at the University of Michigan, "I am so glad that you are unafraid of the difficulty some singers find in the French language and you seem to enjoy it so much."

Yes, monsieur, I enjoy it enormously.

OF COURSE, BEING in the presence of people who have achieved recognition on the world's stage, whose names we know as well as our own, can be illuminating, reminding us that we all have so much more in common than we realize. They need not be heads of state, just those whose work and ways we happen to enjoy.

I find that those well known in their fields are often more interested in meeting people from other disciplines. Just a few years ago, I had the immense pleasure of sharing a dressing room with the much-admired Kitty Carlisle Hart; we were both reading poems that afternoon as part of the annual poets and poetry celebration in New York.

Meryl Streep was across the corridor; I could not have been happier.

I still laugh out loud at Ms. Hart's declaration that she could hardly wait to tell her friends at lunch the following day that we had not only shared a dressing room, but that I had gone to find a cup of tea for her! And later, before I could put my gushing sentence together to greet Ms. Streep, it was she who offered that she was such an admirer!

Marvelous! We all have so much more in common than we have that is genuinely different. We are interested, curious, in admiration of those with whom we are fortunate enough to share this planet.

I AM THE PROUD AND HUMBLE recipient of more than thirty honorary doctorate degrees from colleges, universities, and conservatories around the world, and I have always taken special delight in the fact that the very first school to have invited me to receive such recognition was my very own undergraduate school, Howard University. I could not have been more surprised when in late 1981, only fifteen years after earning my degree, I received the beautiful letter from the university's president stating that the board of trustees and others involved in such a selection process had voted to offer me this recognition at the commencement exercises of May 1982. I was thrilled. The occasion was made all the more special when I was presented with the opportunity to gawk at one of the other honorees that year, the great Sarah Vaughan. I cannot say that she was full of conversation, but it was still rather special to be with her.

Only a few years later, it was such a pleasure to find myself in the company of the Duke of Edinburgh in a ceremony on the campus of Cambridge University, where I received an honorary doctorate degree. I was an honorary fellow of two of the colleges, Jesus and Newnham, already, and I was deeply moved to be asked to return to receive such a prestigious honor. I was so very happy to have been invited to spend the evening prior to the day's celebration on the campus, in the home of the headmaster for Jesus

College, Colin Renfrew, and his wife—a night made all the more special by the events of the following morning. The joy-filled day began with my being serenaded awake by a choir of young men from Jesus College, who sang just outside the window of the room in which I slept. It was a complete and captivating surprise, but only the first of the many wonderful ways we honorees would be feted on that glorious, sun-drenched day. The procession was delicious: as we honorees made our way to the extraordinarily beautiful building in which the ceremony would take place, we walked along one of the campus streets, past student housing, only to be celebrated by students playing a catalog of my music through their open windows.

My walking partner and fellow honoree that morning was Javier Pérez de Cuéllar, Secretary-General of the United Nations. Yes, I was having quite a moment!

Then there was the ceremony itself. At Cambridge, the music/arts robing is beautifully distinctive. Rather than a black robe, as at so many schools, this one is white silk brocade. Tremendous! To wit, the arts chairman, whose job it was to do the actual presentation of the degree, used quotes from various ancient poems and prose, all in praise of music. It was a remarkable afternoon.

At the luncheon, attended by all honorees, our guests, and members of the faculty from each of the colleges at the university, I had the pleasure of being seated next to the Duke of Edinburgh, the patron of Cambridge University at the time. He proved to be a marvelous luncheon companion. We talked about all manner of things, including that I was scheduled to take a plane that afternoon to Vienna, where I would sing a recital the following day. I was quite amused when His Highness proceeded to advise me as to which route I should have the driver take from Cambridge to Heathrow Airport in order to join the M25, which was all the rage among drivers, who believed that this new motorway would save travel time in this southern part of Britain. I recall saying something like, "But sir, I cannot imagine that you have ever actually driven yourself anywhere in this country," whereby he suggested —I am not altogether sure whether in jest—that as long as he took a regular-looking vehicle, he actually enjoyed driving himself from place to place, with the general public unaware of his presence. To this day, I am not absolutely certain that he was not having a little fun with me on that issue. But the conversation certainly ranks high in my memories of honorary-degree experiences.

Of course, there are other unusual opportunities that can arise from this profession. In the early 1980s, I was enjoying a short break doing something that has always been soothing, inspiring, and totally rejuvenating: taking time for walks on the beach. It was October and I was in Falmouth, Massachusetts, when I received a message that I was to return a call from a telephone number in Washington. It turned out to be that of Senator Charles "Mac" Mathias. I was being invited to sing for the coming presidential inauguration in January. Let me say straightaway that as I was certain that Senator Walter Mondale would become our President, I was not hesitant at all in thanking Senator Mathias for his generous invitation and that I would be absolutely delighted to accept the invitation.

When November rolled around and the votes were counted, I was not sure of how I should proceed, having already accepted the invitation for the inauguration. After much thought and consultation with my family and close friends, it was decided that I should move forward, and that it should be made possible for me, in an appropriate forum, to state my political and social beliefs and my affiliation with the party of Senator Mondale, not that of President-elect Ronald Reagan, who had now won his second term in the White House.

Senator Mathias, a Republican of the type that has all but disappeared from our political discourse, was sensitive enough to the situation to arrange an interview in the then-new national newspaper, *USA Today*. I was grateful for the opportunity to make it clear that I would take enormous pride in singing for the U.S. presidency, and that as a "dyed in the wool" Democrat, I would hope that others would view this participation as I did: as an act of citizenship. All was well.

That period in January 1985 proved to be one of the coldest ever recorded in Washington, and less than forty-eight hours prior to the inauguration, changes had to be made out of health and safety concerns for the parade participants, many of them musical groups from schools around the country, as well as for the spectators. The temperatures were far below freezing.

The inauguration would be moved from the outdoor area of the Capitol Building to the Rotunda, inside the Capitol Building. As a result, marching bands would not be able to take part in the ceremony. Family members and friends who had traveled to Washington would now have to view the event on television, as I would not be offered any tickets for seating in the Rotunda. Members of Congress and the Supreme Court and such would be accommodated in this now much smaller space, but the general public would not be admitted.

I was assigned an assistant for the day and, although well-meaning, she was rather at a loss as to what it was she was meant to do on my behalf. At my request, she accompanied me from the hotel to the Capitol Building that early morning. Upon arriving finally at the correct entrance and presenting ourselves to the bevy of security guards everywhere, I asked her to state that we were there early because I was to sing and had been offered Senator Mathias's office as a holding space as well as a place where I could manage the preparations for my performance. Because my kind assistant had not the faintest idea of what I meant by this—I had told her that one of the main things I needed to do was to "warm up" my voice, having spent too much time outside this very large building looking for the proper entrance—she stated to security that "I needed to get warm." General confusion abounded until it was possible for me to explain my predicament. Soon, we were allowed into the building and I thought all would proceed as intended.

At the ceremony, I sang the Shaker hymn "Simple Gifts," as had been requested by President Reagan. At the close of the event, I stood waiting for the assistant to reappear; she never did. The Rotunda was now completely empty; even the security guards were not in evidence. To this day, I have not the slightest idea what happened to her or why she abandoned her duties with me that day. Perhaps she thought she had completed all that she was charged with doing.

In any case, I found myself wandering around those marbled

halls trying to get back to Senator Mathias's office to retrieve my belongings, and then to find the car that would return me to my hotel and my family. By the time desperation was about to set in, who should bound down a flight of stairs but the Speaker of the House, Thomas "Tip" O'Neill. I was happy to see him and thoroughly amused when he introduced himself to me. I stated: "Mr. Speaker, only a visitor from another planet would not know who you are." I can still hear his wonderful laughter resounding through those great and grand halls. He was most gracious about my singing and asked where I was headed. I explained my predicament and in true "gentleman of the old school" fashion, he directed me to my intended destination, made sure I had understood the instructions, thanked me again, and continued on his way. A few moments later, I bumped, quite literally, into an actor whom I just adored, Telly Savalas. He was as lost as I had been. Together, we escaped our confinement, joking about it all as we found our way.

Yet another memorable opportunity arose when I was asked to perform at a state dinner for NATO leaders meeting in Washington. Of course, state dinners are planned many months in advance at the White House, due to the nature of our world, the obligations of our world leaders, and the schedules of all those involved. But with the participants gathered in Washington and the war in Bosnia having taken many devastating turns, President Clinton and our First Lady decided that instead of the long-planned luxurious evening at the White House, the working sessions would conclude with a concert. I agreed readily to the new arrangements.

It is hard to describe adequately the feeling that enveloped me, coming into what had for their time in Washington been the workspace of these nineteen heads of state, who now, for this evening, along with their spouses, were seated in the same semicircle of their workdays, awaiting a musical performance. I felt a privilege beyond expression in words. Dan Saunders, my piano accompanist, and I presented music that we thought would have meaning for these world leaders and to offer some of what music is able to do: soothe, inspire, comfort, and, yes, give pleasure. Our purpose was clear.

The first song was "Somewhere," from Leonard Bernstein's *West Side Story*.

> *There's a place for us, somewhere a place for us,*
> *Peace and quiet and open air wait for us somewhere.*

The East Room of the White House became an intimate space for sharing music, words so full of hope, so full of meaning, that I was as glad as ever to be a part of this profession. One of the world leaders had lost a member of his family in the recent past and he stated that he had been so shattered by this that he had not been able to grieve properly. That he had not been able to weep—not until, that is, that evening, in the quiet of that space, with those around him who shared the same kind of responsibility in our world, with a small amount of time away from the cares of governance. In that moment, he allowed himself to feel. The President stood by as this personal story was relayed to me, and nothing needed to be said. I broke protocol completely and offered an embrace as my means of saying thank you.

I LOVE TO TELL the story of being in my kitchen at home, having my private line ring and hearing a very familiar voice on the line, but not one that I had heard on a telephone previously. I was being asked to sing for the second inauguration of President Clinton, and he was making the call himself!

There are some very good practical jokers in my family, so I needed to be sure that it truly was the President. The validation was swift in coming. I was being asked to perform with the United States Marine Band, and to come back with a plan as soon as I could.

By now, I had learned a thing or two about appearing at such wide-reaching events, and this knowledge was most helpful in arranging all aspects of my participation on this occasion. I asked a great friend, Bruce Saylor, to compose a medley of music that I knew to be some of the President's favorites, and thus *Oh, Freedom,* had its creation, a medley consisting of "My Country, 'Tis of Thee," the Spiritual "Oh, Freedom," and "Amazing Grace," ending with "America the Beautiful."

As a choir and the Marine Band would be involved, I was happy that we were able to rehearse properly.

On the day, I was so very happy to have been in the holding area with our First Family, where the ease of conversation and amity was at once inspiring and inspired. I would remain in the holding area until the moment of my performance, due to the winter temperatures; I found those few moments alone to be just perfect prior to going out to sing for those assembled on the platform, the thousands in the seating area on the grounds, not to mention the millions via radio and television. I would sing from the same lectern used by those speaking, including the President, and I would be able to see the conductor via the teleprompter screens positioned on both sides of the lectern, exactly as we had rehearsed. I took my place at the appointed time, greeted the crowd, and looked down at the lectern, only to find completely dark screens! There was no way for me to view the conductor; the choir, Marine Band, and conductor were all well behind where I stood.

I decided against allowing panic to enter the situation and relied on listening as well as I could and going on from there. In the end, all was well, save a few extra heartbeats on my part.

EVENTS IN WASHINGTON, D.C., have provided some of my most memorable experiences, including my visits to the Kennedy Center Honors. The first visit, in 1995, was wonderful, as I was the surprise guest for Sidney Poitier. It was as a fairy tale to have rehearsed in secret with the orchestra, and to have had to stay well out of view during the activities of that Sunday evening in the concert hall of the John F. Kennedy Center for the Performing Arts. Senator Ted Kennedy would welcome the crowd and speak to the need of the arts in all of our lives, and of his brother's particular respect for and fostering of all art forms.

I sang "Amazing Grace" for one of the people on this earth that I adore without bounds.

Then came the late summer of 1997, and the world was in mourning at the sudden death of Diana, the Princess of Wales. The tragedy seemed to penetrate the spirits of those who knew her only by name as much as it seemed to affect those who knew her well. Ceremonies took place all over the world in Her Highness's memory, and I was privileged to participate in New York City's commemoration held in Central Park.

A very special invitation arrived by courier in this same period. My delicate spirit was in need of a boost of some kind, and the return address indicated the origin of the envelope. I imagined that I was being invited as a guest or program participant for the Kennedy Center Honors again that year. As it happened, the news was quite different: I would receive this recognition myself. This was such a blessing to me that early September of 1997, that on those occasions when I need a bit of lift, I just think back to the lightness, the joy that I felt upon reading those words.

The events of that December weekend were overwhelming in the elegance and attention to detail that were present at every turn. My fellow honorees, Lauren Bacall, Edward Villella, Bob Dylan, and Charlton Heston, made for quite an impressive group, to say the very least. I was overjoyed to be among them.

I had had the pleasure of meeting Miss Bacall previously and so it was a special delight to share this marvelous weekend with her. We were both surprised at how shy our new friend Bob Dylan was; it was at once amusing and puzzling. It soon became clear that he was utterly at ease in a small group, but that the glad-handing and all with fans and huge crowds was truly not for him. The great Villella was always eager to speak about Florida and his dance company and countless experiences. Personally, I was happy to have been able to avoid any discussion of politics with Mr. Heston, who gave the impression of being as delighted with being there as the rest of us. Politics would remain unspoken.

It was a weekend of grand memories to forever cherish and, I tend to think, never to be duplicated—the luncheons and the special dinner at the State Department, the visit to the White House on the day, and the thrill of being seated in the box next to the First Family at the Sunday-evening event.

My family and friends from near and far were with me; it was a wonderful time. And to my utter delight, Sidney Poitier and Secretary Colin Powell spoke on my behalf. Reality was rushing ahead of my dreams.

OUR NATION'S CAPITAL holds so many wonderful memories for me, from my days at Howard to all that has come after those years. Other capital cities have their own grand and glorious presence. There are so many beautiful buildings in Vienna, for example, that it is rather difficult to know which of these is an actual palace or was, indeed, a palace in previous times. The musical history of this city vies easily for the most outstanding of all.

My first visit to Vienna was not to witness a musical performance but to see this new sensation in the classical dance world about whom everyone was talking: Rudolf Nureyev. All that one had read of his artistic strengths were on view that evening on the stage of the Vienna Opera, and I wondered if his homeland would actually permit his remaining in the west. It did not cross my mind that much later in both our performance lives we would become acquainted—become pals.

My attraction to Vienna was enhanced quite quickly by being invited to sing a recital soon after having been awarded first place in the Bayerischer Rundfunk International Music Competition in 1968. Imagine: I was yet a master's degree student at the University of Michigan and would sing a recital in the Mozart Hall of the Konzerthaus in Vienna, all in the same period. Peter Weiser was director of the hall and had witnessed part of the Munich competition. I was thrilled, and so began my courtship with this beloved city and this country.

One beautiful autumn afternoon, decades after my very first singing visit, in the Hofburg Palace, now home to Austria's governmental offices, President Heinz Fischer would award me the highest recognition for the arts of his country, in the most beautiful of surroundings. The ceremony was preceded by a luncheon the likes of which one hardly thinks exists, and there, with my sister, Elaine, having come over from the States and with cherished friends from years of performances in this country, I would be able, in the confidence that comes from the experience that the years can give us, to respond to this wonderful moment in the language of that country. I held the beautiful red box containing the lovely red ribbon and medallion quite close to my heart as I did so. It did not seem as though so much time had passed—that truly I had been a guest of the Salzburg Festival for twenty-five years, or that I had lost count, actually, of the number of recitals in Vienna in the

Konzerthaus and in the Musikverein, the concerts with the Vienna Philharmonic. It was all a glorious fantasy.

WITH THE EXPERIENCES that are mine to enjoy and hold dear forever, it seems churlish, indeed, to offer complaints. One close friend, bless his heart, said to me, "Your trouble is you're just too simple. You don't have enough allure. You could do well with some eccentricities." I laughed and said, "This may be true." But really, when it comes to "getting on with it," I don't require a great deal from others. We've all heard of pop stars whose contracts have riders—a list of dressing room accommodations, meals, and specifications for stage design, sound systems, and lighting—that can stretch thirty pages long, single-spaced, for every appearance they make. They want the brown M&Ms removed from the bowls of chocolate delights sitting in each of their dressing rooms, six-hundred-thread-count Egyptian linens for their trailers, and enough fanciful, expensive foods to feed a small nation—or rather, their entourage of thirty band members, backup dancers, roadies, and Men of Unclear Purpose. The demands can be quite stunning; I have seen copies of them for myself. I cannot think of enough things that I could possibly need in order to fill such a number of pages.

And I suppose it helps, not being a pop star. Surely, my requests are simple to a fault. I need only those things that will help me keep my vocal mechanism in top form: unscented soap, unscented tissues, fruit and fruit juice that are not citrus, room-temperature bottled water, and paper cups. Voilà! My pals laughingly insist that I should ask for African violets and orchids flown in from who knows where, just to mix it up a bit. Maybe a crystal bowl with five red jelly beans. But really, none of those things have anything to do with my ability to perform. It takes a lot of energy, a great deal of concentration and determination to present the kind of performance that one wishes to on a stage in front of thousands of people at a time. I find my energy better spent in pursuit of that prize: the performance!

This is one of the main reasons for my wholehearted commitment to the rehearsal process. I believe in rehearsals—not runthroughs, but real rehearsals so that one has a basis from which to be comfortable and spontaneous on the stage. I believe that a quality of spontaneity in the arts results from having prepared, having rehearsed adequately, so that at performance time, the concentration is placed squarely on the job at hand and one can relax and allow the work to unfold in grace.

Unfortunately, adequate rehearsal time is a luxury we do not always enjoy. Opera, after all, is such an expensive affair that a new production rarely has more than four weeks between its first preparation in a rehearsal room and opening night. Four weeks!

We do not practice the ritual that I find so marvelous in the spoken-word theater, where at the beginning of the rehearsal period, all cast members meet together with the director for a readthrough of the entire play. In opera such a procedure is termed a *Sitzprobe* (a seated rehearsal), and it comes much later in the rehearsal process, normally just prior to the first stage rehearsal with the orchestra, which occurs rather close to that one week of rehearsal onstage prior to opening night.

Costumes, sets, lighting, all this is realized without the singers being present and often months prior to a production's presentation. I recall stating to a director of one Wagner production that since the long aria of one of the characters elucidates what my character knows already, without upstaging my colleague and his aria, that my character should not seem as though having a rest at the time, as her sleep would be anything but peaceful. The core of her being is revealed, and I felt there needed to be some indication of this uneasy spirit. The director listened, and then stated, as if patting the silly singer on the head, "But my dear, the lighting was set in our technical rehearsals last summer and there is no light at all on your character during that aria, so your reactions would not be seen!"

That the director considered this to be not only correct but a sufficient response to my concerns was amazing. Can you imagine anyone mounting all of the lighting for a production of *King Lear* without so much as stand-ins for the characters?

In another departure from the habits of the spoken-word theater, at the conclusion of the dress rehearsal for this new Wagner production, no notes were given to the singers, as the director had to leave for the airport to take his plane back to Europe. Amazing.

I HAVE FOUND that in order for me to remain concentrated and focused throughout performance periods, I must be prepared from the first moment. I do not know how other singers manage their lives, but I have always felt that in order to absorb the rehearsal process, I need to arrive at the first rehearsal having memorized

my text, my part, and everyone else's part. You would be surprised
how often I have found this not to be the case. It is astonishing to
me that anyone would even think of arriving at the first rehearsal
dependent upon looking at the score. But believe me, it happens.

I believe that if we are doing our jobs properly, the essence of
what we are singing should be clear. Audience members should
not have to rely on a translation on a screen in front of their seats or
projected over the top of the proscenium in order to comprehend
the story. I study the text until it feels organic. In fact, in poring
over a text, I often find myself wanting to wake someone up at
three o'clock in the morning to say, "I have finally worked out the
arc of that phrase! Heaven be praised." (I have learned to resist this
impulse.)

I remember two distinct occasions at the Metropolitan Opera
where my peculiar dedication to words made for some interesting experiences. One was a production of Béla Bartók's *Bluebeard's
Castle*. Based on a French fairy tale, it is written in Bartók's native
tongue, Hungarian, and the text for our performance was a third-
generation translation, first from Hungarian to German and then
from German to English. I had not yet studied Hungarian, but it
became clear rather quickly that there were meanings, syntax, and
contexts lost in the double translation. This would not do. I bor-
rowed Hungarian-English dictionaries and set about retranslating
the opera. I was also very lucky to have had made the acquaintance
of a trumpet player in New York City who was Hungarian, and
one of the families in our village up the river from the city was
also from Hungary. I had great support, and for days and days, I

worked on the score, retranslating the text so that we could convey this sensational tale in English with rhythm and cadence that I hoped would do justice to the narrative.

Several years later, I was preparing to sing Leoš Janáček's *The Makropulos Case,* written originally, of course, in Czech. The libretto had suffered the same fate as *Bluebeard's Castle:* translated into German and then into English. Again, I had a dictionary and support from Czech-speaking friends who helped me understand and translate the original text of the entire opera.

One scene was a particular challenge because it required me to choose from among subtly different shades of meaning. *The Makropulos Case* tells the story of an opera singer who drinks an elixir that preserves her youth for 250 years. Our stage set was pure 1950s Hollywood. At one point in the opera, my character, Emilia Marty, is recognized by a man who realizes that he had had a close relationship with her at some other place and time. He angrily calls her a word that had been rendered in English as *slut* in the translation we were all meant to use, the one supplied by the opera house. My colleague singing that part had not written the few wording changes I had offered into his score. I decided to bring it up with him during a break period when it was possible for us to speak. I told him I understood that he was using the translation we had originally received, but that the word *slut* was too modern for both the time of the opera's composition (between 1923 and 1925) and the period in which the director had set the opera, the 1950s. The word *whore* would have fit the time period, but that word could prove difficult to enunciate in singing and might have been hard for the audience to understand. So I had proposed we use a word that was definitely 1950s Hollywood: *tramp*.

"Try singing that," I suggested, "and see if that does not make more sense to you. It means the same thing but is more appropriate for the time period in which the opera is set."

My colleague made it clear that he did not wish me to bother him with my feelings about the translation; he simply wanted to sing his part as it was. Years later, I would learn from a music critic, of all persons, while offering an interview, that this colleague had relayed the story to the journalist, adding the fanciful detail that I had wished to have him change the word for religious reasons. *Religious reasons?* Wondrous!

I AM ALWAYS grateful for the opportunity to make updated translations of many of the songs I sing, some of which were already a bit arch when they were translated from German or French in the 1920s. I do this because I want everyone to have a true understanding of the song. Certainly, with some opera libretti, we may simply shake our heads and say, "If this were not an opera, I don't know how we could possibly present this story on stage." Some operas force us to totally suspend our disbelief and, perhaps, they are not always the very best of literature. But these operas have survived for a reason: their sheer beauty. And even though the words may not be the highest form of literary art, the music has kept them all alive. No one can explain the story of the sensational Verdi opera *Il trovatore* with a straight face, but there is no danger in these great and grand arias leaving the public's ears . . . ever!

It is a fine idea to study past performances so that one can truly have a basis for reinterpreting a work of art. Take, for instance, George Balanchine's renowned choreography for the New York City Ballet. I am told it is most instructive to be able to look at his notes and to see what he changed along the way and with whom he worked. Those times when he created choreography for a certain ballerina who could perhaps do more turns in one minute than most other dancers of the time. A choreographer today might have to adjust for that. But without knowledge of what Balanchine intended and the artists who were able to achieve that intention, we might not be able to give his work continued life and allow for its continued growth. Special gifts of past performers merge with other, equally special gifts of today's performers. This, for me, is the true meaning of art itself: newness, rebirth, with each new interpretation grounded in the knowledge of its creation and development.

I believe one must be a student of life, that learning and searching should never stop, and that scholarship produces wonderful rewards. I enjoy this perpetual search for information and inspiration and find both everywhere. For example, an Ella Fitzgerald scat might trigger a new way for me to look at a John Cage composition. Or the proper pace of a song by Brahms might reveal itself in the quiet spaces of a staged performance of a Shakespeare soliloquy. Tell the story. Don't rush. Perhaps the pace needs to be picked up here. It's a long story—take your time. A wonderful song of Brahms comes to mind: "Von ewiger Liebe" ("Of Eternal Love"). Walking in the darkness, a lover questions the fidelity of the other. Pacing and time are essential.

I enjoy watching stage plays, as the words presented are neither confined nor supported by the tempo of music. An actor might take the text very fast one night and slower the next, taking time after the first paragraph because it is possible; she is not obliged to complete a sentence so that another actor may come in on time with the music. The work of really good actors demonstrates the importance of good phrasing, which can make even the most complex thoughts understood. The best actors listen to one another: collaboration at its best. It is wonderful to develop an intimate relationship with one's text. This makes it possible for the audience to come closer and understand that this particular moment is the essence of the play—the essence of the evening's presentation. To me, this is the most inspiring achievement of all: to truly communicate all that the words portray.

I never tire of preparation, and I think it is fine indeed if I form an opinion about the work at hand in the process. Remember that my parents taught my siblings and me at an early age that "I don't know" was not a good answer and that opinions were not only welcomed, but required. At this point in life, I have neither fear nor doubt in expressing an opinion as regards my work.

Of course, tact is essential when imparting a performance idea, especially, I feel, with conductors, some of whom might find the spirit of collaboration difficult to master. There was the time, for instance, when an American orchestra invited me to sing the wonderful dramatic scene *The Death of Cleopatra* of Berlioz. I was not given the all-important piano rehearsal prior to the orchestral rehearsal and this proved difficult. Getting together with a piano and the conductor prior to the first orchestral rehearsal ought to be written in law. Many concerns can be worked out so easily between the two of you. No egos need to be challenged or injured. The Berlioz was new to this conductor and he gave the downbeat to the orchestra much slower than is written in the score. So in a good moment, I leaned forward—out of earshot of the concert master so as not to embarrass the conductor—and said, "I am very sorry, but the first few bars are normally at a tempo about three times as fast as you have done it." The conductor leaned toward me and said, "I think the slower tempo is better." I said, "But it was Berlioz's idea to have it faster. What do you think we ought to do—your idea, or the allegro that is written in the score?" The conductor was not thrilled.

I recall another such instance at the opera house in Berlin as I was preparing to sing one of my first performances of *The Marriage of Figaro*. The beautiful aria in the second part of the opera where the Countess Almaviva sings "Dove sono i bei momenti" ("Where are the joys of yesterday?")—a long phrase that upon its repeat takes considerable breath control. I was working with a conductor who was new to me and who stated that singers more experienced than I would take breaths in various places within the phrases. I replied that given how Mozart had written the score, and how the text was constructed, I thought breaths in the middle of the phrase to be inappropriate. Moreover, I had the breath control to sing the aria as it was written. I think he thought I was being a silly upstart, but I was not bothered by his attitude or suggestions, and performed the phrases as Mozart wrote them.

I still do!

OF COURSE, THERE are several orchestral conductors who, if asked, would agree that the offstage relationship that we share is that of an abiding, respectful, warm friendship. This does not mean that when it comes to our artistic presentations we can never have a difference of opinion, one from the other. But as everyone surely knows, and this holds true for any profession, in any kind of relationship, if you are building on a foundation of mutual respect, comity, and the desire to produce the very best of which you are capable, any difficulty is but a problem waiting to be solved. We are colleagues, with the kind of long-standing interaction that is, in itself, comforting.

I have found great joy in working with several conductors who are true collaborators. James Levine, most certainly. Singers love him! Jim involves himself totally in the rehearsal process and we have gotten on like a house on fire from the very beginning of our work together. I acknowledge that I can bore a conductor to tears wishing to rehearse a phrase or a page more often than he (and even today, the conductor is still more often than not a "he") feels necessary. Jim always gives space. He is interested in seeing how far a singer or instrumentalist wishes to take a phrase, a musical point, and then he'll accompany us to that place, willingly. Making music with him is always a pleasure, and when it is a challenge, it is an incredibly rewarding challenge. Whether he is accompanying me at the piano or conducting a full orchestra, I never feel that it is a contest of wills: our only goal is to do our best for the music. It is a privilege to work with him, and I know I am not alone in saying this. He is so comfortable in himself as a musician and so thoroughly encouraging as a collaborator.

The same is true of the late Herbert von Karajan, with whom I had the privilege of working on both a performance and a recording of the "Liebestod" from Wagner's *Tristan und Isolde* in the late 1980s, with the Vienna Philharmonic Orchestra and then with the Berlin Philharmonic. I remember spending a lot of time sitting in his spacious office in Salzburg during the summer festival simply discussing the role of Isolde. And he had much to say—by that point he had conducted the opera forty-seven times! A photograph of him steering a magnificent-looking yacht was a prominent part of the collection on the walls of his workspace, and we spoke about that particular joy of his often, as well.

For the first rehearsal of the "Liebestod" in Salzburg, von Karajan asked me to come and listen to the orchestra play the entire aria without my singing at all. It took me a moment to understand what he was doing. He wanted me to really hear the orchestra, and I became aware that as a conductor he was going to be completely supportive of my singing, and that the orchestra would be equally so. Wagner's orchestration was conceived with the special, covered orchestra pit of his opera house at Bayreuth in mind, and there was little danger of the instrumentation overpowering the human voice in such circumstances. But standing onstage with the full orchestra right behind me, I was confident that, through von Karajan's efforts, the right balance would be achieved. It is such a pleasure to work with conductors who are so secure in their own work that collaboration is a given. They are happy to provide the thrilling support of all else that takes place. In fact, von Karajan and I spoke about this after our performance on New Year's Eve in Berlin: the necessity of true collaboration. I do not know if he worked with other singers in this way, but it was an experience that helped to solidify my own thoughts about orchestral accompanying and how it is truly worth the time to achieve that elusive thing: proper and comfortable balance among performers. Everyone is happy to arrive at the point when we come jointly to conclusions about how to proceed—when we are so well rehearsed that we have the freedom onstage to offer something that has not been rehearsed at all, being at one with the music and with our fellow musicians. That is where the magic lies.

His Eye Is on the Sparrow · CHARLES H. GABRIEL

Why should I feel discouraged? Why should the shadows fall?
Why should my heart be lonely? And long for Heaven and home.
When Jesus is my portion, my constant Friend is He
His eye is on the sparrow and I know he watches me.

I sing because I'm happy,
I sing because I'm free.
For His eye is on the sparrow
And I know He watches me.

"Let not your heart be troubled"
His tender words I hear
And resting on His goodness, I lost my doubts and fears
Though by the path He leadeth, but one step I may see,
His eye is on the sparrow and I know He watches me.

Whenever I am tempted, whenever clouds arise
When songs give place to sighing, when hope within me dies,
I draw the closer to Him, from care He sets me free
His eye is on the sparrow and I know He watches me.

10

And the Journey Continues

"HE'S GOT THE WHOLE WORLD IN HIS HAND"

> He's got the whole world in His hand,
> He's got the woods and water in His hand,
> He's got the sun and moon in His hand,
> He's got the birds and bees right in His hand,
> He's got the beasts of the field right in His hand,
> He's got the whole world in His hand.

The ride from the airport in Frankfurt, Germany, to Baden-Baden, little more than a hundred miles, is restful and lovely. Even with all those marvelous German-made cars whizzing by, it is a beautiful ride, as so much of the landscape is a picture postcard. Peaceful and joyful, if one takes the time for it, with the addition of splendid sunsets. Witnessing one of those sunsets in the summer of 2012, during a concert series that stretched from halls in Austria and Germany to London, it was as though the sun danced across the entire side of a hill, blue at the top and full of oranges and reds and corals and pinks at the bottom, the kind of weather that happens when part of the earth is warm and the sky is cool, with Mother Nature showing herself to be the best lighting designer ever. I could not resist having our driver pull to the side of the road just for a moment, so that we could enjoy that glorious display. "Let's just take two minutes and look at this," I said.

It was a dear friend of mine who spoke to me of the importance of taking the time to savor such moments, at a period in my life when I was perhaps too unsettled in adulthood to appreciate fully what she wished me to understand. Her father had been a general in World War I, originally from the region that would become Czechoslovakia. His duty was to lead the fight against the Austro-Hungarian Empire. For his trouble, he was imprisoned. She spent many of her young years visiting her father in prison, which made her understand early on the value of both freedom and an appreciation of the simple things of life. A loaf of fresh bread pressed through the wire fence that divided her from him, a piece of fresh fruit. "Take time in your life," she implored. "Enjoy your profession, but do not ever become too busy to laugh with your friends, your family; fulfill these needs of your spirit and your soul." She went on to say, "You are not going to find yourself sitting somewhere at age eighty-five, thinking, 'Oh, I wish I had sung a few more concerts.' What you will more likely think is, 'I wish I had actually gone to Kashmir with that group of friends. I could have taken that camping vacation with my sibling's children. I should have spent more time with my friend when he fell ill.' Those are the things that will come to mind; the simple things, the underpinnings of life itself."

Of course, it took me a little while to understand the import of her words, to understand that time taken for myself was not time without a purpose. And I have none other than Albert Einstein to reinforce her words. He wrote once: "Creativity is the residue of wasted time." Creativity. Life.

I take this wisdom to heart, as I know from experience now that growth and understanding can reveal themselves in those moments when thoughts are allowed to run freely. It was this state of mind that made me grab with both hands the sterling opportunity to curate the festival in 2009 under the auspices of Carnegie Hall, *Honor!*

It is a fitting name. We are honored to pay homage, honored by the work, the tenacity, the determination, the courage of those who went before us, honored to be their progeny.

This festival responded to a need that first arose in me as early as my student days at Howard University, during a two-year music literature course with the grand title A History of Western Music. In the textbook for this course, thick with details, there was not one mention of an African American composer—not one.

It was therefore a dream come to reality for me to be a part of this celebration of the African American cultural legacy. The three-week-long, fifty-two-event celebration in March of 2009 took place in many different venues in the city of New York, with immensely talented singers, instrumentalists, dancers, actors, scholars, and all who shone a bright light on the contributions of a people and a heritage of which I am rightfully proud. We were fortunate in having Mellonee Burnim and Portia Maultsby's 2006 compilation *African American Music: An Introduction* as a marvelous guide: a timeline for the development of music ranging from the Spiritual to the blues, on to bebop, into jazz in all its variations, and rhythm and blues with all its machinations, on to pop and off to hip-hop and whatever comes next. We presented and celebrated it all. *Sacred Ellington,* my production of music taken from the three different sacred concerts composed by Duke Ellington, employs jazz band, jazz combo, piano, string quartet, gospel choir, a tap dancer, a spiritual dancer, and yours truly. It was a blessing to be able to present this production in the very same place where the Duke himself performed his sacred music concerts: the Cathedral of Saint John the Divine.

At Carnegie Hall, the premiere of a multimedia extravaganza, *Ask Your Mama! Twelve Moods for Jazz* by Langston Hughes and with music by Laura Karpman, was presented as part of the festival. At the Apollo Theater, a gospel fest for the ages was offered. The wonderful Shirley Caesar was in rare form. It was also tremendous to hear a children's gospel choir.

From the time its doors opened in 1891, up until the *Honor!* festival in 2009, Carnegie Hall had welcomed some nine hundred African American musicians, actors, lecturers, and more to the stage. During the festival, Toni Morrison, Cornel West, Michael Eric Dyson, Derrick Bell, Maya Angelou, Terence Blanchard, Harolyn Blackwell, the Roots, and many more would take the stage at Carnegie. What splendor. What a gift to us all!

I thought of the enduring strength and genius of Louis Armstrong, who, invited to offer a performance somewhere in the South, found that his audience would in fact be segregated and that neither he nor his band would be permitted to enter the premises via the front door. His integrity led him to refuse to perform, and to pay his band out of his own pocket. It would be Bing Crosby who would insist that such a talent as rarely walked this earth should enter through the front entrance of anywhere in this world. Crosby insisted that Armstrong walk with him through the front door, which Armstrong did, on the condition that his band members be invited to do so, as well.

That was just one of the incalculable number of incidents of intolerance, but it was conquered by a higher degree of humanity and the simple wish of an African American to offer a gift, a talent. Armstrong played Carnegie Hall, as did Miles Davis, John Coltrane, Duke Ellington, Cab Calloway: the list is long and wonderful.

It was pure joy to stand on this stage, Carnegie Hall, and speak their names, and honor them as they honored us.

BY NOW, I UNDERSTAND completely that life does not occur in straight lines and that thinking of it as such only establishes the perfect environment for disappointment. The reality of peaks, valleys, and curves becomes clearer with experience, with time, with living.

I think that growing older in grace and with grace has a great deal to do with one's attitude toward life's progression and exactly what that means. I have decided that time has something to teach me. That I might now implement ideas that for various reasons were left by the wayside of life.

There will always be the various camps of music enthusiasts, some who feel that the works of Mozart and Beethoven, for example, are so superior to everything else that one need nothing else. Or the Wagner devotees who offer their sympathy to those who do not possess their depth of understanding or appreciation of Wagner's music. And let us not forget the camp that feels a trained opera singer is somehow "breaking ranks" by adding the music of different genres to his or her repertoire. Woe unto the opera singer who finds joy in the music of Rodgers and Hammerstein!

Such opinions are not a part of my choices in life. As has always been the case, I sing the music of my heart.

Roots: My Life, My Song is an example of breaking ranks. I absolutely adore singing such classics as Harold Arlen's—but really Lena Horne's—"Stormy Weather." When I was considering including this song on the CD, I called Miss Lena (I always called my pal "Miss Lena," which always made her laugh) to ask her permission. She responded, as usual in her goodness, "Oh, girl. That song does not belong to me. Go ahead and sing it and have a good time." And that is what I am doing with this music, having a good time!

I THINK, TOO, that the passage of time can be so instructive and rewarding if we allow the respect and space for it. And I wish that we women could somehow relieve ourselves of the notion that at age sixty, we need to look like we are thirty-five. Time settles in and your hair changes and your skin becomes a little less firm and wrinkles settle in and your body does not sit easily in the same positions it did when you were young and spry, but there is beauty there, if you let it be. I suppose it is pop culture and our own sense of mortality that lead so many of us to think there is something wrong with letting it be, but I disagree. I say always that fine wine becomes even better in the bottle over time. I have decided to be a Pomerol.

One of the things that gives me joy is the sheer look of flowers. When one considers the many hundreds of books written on the subject and the number of gardens everywhere, it is clear that a love of flowers is universal. I am drawn particularly to orchids. I had no idea of the thousands of varieties of this flower until I visited an exhibition in Tokyo some years ago. Some orchids grow only in Africa, others only in Malaysia, others only in the Amazon, and so forth.

With this knowledge now under my belt and with my love for this flower only increased, you can imagine that I was floored when the French National Museum of Natural Sciences and the National Botanical Garden invited me to be present at a ceremony at which an orchid would be named for me. My reaction upon hearing this amazing news was stunned gratitude.

On a beautiful, sunny morning, we found ourselves in the warm and humid home of the orchid garden of the National Botanical Gardens of France, which is in Versailles. Live music played quietly and everyone spoke in lowered tones, which somehow seemed to fit this atmosphere completely. I was transported.

It was there that I would learn that an orchid grower in the South of France had given seven years to the development of this perfectly gorgeous Phalaenopsis: a beautiful ivory flower with a tinge of light purple at its head. I was presented with a specimen in the loveliest of ceremonies, with poetry from one of my all-time favorites, Paul Verlaine.

A specimen of this plant can now be found in the New York

Botanical Garden in the Bronx, in the Enid A. Haupt Conservatory.

Amid such beauty, the spirit floats, soars a bit, and rests again in complete joy. Flowers make their own music.

I listen to a good deal of instrumental classical music and jazz and allow it to calm me and lift my spirits, and on occasion to teach me. There is great value in listening to such giants as Ellington and Fitzgerald, Monk, Coltrane, and Vaughan, among countless others. The phrasing, the wonderful use of blue notes, the pleasure that seems to spring from an Ella Fitzgerald CD, serve to nourish the spirit. By contrast, I seldom listen to opera, as it is nearly impossible to listen and not sing along. This is not relaxing as it is nearly impossible to simply listen and not jump in to sing a phrase or two.

I derive great pleasure, though, still and forever, from my work. I am so grateful and so very happy that my voice and I are enjoying a fine relationship at this time of life, a time when our voices are subject to the same vagaries as the rest of our bodies.

Living changes the voice, and it can be in a positive way. Life changes the way we think about a song, or an aria, or an entire operatic role. Living gives us more information.

I had the experience recently of working with a conductor who, in preparing for our performance, listened to a recording that I had made twenty years ago.

It took me a moment to explain that "love" is one thing at age thirty-five or forty, but it is a different thing, perhaps a more urgent wish, at age sixty—and that my singing of this song has changed with me. Life had intervened and taught me much more about love and longing.

My conductor understood and we had a beautiful time together.

THE EXPERIENCE OF LIVING can be wonderful in the insight we are able to offer those of fewer years. I am so grateful to have been blessed with a group of women a generation and more ahead of me in years, on whom I rely for wisdom. My aunt Louise is about to celebrate eighty-seven years, with the brightness and keen-minded sense of life and living that have only expanded with her years. She still has one of the very best collections of hats around, and wears them, with her jewelry and high-heeled shoes! She does not fret about things over which she has no control. One seldom sees a frown in that wonderful face.

I would like to be an Aunt Louise.

My pal Christine, in her twinsets, pleated skirts, pearls and all, is another one to emulate.

She is so circumspect in the way she carries herself that if the word *damn* passes her lips, as it did when we spoke recently, the world practically rocks. She stated that when you have managed to reach a certain age, you do not give a *damn* what others think about what you feel, say, or do. I have come to some conclusions about life, she said, and I am comfortable in speaking to those conclusions. Why suffer fools if you do not have to do so? she asks. Why do anything that you do not really wish to do, if it is not going to cause harm to another person? I embrace these sentiments.

From my own ancestry, there are stories of strong and wise women. I saw a photograph of my great-grandmother once, which is odd enough, considering where she lived and when she lived.

Somehow, in its early decades, the art of photography found its way to Georgia, to her little corner of the world. She lived to be nearly ninety years old. I remember looking at her face and then back at my mother's, searching for evidence that the two were kindred. My mother explained how an African American woman living deep in the backwoods of Georgia at the turn of the century, in the midst of the danger that came with simply being African American, could not only live to see ninety years, but look as beautiful as my great-grandmother did in that picture. For one, she had a very healthy lifestyle. She spent a lot of time outdoors, much of it exercising. Except no one really called it exercise. She walked the hillside, carrying water, searching for berries, moving with great ease as she worked the land. My great-grandmother washed her face with red clay, too, which, when I was very young, seemed very odd. But of course, we all know now that you can buy such products in small bottles these days for great sums in our fancier stores. The water my great-grandmother used with that clay was also free of pollutants and acid rain: pure. No doubt, as people in the country in those days tended to get up with the sun and go to bed at sunset, she had gotten plenty of rest and, living on a farm, the blessing of an abundance of vegetables and fruit. All these things I am rather sure contributed to her looking simply terrific in that photograph, which, in fact, had been taken near the end of her life. She lived a wholesome lifestyle free of the vices that consume all too many.

The same is true of my grandmother, who was beautiful, strong, and independent well into her many years on this earth — well after her twelve children were adults and had left the farm to forge their own lives. There was a considerable amount of time and effort poured into trying to convince Grandmother to leave the farm and move in with someone who would be responsible for taking care of her. My uncle Floyd, whose farmland was contiguous to hers, thought he would be successful in convincing her to leave the farm and live with him, as she would not have been leaving familiar surroundings. But Grandmother would have none of this. Now well into her eighties, she made it clear that this farm was her home. She had lived there happily with Granddaddy and all those children, working their own land in grace. She remained there to live out her years.

WHILE I MAKE MYSELF comfortable on a daily basis with the passing of time, I would not mind fewer bits of correspondence from the AARP. Those envelopes with the big red letters that appear as if by magic on such a regular basis can put a damper on your thought of using that new blue eye shadow! When that correspondence began arriving, I thought surely there must have been some mistake. Some days, I still think someone must have made a clerical error somewhere along the line.

This brings me to the subject of love, friendships, families: life. The sensations of romantic love make us think there must be extra air to breathe—that the world has righted itself on its axis and that the sun shines only for us. I live in love and in passion practically every moment. Still, it is simultaneously amusing and perplexing that because I have not married or had children, casual, and may I say insensitive, observers relate that I cannot possibly have a "full life" since my life most probably does not resemble theirs. It is a most false assumption. The truth is that life is full to overflowing, satisfying, generous, and most assuredly blessed. Those with whom I share my personal life know this well. We celebrate it. And if we find that in order to keep our relationship safe, we must keep ourselves and the way we feel for one another out of the view of the curious, then so be it. Friendships of all kinds are to be cherished and nourished—wrapped in limitless love that glows and grows from that deepest part of knowing that the ones we love walk into a special room in our hearts and minds and sit there with us, content, independent of outside influences, sure that there is nowhere else they would rather be. I like that. It is private. It is personal. May it ever be so.

Of course, when the questions come, sometimes I cannot resist having a little fun. I love the look on the faces of strangers who cannot resist their curiosity in asking me, "Do you have children?" To which I will reply, "Yes, I have ninety-six this year!" I am naughty enough that I enjoy watching their reactions as they process this response. Sometimes I will ease their confusion by stating, "You see, I have a school of the arts for middle school children."

In my youth I learned from my own godparents that it is not necessary to give birth to children in order to have them happily and firmly in your life. They had no children of their own, but lavished their care on the children in their circle. I do the same. It just happens that all of my siblings have produced boy children, so with ten nephews I have had the distinct privilege of being surrounded by tricycles and finding half-eaten jelly sandwiches stuck, somehow, to the back of my jacket. Those who know me well caution others that they should not inquire of my family unless they are sitting comfortably, as there will be a long response! I have always adored these children, and now that they are all adults, most with their own children, it is heartwarming indeed that we have lost none of our naturalness and comfort with one another. I love spending time with them in deep, meaningful conversation that is as inspiring as their earliest offerings were charming and adorable. How could I not feel a special warmth from three little boys, about five, seven, and nine, who wished to take me to lunch with the money they saved up, at a restaurant they said they were sure I'd like because, as they so proudly pointed out, "It has pictures of the food on the menu"? How could I not adore the delicious demeanor of these children when they attended their first Detroit Tigers game? My nephews were raised around a lot of celebrated musical artists, so they were accustomed to enjoying live performances by these friends of their parents as well as my own, of course. At this Tigers game, they were sure that they understood how the "audience" is meant to respond. Imagine, then, when, at the baseball game, they found the crowd yelling their approval at something that happened on the baseball diamond, and, as they knew no better, the three of them rose to their little feet to yell, "Bravo!" Priceless.

Who would not find these now adults simply wonderful in taking some of their vacation time of late to travel to New York to try to usher their Aunt J into the twenty-first century, with all the newest technology available, and providing a bit of a tutorial prior to their departure? When one thinks of all the other things that could occupy the time of beautiful, marvelously educated, sophisticated young men, how can I not love them fully and deeply?

Love, ease, joy, friendship—they all grow with the years and plant their roots around me with the sure and always-present power of enduring devotion. I love my men friends. Every single one.

Marriage proposals come in all shapes and sizes, don't they? From "Why don't we marry?" to "I think we would make a great team," to a drive into the French countryside on a glorious summer's afternoon for lunch that seems too magnificent in its deliciousness to be real, followed in the most leisurely fashion by the presentation of a family crest from Louis XIV, and the most romantic of poetry. Resistance is presented its greatest challenge yet.

The thought of being titled oh so enticing, and with the beauty of that very special day still so alive in my spirit, I rejoice in knowing that I am sensible enough to be thrilled at "the invitation to this particular dance of life," while at the same time aware of that little streak of Carmen in me—that bird in flight, that freedom that I so cherish.

THE STRONG SPIRITS of the great women in my own family inspire me. My mother remains the central heroine of my life. The inexorable risings and settings of the sun become a topic not of intellectual discourse, but a part of my own reality. They set the example for me, these ancestral women, by making it clear that the passing of the decades can be a beautiful part of life. But it is surely not for the faint of heart. Aside from the fact of losing those who have offered long-term friendship, love, and companionship, one's own body can present a plethora of health-related concerns. Even with the acknowledgment of such considerations and changes, we are wise to remain independent in mind and spirit as we strengthen even further those wonderful "ties that bind"—the support that true love and devotion offer us.

A close friend, one who is reaching for age ninety and still travels the world, full of interest in absolutely everything, said to me recently that she looks in the mirror sometimes and wonders, *Who is that old lady?,* as it surely cannot be her, with her fabulous attire and an interesting companion waiting to take her arm. She is one of the very lucky ones. She says she has treated her health always with the respect and care that it deserves. I feel as well now as I did in my forties, she says, as she sweeps out of the door for another evening in her magnificent life.

Still, here in our youth-obsessed world, where popular culture swallows its starlets whole and discards them long before they can blow out the candles on their thirtieth birthday cakes, society would seem to wish only to have the next youthful loveliness to admire. Why not be grateful for those indications of life and living that find themselves on our faces? The wrinkles and lines make a statement of the good and then the not so good that make up our experiences to date.

Besides, what folly it is to dismiss all that comes with these experiences, with living; we should be grateful for every moment. I draw strength and guidance from thinking of the experiences of those who preceded me in this profession. Those ancestral monuments to courage and determination enabled me to consider how I could allow my audiences to know that I realized fully that 1995 was a special year for remembering some of the most shocking displays of inhumanity: fifty years since the end of World War II and the Holocaust that defined that war, that defamation to the soul of the world.

I had programmed the Maurice Ravel setting of a version of the Kaddish in various places prior to 1995, but decided that this would be my statement. I would sing it in all recitals that year and would not need to say more.

Kaddish

Yitgaddal v'yitkaddash sh'meh rabba.	May His great name be magnified and sanctified.
B'alma div'ra chiruteh,	In the world which He created, according to His will,
v'yamlich malchuteh,	may He establish His kingdom
b'chayechon uv'yomechon	during our life and during our days
uv'chayeh d'chol bet Yisrael,	and during the life of all the house of Israel,
baagala uvizman kariv.	even speedily and soon.
V'imru: Amen.	And let us say: Amen.
Y'heh sh'meh rabba m'vorach l'alam ul'almeh almaya.	Let His great Name be blessed forever and to all eternity.
Yitbarach, v'yishtabbach v'yitpaar, v'yitromam, v'yitnasseh v'yithaddar, v'yitalleh v'yithalal,	Blessed, praised and glorified, exalted, extolled and honored, magnified and lauded,

sh'meh d'kud'sha b'rich hu,	be the Name of the Holy One,
l'ela min kol birchata v'shirata,	though He be high above all the
	blessings and hymns,
tushb'chata v'nech'mata,	praises and consolations,
daamiran b'alma.	which are uttered in the world.
V'imru Amen	And let us say: Amen.

My recital-performance tour that year would take me back to Japan to cities familiar to me, as well as some that I had not visited on previous occasions. One such city would be Hiroshima.

I wondered if it was even appropriate that an American should perform in such a year in Hiroshima. I had the opportunity to seek the advice of President Clinton regarding my plans to travel and sing there, just in case there could be any concern from my own government in this regard. Perhaps I was worrying too much.

The presenter was certain that this was precisely what he wished. It would turn out that the presenter had been born just days prior to August 6, 1945, the day Hiroshima became the first city in history to be leveled by an atomic bomb, an American atomic bomb; the city of Nagasaki followed three days later. I would learn from the presenter that his life had been saved because he was yet in hospital on that awful day. He wished the two of us to make this music together in 1995. He joked that unlike him, I had waited until the war's conclusion, even in the Pacific, to make my appearance on earth, and he felt that our lives were somehow connected.

I am not able to describe fully how deeply I took his kindness, the forgiveness to my country that was apparent in all he said, as well as his stated hope of forgiveness for the act of December 7,

1941: Pearl Harbor. This gentle, caring spirit, this muse who took, he stated, the greatest of pleasure in watching Hiroshima's rebirth. There are no trees there that are more than sixty-eight years old; he and everything coming from the earth in his hometown are the same age. Miraculous. Gigantic amounts of replanting have taken place, and the city looks fresh and vibrant and green.

My pianist and I arrived on the stage to a beautiful welcome by the audience and proceeded to offer our program. And almost immediately, I spotted something that I can see as clearly today as I could that beautiful early evening in Hiroshima. In the very first row sat a very young girl of no more than five or six years, dressed from head to toe in red, white, and blue. Her beautiful dress with its full skirt was ivory, and all of her accessories were red or blue or both. I was happy that I had already begun the first song and that my professionalism would take me through until the end, as the vision of this little girl in that time and place was something never to be imagined and surely always to be remembered.

The first part of the program offered the gorgeous harmonies of the late German Romantic period of musical composition, and it was my belief that, given her age and the now later hour in the evening, she would, understandably, be absent for the second part of the recital with Ravel and Messiaen on the program. But no; we returned to the stage after the intermission and there she still sat, smiling from ear to ear, seemingly eager to hear what would come next.

After the performance, her parents told me that they had purposefully had her sleep during the day so that she might remain awake for the entire performance.

She and I shook hands, as I did not feel it appropriate in this culture to embrace a child unknown to me, and to my delight she stated what I can only imagine she had rehearsed hundreds of times: "Welcome to Japan, Miss Norman."

AN OBSESSION WITH the culture of youth is simply not in evidence in some parts of the world. In several countries the mature are revered. Take, for instance, the Living National Treasures of Japan: those masters who have achieved a very high degree of skill and recognition in the arts and humanities. The Japanese government recognizes, protects, and celebrates those whose decades of mastery are so crucial to the preservation of the Japanese culture. These individuals are held up as icons and offered amazing reverence and respect.

It was a great honor in 2004 when it was my pleasure to perform Schoenberg's *Erwartung,* in addition to Poulenc's *La voix humaine,* in Tokyo, with two such Living National Treasures in the audience.

My colleagues and I were thrilled to know that they were there to witness these very modern stagings, the kind of theater that was still rare in Japan at the time, especially for productions on the opera stage. In fact, we had been concerned about the reception that our presentations might receive in Japan as a whole. My experience to that date in performing in Japan quieted my mind, as I had seen audiences express themselves in ways that I had been warned not to expect — "Western-style" outbursts of appreciation from those steeped in a culture that considered such behavior inappropriate, or so I was told. The reality was quite different.

On my very first visit in the mid-1980s, with the great Seiji Ozawa as conductor for a concert of Strauss and Wagner, we were rewarded with a forty-seven-minute standing ovation. There was nothing quiet or reserved in the audience's reaction to our music. Thus, I knew from this experience alone that our audiences could well surprise us.

I had often been moved very deeply by the earnestness with which Japanese audience members would express their appreciation of the music. I still have an exquisite, hand-embroidered handkerchief given to me following a recital in Osaka. I was told at the time that this particular piece had been in the giver's family for more than 150 years. I keep it close.

After the opera performances that evening in Tokyo, it was a lesson in decorum and utter respect to see how beautifully these two actors, these Living Treasures, were treated by everyone. All whom they passed bowed from the waist and remained with head bowed until the actors had passed them by.

It was truly exceptional that these Treasures had chosen to come backstage at all, we were advised. When they came with such kindness and genuine pleasure in their expressions of their appreciation of the performances, we were beside ourselves with joy.

Whereas the physical act of bowing is not at all a part of the culture of our country, would that we could attain such a level of celebration and consideration of experience and wisdom that can come from living: listening, learning, being, and how "living treasures" could inform and help to structure and direct our own lives.

One must not allow the foolishness of present-day habits and preferences to dictate our understanding of life itself. With every passing day, we can learn a little more about ourselves and our relationship to others. The answer to "Why are we here?" can become clearer with each interaction, with each setting of the sun, with each new day awaiting our curiosity and gratitude.

POSTLUDE

$\mathcal{I}$ relish the opportunity to speak in public. When I do so, my audiences are often surprised that I do not restrict my remarks to singing. I prefer to speak about all of the arts, and of citizenship, and of the responsibility that we all have to look beyond ourselves. Lending a helping hand should be a natural part of our lives, as natural as a violinist picking up the violin for a day's rehearsal. Participating in the sociopolitical struggles of our day should not be something that we "get around to one of these days." We must make certain that we join the ranks of our fellow citizens, now. This I believe to my core. I take these words of Simone de Beauvoir as a succinct expression of a philosophy embracing *all* of life:

> *One's life has value so long as one attributes value to the life of others, by means of love, friendship, indignation, and compassion.*

Surely, we need to find ways of loving our neighbors better. We need to offer friendship with more ease. We need to find compassion in our hearts and in our spirits for those whose lives reveal the despair that we, perhaps, have been spared, but whose experiences could be our own, there but for the grace of our Creator. We need, too, a sufficient amount of indignation to insist on decent housing, a living wage, and nourishing food for all our brothers and sisters, all our elders, all our children. The words of George Bernard Shaw come to mind:

> *I am of the opinion that my life belongs to the community. And*
> *as long as I live, it is my privilege to do for it whatever I can.*
> *I want to be thoroughly used up when I die, for the harder I*
> *work, the more I live. Life is no brief candle to me; it is a sort*
> *of splendid torch, which I have got hold of for a short moment,*
> *and I want to make it burn as brightly as possible before hand-*
> *ing it on to the future generations.*

I applaud these words, this sentiment, this full awareness of the reason for being. I applaud it, too, as my ancestors had their own way of saying precisely the same thing:

> *This little light of mine, I'm gonna let it shine!*

Indeed, I preach the sermons I have heard all my life:

The Sermon of Getting On with It. Life is bound to present obstacles that may well have you questioning your own worth, your choices in life, even your faith. But we would do well to adopt the idea that life, truly, is a series of lessons, and we should try as hard as we can to confront our challenges with the same tenacity with which we pursue our pleasures.

The Sermon of Gratitude. Let us not be too busy to say thank you, to offer congratulations, to give a deeply felt handshake, an embrace. We should offer gratitude for the simple things that are packed with meaning for ourselves, yes, but even more so for others. This includes, too, that quiet, still time when we offer the universe thanks for that performance that somehow "took off" from the moment everyone was in place.

The Sermon of Respect. Let us decide to abandon the belief that work with our bodies is somehow less important than work with our minds, or that work accomplished through the magic of our minds is somehow more important than that accomplished purely through our hearts.

The Sermon of Humility. Can we please allow someone else to offer positive commentary on things that have to do with us? Our marvelous family. Our work. That new dress that flatters every part of us. May we come to the understanding that the gifts that we possess are not offered to us out of some magnificent personal accomplishment, but rather are an expression of Divinely ordered coincidence. The operative word here is *gifts*.

The Sermon of Self-Awareness. Those of us who live and breathe our days through the arts are placed uniquely to help treat the malaise of our world. The self-awareness that comes from participation in the arts at any level opens the self to one's own humanity in its fullness. This knowledge of ourselves can lead to wisdom and wisdom to the understanding of others. This understanding, this acknowledgment that every human being has worth, must surely lead to tolerance.

ART MAKES EACH of us whole by insisting that we use all of our senses, our heads, and our hearts—that we express with our bodies, our voices, our hands, as well as with our minds. In Arthur O'Shaughnessy's poem "Ode," he wrote in praise of artists everywhere:

> *We are the music-makers,*
>
> *And we are the dreamers of dreams,*
> *Wandering by lone sea-breakers*
> *And sitting by desolate streams;*
> *World-losers and world-forsakers,*
> *On whom the pale moon gleams:*
> *Yet we are the movers and shakers*
>
> *Of the world for ever, it seems.*

What a thought. Creative spirits, the movers and shakers of the world. Where could this all lead? We might come across the idea that an awakened spirit, this ability to express ourselves through the inspiration of the arts in our lives, could well be the real meaning of life. That the exploration of our own imagination might just be our real life's work.

We each express ourselves in our own ways, with our own gifts and talents. Let us not be afraid to stand up and be an example of the change we wish to see in our world by doing something strong and useful in offering to others the teachings of our hearts and minds. The fullness of ourselves.

And imagine, if you will, the harmony that this could bring to our world.

CODA

I sat going through my mail one February day in 2013, not really paying close attention to what I was doing until I came across a stylish-looking envelope with a logo I had known all my life: the NAACP. Thinking it to be an announcement or an invitation to an event in the New York area, I opened the letter, hoping that my schedule would allow me to attend. I was so taken with its contents that I had to read it twice to be absolutely certain I had not misunderstood it. The letter informed me that I had been chosen to receive the highest award given by this oldest, most storied and revered of American civil rights organizations: the Spingarn Medal.

I thought of those days in the church's annex and meetings of the Augusta Youth Chapter of the NAACP, and of the determination and strength of those who guided our actions and reactions to the laws and habits of the day. I thought of the mass meetings at Tabernacle Baptist in the 1960s, and of how the work of the NAACP is needed now more than ever.

There were a few teardrops on the letter by the time I contacted my siblings and a few pals with the news later that day.

Orlando, Florida, July 17, 2013, is a day that will remain in every detail in my memory. My heroes, Congressman John Lewis and my big brother Silas Jr., presented the Spingarn Medal to me. Both spoke with such depth of feeling that I was not certain I would be able to compose myself in order to offer my own remarks of thanks on acceptance of the award. I was very happy that I had written out beforehand what I wished to say.

The ballroom of the hotel that had housed the many events of the NAACP convention was filled with everyone in their best suits and dresses, full of the goodness of fellowship. The civil rights icon Julian Bond sat across from me at the dinner table.

Was I dreaming?

We took a hundred photographs and I was more grateful than ever for the strong, unyielding shoulders on which it is my greatest honor to stand. The pioneers, the trailblazers, the pathfinders, all those whose names we know as well as our own, along with all those unknown heroes of strength, courage, and faith. My gratitude knows no bounds.

Then, because life just keeps on giving, I had the thrill just two weeks later of being in Statuary Hall of the United States Capitol Building, for the congressional commemoration of the fiftieth anniversary of the March on Washington. My seat faced squarely the newly dedicated statue of Rosa Parks, she for whom I had been given the honor to sing when she was awarded the Congressional Gold Medal by President Bill Clinton some sixteen years earlier. Coincidence? My wonderful aunt Louise, in one of her magnificent hats and looking altogether beautiful, sat next to me.

The representatives of both houses of Congress offered remarks appropriate to the day's celebration. All thanks and honor were offered to our living, breathing, "no thought of letting up now" honoree of the day: Congressman Lewis!

His speech will be a part of the history books. The blessing of singing for him and to him—a man who, with so many others, dedicates himself to helping us all find the "better angels of our nature"—will abide in my spirit forever.

Zueignung • RICHARD STRAUSS • Devotion

Ja, du weisst es, teure Seele,	Yes, you know, my most precious of souls
Dass ich fern von dir mich quäle,	Away from you causes my heart's pain
Liebe macht die Herzen krank,	It is our love that brings such exquisite passion.
Habe Dank.	For this, I thank you!
Einst heilt ich, der Freiheit Zecher,	Once, I thought of a life as a free spirit
Hoch den Amethysten-Becher,	I held high the cup of boundless pleasure
Und du segnetest den Trank,	You came into my life and blessed that cup.
Habe Dank.	For this, I thank you!
Und beschworst darin die Bösen,	All sadness and grief were swept away
Bis ich, was ich nie gewesen	And I became more than I ever believed I could be
Heilig, heilig an's Herz dir sank,	With Divine gratitude, I became yours.
Habe Dank.	For this, I thank you!

ACKNOWLEDGMENTS

$\mathcal{A}$LL TEACHERS in the public schools of Augusta who it was my privilege to have as guides, at C. T. Walker Elementary School, A. R. Johnson Junior High School, and Lucy C. Laney High School.

Those generous parts of the community there that supported the young lives of all of us.

Howard University, for giving me a place to grow into adulthood with my heritage, and responsibility to that heritage, in sharp, vivid relief.

Denene Millner, for her assistance in combining related material for this book into understandable portions that speak to similar thoughts, expressions, and experiences.

Carol Friedman, for the most flattering of photographs always, including the one on the jacket cover of this book.

James Levine, for providing the introduction to these recollections, thoughts, hopes, and dreams; this book.

The many: my musical colleagues, icons, and other inspiring persons who encourage dedication and devotion toward one's chosen profession and active participation in the larger community, the world in which we live.

And after this, as I have stated often, to everyone, everywhere who has ever said, and those who continue to say: "Let's ask Jessye to sing."

> *Oh, I'm going to sing,*
> *Going to sing,*
> *Going to sing all along the way,*
> *We'll shout o'er all our sorrows*
> *And sing forever more,*
> *With Christ and all His army*
> *On that celestial shore!*

INDEX